ÎLE PLATE

ÎLE RONDE

ÎLOT GABRIEL

COIN DE MIRE

GRAND GAUBE

RE

POINTE BERNACHE

ODLANDS

ÎLE D' AMBRE

POUDRE
D' OR

PITON

**RIVIÈRE
DU REMPART**

POSTE DE FLACQ

POINT DE FLACQ

oliere

CENTRE DE FLACQ

oir

ST JULIEN
VILLAGE

MILITAIRE

FUEL

BELLE MARE

BELAIR

TOUESSROK HOTEL

FLACQ

ÎLE DE L' EST

GRANDE RIVIERE SUD-EST

ÎLE AUX CERFS

GRAND PORT

EUE

E VALE

MONTAGNE
DU LYON

UNY

VIEUX GRAND
PORT

MAHEBOURG

PLAISANCE

INDIAN OCEAN

LE SOUFFLEUR

EURE

Equator

AFRICA

SEYCHELLES

AMIRANTE

ALDABRA

FARQUHAR

COMOROS

RODRIGUES

MADAGASCAR

MAURITIUS

REUNION

Tropic of Capricorn

SOUTH AFRICA

N

VISITORS' GUIDE TO MAURITIUS AND RÉUNION

VISITORS' GUIDE TO
MAURITIUS
AND
RÉUNION

HOW TO GET THERE · WHAT TO SEE · WHERE TO STAY

Marco Turco

SOUTHERN
BOOK PUBLISHERS

This book is for Jody ... you know all the reasons why

ISBN 1 86812 531 9

First edition, first impression 1995

Published by
Southern Book Publishers (Pty) Ltd
PO Box 3103, Halfway House 1685

While the author and publisher have endeavoured to
verify all facts, they will not be held responsible for any
inconvenience that may result from possible
inaccuracies in this book.

Cover photograph by Jody Turco
Cover design by Insight Graphics
Maps by Colin Stevenson
Set in 10/11.5 pt Palatino
by Kohler Carton & Print, Pinetown
Printed and bound by Kohler Carton & Print, Pinetown

ACKNOWLEDGEMENTS

Without the assistance and unselfish commitment of many people, this book is unlikely to have ever reached fruition. Writing this guidebook was a team effort. To those many not mentioned below, although I may have forgotten your names, your kindness, affection and hospitality are among my happiest memories of the Indian Ocean islands. I thank you all.

South Africa

Allan Foggitt and Neil Wesselo of Starlight Cruises; Greta Du Bois and Air Austral; Dave Barry and Backpacker for travel-packs and other luggage; Urbans Footwear for leather boots; Maria Barbaressos of Club Med; Winnie Kyriakides and St Géran.

Jody Turco. For being there, always. What addicted traveller could ever ask for a better companion?

Louise Grantham and Southern Book Publishers; Colin Stevenson for the maps; family and friends, for your interest, support and encouragement.

Mauritius

Pradeep Ramrekha and the staff of the Maritim Hotel; the European management of Club Med; Philippe LaMothe and the Hotel PLM Azur; PR Prayag and the Gold Crest Hotel; Nicolas de Chalain and Le Paradis Hotel; Patrice Binet-Decamps and the Belle Mare Plage Hotel; management and staff of St Géran Hotel; Nico Kux at Kuxville Beach Cottages; Cecile Ah-Yu Leong Son, management and staff of the Royal Palm Hotel.

Réunion

Réunion Tourism Board for brochures, pamphlets, maps and contact numbers; Air Austral; Nathalie Hoareau and Apavou Hotels; Raymond Demeaux and Demotel; Michel Wilken of Hotel Lallemand; Pasqual Porcel and Hotel Sterne; Mme Forest of Hotel des Thermes; Pascale Moreau and VVF; Jean Durand and Le St Alexis Hotel; Didier Lamoot and Hotel Coralia; Michel Boulet and Ascotel.

CONTENTS

HOW TO USE THIS GUIDE

Both Mauritius and Réunion are primarily package tour destinations. This inevitably means that visitors' air and land travel arrangements are organised by the tour company, hotel or travel agent. In recent years, however, there have been a growing number of tourists who prefer compiling their own itineraries, only leaving accommodation and flight schedules to a travel operator. There is a definite allure to planning your own trip around one of the islands in the south-western Indian Ocean.

Having chosen which island you would most like to visit, the next step is the time-consuming task of contacting the relevant tourist boards. Give yourself at least four weeks from writing the request to receiving the information. All prospective visitors should then get hold of a detailed map of the island. These are usually obtainable from good bookstores, and directly from the tourist authority or embassy. With a copy of this guide at hand, you can now start planning a route, the things to see, places to stay at and things to do.

Chapter 1 offers a broad spectrum of general information that is useful before departure. It is divided into subheadings that include: planning, money, suggested length of visit, health and photography. The islands detailed in this book are discussed in separate parts. Part 1 deals with the beaches and plantations of Mauritius and Rodrigues. Part 2 provides all the necessary information for touring the Indian Ocean's best adventure destination, Réunion.

These parts are split into various chapters. An introduction is followed by facts about the country, with information on its history and government, geography and climate, festivals, holidays and wildlife. Facts for the visitor are arguably the most important to study prior to arrival on the island. They are also, however, the most likely to change. If you find things so different as to affect future visitors, please write to me care of my publisher. This information will be used in updated editions. All letters will be answered.

The section on getting there provides information on international transport to the island of your choice. Remember that as Mauritius and Réunion are so near each other, crossing to another island can be done in a short time, either by aircraft or boat. Getting around is aimed at travellers who prefer finding their own way about. There is detailed information on local transport, hiring vehicles and a list of tours visitors may wish to take. A commentary on the island's capital city then follows. Both Mauritius and Réunion have exciting, vibrant and enchanting capital cities. These chapters offer readers a basic street map and where to find banks, post offices, tourist information and embassies. A section describes a walking tour of the city, using the map supplied.

Once you have gathered as much initial planning information as possible, turn to the specific regions of the island. There is advice on local and tourist accommodation, where to have meals, where to find the best curio shops and the most interesting things to see and do.

Both these islands are magical. To those who are vacillating between a sedate holiday at home or adventure to the Indian Ocean islands, the immortal words of Ibn Battuta (1304-1377), the greatest traveller in the history of the world, should be your guide:

"I would walk with all those who walk. I would not stand still to watch the procession passing by."

1 GENERAL INFORMATION

PLANNING

Although many of the tourists who travel to Mauritius and Réunion do so on fully inclusive tours, recent surveys, by both the Mauritian and Réunionnais tourist boards, indicate that an ever-increasing number prefer the cheaper option of independent travel. Those who prefer the comfort and security of an organised tour can happily leave all the preparing and planning to their travel agent. But for the visitor who wants the freedom of choosing to go where and when he pleases, planning is essential.

The differences between Mauritius and Réunion are astonishing. Mauritius is undoubtedly the place for beach holidays, while Réunion is more suitable for outdoor adventure activities. Both have beaches, though those on Réunion are far from idyllic. Mauritius is a gentle island, with soft-spoken, gracious and friendly people. Réunion's landscape is dramatic and inspiring, its people somewhat reserved, more influenced by Europe and therefore not as spontaneous as the Mauritians. Mauritius has the most developed tourism infrastructure in the Indian Ocean. This translates into one of the best island holidays available. The beaches are lined with tourist hotels, restaurants, water sport facilities and curio shops. Réunion, on the other hand, is geared at visitors who prefer exploring wilderness areas and communing with nature in places of great natural beauty and sparse habitation.

In view of the vast differences between the islands, visitors should carefully consider what they want from their vacation. If you just want to relax, suntan, enjoy good seafood and occasionally raise yourself to see a few sights of particular interest, then Mauritius is definitely for you. However, if you are one of those people who enjoys being busy while on annual vacation, then the mountains, volcano, rivers and forests of Réunion are recommended.

Because Mauritius and Réunion are so close to each other, visitors should consider visiting both, crossing to the other island even for just two to three days. The price differences, however, need to be borne in mind when planning. Mauritius is probably the cheapest island in the region, after Madagascar. Réunion is one of the most expensive holiday destinations in the world. Budget travellers are unlikely to be able to stay longer than a few days. If this is your situation, then simply take a short hop to Mauritius, where your tourist dollars will have as much as six times the value that they had on Réunion. As a brief guide, the following should help:

Mauritius: Low to moderate prices. Well-developed and supported tourism industry. Long white beaches. Friendly people. Extensive water sport facilities. Excellent standard of accommodation, from five-star hotels to palm-frond beach huts. Handicrafts. Tea and sugar estates. Hindu culture and traditions. Delicious cuisine. Wilderness reserves. Rare wildlife. Good public transport network.

Réunion: High prices. Hiking and walking. Adventure sports. Helicopter rides. Active volcano. Rainforests. Mountains and cirques. French food. The island with the most European culture in the Indian Ocean. Deep-sea fishing. Remote mountain villages and culture. Satisfactory high to medium-priced tourist accommodation. People reserved. Predominantly French life style and standard.

Having selected which island to visit, get hold of the relevant map and start planning your route, taking into consideration what you want from the destination. Consult the geography and climate section of this book when deciding at which time of the year to go. If you are only going to Mauritius, the season hardly needs consideration. Réunion is a different matter, though.

Visitors hoping to hike in the isolated regions of Réunion are advised to commence getting themselves fit about two months before departure. The steep hills, humid forests and inclement mountain weather demand a high price in return for the magnificent visual rewards that they offer. Make sure that you have made medical and dental visits no more than five weeks prior to departure. Applications for visas and driving permits need to be made about six weeks before leaving. Get your necessary vaccinations done a minimum of six weeks ahead; this will allow you time to cope with the infection and build up sufficient immunity.

DURATION OF STAY

Tourist industry surveys show that most visitors to Mauritius spend 10-14 days on the island. On Réunion, 10 days is the norm. These statistics are good indicators of what tour operators and travel agents suggest to their clients. Trying to see both islands adequately within this time, however, is really difficult. With the array of sights to see on the islands, visitors should perhaps consider either extending their trip or concentrating on covering one island at a time. Two weeks on each is suggested. By allocating yourself this time, it is quite possible to visit most of the places of tourist interest, plus allowing yourself time to simply relax and soak up the atmosphere of the islands.

Transport to these islands from abroad is costly and going for anything less than 10 days is not economically viable. For independent travellers, it is recommended that you spend at least 18 days on each island. This offers the opportunity to leave the tourist trails and go wandering into the isolated villages and rural districts where the people are still largely unaffected by the trappings of modernisation.

BEHAVIOUR

Your conduct can have a marked effect on how people react to you, and therefore on your enjoyment of your visit. While on Réunion it is legal to swim and suntan topless on all beaches, on Mauritius this is only allowed on beaches in front of tourist-class hotels. At hotels on Mauritius, where the staff is mainly Muslim, going topless should be forgone in deference to their Koranic laws.

Consuming alcohol in public places is permitted, while staggering about drunk beyond the confines of the hotel is likely to have you sleeping it off in the musty cell of some island gaol. Budget travellers are not encouraged on Mauritius or Réunion. As a result, backpackers' behaviour needs to be exemplary. Start off by arriving at the airport in clean, presentable clothes. Ethnic African dress, tribal trinkets and glazed eyes are guaranteed to get all your bags thoroughly searched and a long list of probing questions asked. Even if you are backpacking around the island, keep a set of smart clothes for arrival, departure, government and official encounters and occasional forays into top-class hotels and restaurants for meals and to watch entertainment. It is amazing how much you can get away with by being dressed "correctly".

On both Mauritius and Réunion, independent travellers will run into petty government officials. This is one of the most distasteful parts of travel. For some unknown reason, the island officials, on Réunion in particular, are consistently unpleasant to foreigners – woe betide visitors who cannot speak any French! On Mauritius things are not as bad. Remain calm. Be polite but firm, and things will get done. Threatening to speak to their superior has a negative effect, but saying you will contact the tourist board about poor treatment has a positive influence.

Off the beaches, men should not go around without shirts on, or barefoot. Women must avoid short shorts or see-through clothing in public places – especially on Mauritius, where the strong Hindu culture frowns upon overt displays of exposed skin. Be sensitive to each of the islands' culture. Each is unique, with subtle nuances that are not immediately obvious. Spend the first few days simply watching and learning. You will soon feel comfortable and be able to understand the unwritten rules and codes of island behaviour.

PHOTOGRAPHY

Mauritius and Réunion both offer photographers a veritable feast of photographic possibilities. Before departure, page through a few books that feature island photography. In this way you will have a clearer idea of what to expect and possible slants to pictures. The serious amateur photographer would do well to attend one of the many courses that are offered by adult education centres.

Use a camera that has a built-in flash unit, which can be turned off, and take along a hand-held or horseshoe flash unit. Suggested lenses are: a fast 55 mm lens, normal macro lens, a fast 28 mm wide-angle lens, a fast, short zoom lens of 35-70 mm and a longer zoom of 80-200 mm. Photographers may also consider taking along a 2X tele-extender to double the focal length of tele lenses. (Remember though that this will cause you to lose about two stops in exposure.) Although very few people still use them, a hand-held light meter, which reads daylight and flash, will prove very useful when taking photographs in the intense light of the islands. Add a "bounce" flash unit and PC cord. A collapsible tripod will prove useful when taking photos of floor shows and people. Finally, a padded camera bag or padded day-pack should complete your equipment.

Choosing film is not often a problem for the tourist who just wants to take snapshots. For the visitor hoping to capture more than just the holiday, selecting the film requires consideration. The best colour negative print films available are Kodak Gold and Fujicolor. The big advantage of these films is that you do not have to worry about taking filters along, as colour correction can be done during printing. If you are hoping to sell your pictures, then a colour transparency film must be used. The best colour slide films are: Kodachrome 25 Professional, Kodachrome 64 Professional and Ektachrome 64X Professional.

Due to the concentrated light that photographers encounter on Mauritius and Réunion, you should take along a selection of filters with which to reduce the washed-out appearance of many island photos. A UV clear to pale yellow is recommended for reducing the blue haze that often occurs in the highland areas. Use a 30M magenta filter to produce dramatic sunset effects. For taking effective photos of the beautiful moonlit nights, you will need a 80A deep blue filter. Add a polarising filter to eliminate certain light rays and redirect others. This filter cuts down glare off the sea and darkens an over-bright sunlit sky.

Every person taking a camera to the islands needs to be aware of the damaging effect that sun, sand and humidity have on the equipment. Get yourself a cleaning kit, available from any reputable photographic dealer. To make sure that your equipment does not malfunction at that critical moment, spend a few minutes each evening dusting off and cleaning it. There is no need to carry huge amounts of film or batteries with you. Both the islands have excellent photographic shops that carry most makes of film and camera batteries.

Damage to film by airport X-ray equipment is a concern to photographers. Carry all your film, whether exposed or not, in a hand-held bag. Check in early and get the officials to hand-check the film. There have been reports from Réunion that airport personnel insist that film go through X-ray equipment. In this case, put all your rolls of film into a lead-lined bag. It is also an advantage to get a letter in French stating that you are a photographer (if possible state agency or publication), and requesting that your film and equipment be examined by hand.

HEALTH

The majority of visitors to Mauritius and Réunion will return home sunlanned, healthy and rested. Very few tourists ever get seriously ill. The worst thing that is likely to affect a traveller is an upset stomach – mainly due to the change of diet. Both islands have good medical and hospital facilities. On Réunion, the clinics equal any found in Paris. All visitors must be in possession of a current International Certificate of Vaccination. These are obtainable, free of charge, from your local department of health. Stamped into this booklet are the details of your having received the following injections: yellow fever, cholera, infectious hepatitis, typhoid and tetanus. Smallpox and polio should already have been administered to you as a child. If not, have them done through the department of health.

The yellow fever immunisation is valid for 10 years. For cholera, it is recommended that you have it redone every six months. A booster for the polio vaccine should be done every five years. Although immunisation against typhoid and hepatitis is not essential, it is advisable for all those visitors who are likely to be staying and eating with locals in rural communities.

Visitors who are planning on travelling to other islands of the Indian Ocean should get hold of a copy of *Travellers' Health*, by Richard Dawood, Oxford University Press.

The greatest danger to tourists is the sun. Four types of sun-induced conditions present themselves: sunburn, prickly heat, heat exhaustion and heatstroke.

Sunburn

Expect to get sunburned very quickly. The harsh sunlight causes secondary rays to bounce off the surface of the sea. This means that even when sitting in the shade of a tree you are likely to be reached by the sun's rays. Use a high factor sun cream for the first few days, reducing the factor and finally changing to an oil. Protect your feet, back of the legs and the top of your head. A hat and sunglasses are highly recommended. If riding about on a bicycle or in a boat, lather sun-block cream onto your arms and legs.

Prickly heat

This is caused by perspiration being unable to exit via the pores. It gets trapped beneath the skin and develops into an itchy rash that stings when the blisters pop. Keep yourself cool by taking cold showers, wearing lightweight cotton clothing and covering any open blisters with a zinc or sulphur powder.

Heat exhaustion

This is a common health hazard, especially during the first few days on the island. It is caused by the loss of body salts through perspiration. The first signs are usually a severe headache, apathy and increasingly frequent muscle cramps. Keep your intake of fluids high, but avoid alcohol and soda drinks. Rather consume fruit juice or cold water. Add salt to your meals or take salt tablets.

Heatstroke

This is a serious health problem that could quite easily result in death. Unable to cope with regulating your internal heat, the body's temperature starts to rise. Travellers should be aware of the first signs of heatstroke. Sweating stops, a reddish colour spreads from the head downwards, a migraine headache develops and coordination becomes difficult. When any of these symptoms become obvious, get the patient to a medical facility as quickly as possible.

Apart from the sun, the only other health problems visitors are likely to encounter are diarrhoea and possibly malaria, though malaria is reputedly rare on Mauritius and non-existent on Réunion.

Diarrhoea

This is usually attributable to a change in food and water. Diarrhoea is more of a nuisance than anything else. Keep your liquid intake high, don't eat the spicy Creole food for a few days and stick to bland meals. If the situation persists, or you begin to notice blood in your stools, consult a doctor. Should you find yourself high in the mountains or deep in the forests, resort to using Lomotil until you can reach a doctor.

Malaria

Visitors do not have to worry about malaria on Réunion. On Mauritius, however, even though its department of health claims the island is malaria free, you should avoid the risk and take a course of anti-malaria tablets. Consult your local doctor or clinic on the current anti-malarial programme – these change frequently, as the anopheles mosquito develops rapid immunity. In 1995, the schedule of prevention included the use of chloroquine tablets, to be taken once a week. In addition to this, it may be advisable to take proguanil daily. This programme should start at least 14 days before departure, and continue three weeks after your return.

WHAT TO TAKE

Along the coast, on both Mauritius and Réunion, visitors will find the climate hot and humid throughout the year. Guests at tourist-class accommodation should include at least two changes of evening wear. You need not cart along a ball gown or black-tie outfit, but take something that includes a light jacket and collared shirt or skirt or dress reaching to below the knees. Linen and cotton clothing are the most suitable. Travellers, as opposed to tourists, can get away with shorts, T-shirts and sandals. Take along at least one set of smart clothes for the odd special meal at a fine restaurant or hotel. Hikers and budget travellers should pack all their clothing into soft backpacks. If you are planning on trekking only, then a straightforward internal frame pack is ideal. However, if touring rather than hiking, then rather select a travel-pack, which is a combination of suitcase and backpack. Visitors on an organised tour can get away with suitcases and shoulder bags.

For Mauritius, a suggested list of clothing would look something like this:

one smart set of clothes and dress shoes, a lightweight jerkin, raincoat or umbrella, swimming costume, a pair of denims, two pairs shorts, two T-shirts, a pair of training shoes, a pair of sandals, hat and sunglasses, windcheater.

For those visitors who are venturing up into the cold mountains of Réunion, add to the above list:

one pair light woollen gloves, two pairs socks, sleeping bag, a heavy jersey, adequate wet-weather gear to withstand the cyclonic climate, one pair hiking boots, warm (corduroy) trousers.

In conclusion, remember to pack those little things that never seem necessary at home, but always are when you travel:

multi-function penknife, sewing kit, four small locks and spare keys, length of cloth (such as worn by Comorians and Malagasy) which is big enough to sit on, lie under or wrap yourself up in. Add to this list a washing and toiletries kit, small towel, length of clothesline and pegs, and clothes washing powder.

Part 1

MAURITIUS

2 INTRODUCTION

In the spring of 1897, Mark Twain arrived on Mauritius during his epic journey along the equator. Almost 100 years later, his words of praise for the island have lost none of their relevance. "You gather the idea that Mauritius was made first, and then heaven, and that heaven was copied after Mauritius."

Many of its beauties and sights are not immediately apparent to the casual eye, but, beyond large-scale tourism and industrialisation, the authentic Mauritius patiently awaits discovery. With the most developed tourism industry in the Indian Ocean, Mauritius is beginning to stagger under the sheer numbers of annual visitors, not to mention its huge problem of overpopulation. Despite the hardships, the Mauritian people remain the friendliest of all Indian Ocean islanders. You will not meet them by spending every day on the beach, or at the same hotel. To see the face of the island, visitors must get out into the villages and rural districts. There, you will find gentle people, carrying on in the traditions of their ancestral countries.

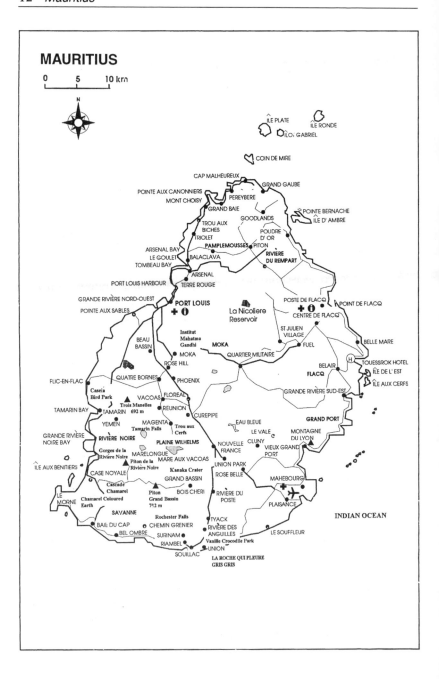

3 FACTS ABOUT THE COUNTRY

HISTORY

From seamen to slaves and pirates to princes, the history of Mauritius is inextricably interwoven with legends and myths. In the latter part of the 10th century, Arab seamen, trading far from their native ports, discovered the island and named it Dinarobin. They were not interested in settling on this remote island in the Indian Ocean. In the wake of the Arabs, the Portuguese arrived in 1511, Domingo Fernandez renaming the island Ilha do Cerne (Swan Island). At that time Swan Island was grouped with the other recently discovered islands of Réunion and Rodrigues. Collectively known as the Mascarenes – in honour of Admiral Don Pedro Mascarenhas – the islands remained uninhabited, being used only as a replenishment stop on the Portuguese trading routes. Soon, Portugal found other, more hospitable islands with ports for her ships and Ilha do Cerne became little more than a name on a navigation chart.

Then, in 1598, Vice Admiral Wybrandt van Warwyck landed on the south-east coast, and promptly claimed the island for the Prince of Orange and the Netherlands. He named the island Maurice – the name of the Prince of Orange. The Portuguese put up no claim to the islands and the change of ownership occurred without opposition. It was another 40 years before the Dutch decided to settle Maurice permanently. They set up base stations for their Dutch East India Company ships, established gardens and started farming sugar cane and tobacco. Their occupation also brought disaster and suffering. The flightless dodo bird disappeared, mercilessly hunted for sport and occasionally for food. Slaves were transported from Africa, many dying at sea or at the hands of cruel plantation owners. Java deer were introduced from the Dutch colonies in Southeast Asia, as were wild boars which hastened the extinction of the dodo by eating its eggs.

By 1710 the Dutch East India Company had lost interest in Maurice, and the settlers began to look to more profitable territories such as Indonesia and the Pacific isles. Meanwhile, the French had settled the nearby actively volcanic island of Réunion. Five years after the Dutch abandoned Maurice, Captain Guillaume Dufresne d'Arsal arrived from Réunion and raised the French flag, renaming the island Île de France.

Once again, the island became a way station, this time for the French East India Company. From about 1721, French immigrants began to arrive and re-established sugar cane and tobacco plantations. Things moved slowly, and it was not until the arrival in 1735 of Governor Bertrand Francois Mahé de Labourdonnais that the settlements began to flourish. He commissioned the building of the first sugar mill, extended the port facilities, established a hospital and commenced work on the island's extensive road network. He left Île de France to go and fight the British in India a few years later. Visitors to Réunion can see a statue of the legendary man near the seafront cannons in St-Denis.

By the late 18th century, the mighty British navy had claimed numerous islands in the Indian Ocean for the English crown. On land, the French had been routed and their failures were quickly exploited by the British. The French East India Company collapsed, and those in its outposts were left to their own devices. Pirates and corsairs arrived to replace the law and order that were once maintained by French troops. Robert Surcouf established himself as buccaneer king and set up court in Port Louis. Soon word spread of the sanctuary to be found on Île de France, and pirates who had been plundering Indian Ocean trading vessels began to use the island as their base. There was still a token administration on the island, but after the revolution in France, the governor was literally thrown out. The pirates had strange principles, often at odds with their bloody careers. It was they who in 1789 set the last of the French-owned slaves free.

By then the British had started taking over the remaining French islands, and, in 1810, they initiated a rather half-hearted attack on the pirate-held island, near present-day Mahébourg, in what became known as the battle of Grand Port. The British were repulsed. This is the only French naval victory to be commemorated on the Arc de Triomphe in Paris. Not a little bemused, the British laid more careful plans for the next attack. Royal Marines landed on the north coast – near Cap Malheureux – and the troops quickly overran the island. The planters and the pirates, who were powerless without their vessels, quickly surrendered. Many were publicly executed, and many French settlers were deported back to France.

The 1814 Treaty of Paris gave Britain, as "spoils of war", Île de France, Rodrigues, and the Seychelles, but returned Réunion to the French. In typically British fashion, they changed the island's name back to Maurice, or Mauritius as the English insisted on calling it. Slaves were reintroduced to work the estates and plantations. Tea, imported from India and southern China, was planted in the cooler highlands and sugar mills sprang up all over the island. Reluctantly obeying colonial orders, planters set their slaves free in 1835. To replace the slaves, thousands of indentured Indians and Chinese arrived to cut cane and work the plantations. Part of their incentive was that they had the option – at the end of the contract – to remain on the island permanently. Given the overpopulation, lack of work and poor living standards in India and China at that time, most of the workers chose to stay on Mauritius. This has led to the large number of Indians still on the island today. They comprise over 70% of the population, and have the largest contingent in government.

A powerful Labour Party was founded in 1936, with most of its members coming from the sugar cane estates. Instigating workers' action, the Labour Party was responsible for labour unrest and strikes in 1937. Led by the capable Dr Seewoosagur Ramgoolam, the party's following grew ever stronger, especially during the turbulent pre-independence era of the 1950s.

Another party, in opposition to the Labour Party, soon appeared on the Mauritian political scene. Known as the Parti Mauricien Social Démocrate (PMSD), this party stood for the minority Europeans and Creoles on Mauritius. With their wealth, tight cliques and ownership of land, the members of the PMSD wielded strong influence in the country. But with a history of oppression, exploitation and elitism, the PMSD remained small and no real threat to the Labour Party, with its vast workers' adherence.

Finally, on 12 March 1968, Great Britain granted Mauritius independence. Dr Seewoosagur Ramgoolam, who had been knighted, was inaugurated as the island's first prime minister. For almost 13 years, he played a wily game of international diplomacy and internal integration that resulted in his ending his term of office with a coalition government that included the PMSD.

From 1982, with Seewoosagur out of contention, two relatively new parties, the leftist Mouvement Militant Mauricien (MMM), led by Paul Bérenger, and the socialist Parti Socialiste Mauricien (PSM), under Aneerood Jugnauth, entered the arena. These two parties combined and came to power in a landslide victory. One of the first things the MMM did was to nationalise the flourishing sugar industry. Estates, factories and nurseries were all gathered under one department in a grand socialist scheme. Trade links with South Africa were severed, and almost immediately a country on the edge of entering the First World crashed.

The economy crumbled and Franco- and English-Mauritian planters and business people clandestinely transferred their fortunes to overseas banks. Mauritius's future looked bleak. The two parties in power could not agree on a suitable remedy, and in a desperate bid to rescue Mauritius, Anerood Jugnauth split from the MMM. Never confident enough in his party's popularity, Jugnauth joined forces with the Labour Party and PMSD.

As expected, this coalition swept to victory in the August 1983 general elections. Jugnauth was appointed prime minister and immediately set about restoring the country's economy. He reopened trade links with South Africa, returned sugar mills to their original owners and allowed limited free enterprise for the sugar, tobacco and tea planters. The political scene in Mauritius seemed peaceful, successful and dynamic. It was not to last.

In 1986, a government-instigated enquiry found several senior government officials implicated in drug trafficking. Suspicion, intrigue and accusation dogged the cabinet until the deputy prime minister, Harish Boodhoo, resigned. Seeing its opportunity, the MMM demanded another election, which was held on 30 August 1987. The MMM, however, misread the islanders' mood, and once again lost to Jugnauth, who remained prime minister.

GOVERNMENT

On 12 March 1992, Mauritius declared itself a republic. However, it did not do what many other post-colonial countries have done: renounce all ties with Great Britain. Mauritius retained her seat in the British Commonwealth and continues to play an active and important role in that organisation. There is a Westminster-based constitution in effect on the island. Political power rests in an elected cabinet, which consists of 21 ministers including the prime minister, who is voted into the position at a general election held every five years. A legislative assembly enacts laws and procedures for the island. There is a speaker, 62 elected members, eight additional members and an attorney general.

GEOGRAPHY

Of volcanic origin, Mauritius is 47 km wide by 58 km long. With almost 160 km of coastline protected by offshore reefs, the island is typical of what geographers call a retrogressing island. Although there are no active volcanoes on Mauritius, the remains of extinct craters can be seen at several locations around the island. Craters that are worth a visit are Grand Bassin, which is now a sacred Hindu lake east of Macchabée forest, Kanaka crater, surrounded by sugar cane, bush and tea estates near Bois Cheri, and the smaller Trou aux Cerfs depression south of Vacoas.

While the coastal areas are flat, with long white beaches, casuarina trees, hot humid weather and lots of sunshine, the inland regions are very different. Tall mountains dominate the southern and south-western reaches, with peaks such as Le Morne, Piton de la Rivière Noire, Pieter Both and Mt du Rempart testimony to the savage fury of the island's fiery birth. Central Mauritius is highland country, with cool temperatures, frequent mist and light rain. The highlands are a good place from which to flee the often oppressive heat of the coast. From the central highlands there is a steady flattening of the countryside to the north and east, until, by the time visitors reach Grand Gaube, the land is flat and prone to flooding. You do not need to be a geographer to appreciate the powerful forces which created this beautiful island.

Mauritius is about 6 000 km west of Australia, 1 400 km east of Africa and 4 000 km south-west of India. Surrounded by the warm waters of the Indian Ocean, Mauritius is 180 km north of the Tropic of Capricorn, within that balmy band of sunshine and coconut glades known as the tropics.

CLIMATE

Without clearly defined wet and dry seasons, Mauritius is a year-round holiday playground. Despite its small size, weather patterns throughout the island are not uniform. Often, in the highlands, travellers will encounter light rain and cool temperatures, while at the same time, on the coast, there will be brilliant sunshine and clear skies. A word needs to be said about what are considered low temperatures on Mauritius. Any temperature below 16 °C is termed cold by the islanders. Even when the yearly cyclones sweep across the island from about mid-December to early April, the air temperature remains high.

Mauritius has at least 12 hours of daylight each day, with an additional hour during the summer months of November-April. February can become unpleasant for visitors from colder climes. Midday temperatures range around 38 °C, and even during the night the thermometer never drops below 25 °C. It is not really the heat that bothers foreigners, but the high humidity. If you find the coastal regions too unpleasant, sleep up in the highland areas, travelling to the beaches which are never more than 30 minutes away. Autumn and spring hardly exist. Mauritians maintain that summer and winter are the only seasons experienced on Mauritius. Winter, which lasts from about May-October, is something of a misnomer by temperate standards. Nothing really changes, except that no cyclones howl across the island and you may require something warm if sleeping in high-lying areas.

Mauritius can be visited throughout the year. Choosing a season to visit hardly needs to be considered. Cyclones, which occur annually in the area, do not cause undue problems and the storms from their passing seldom last more than three to four days. Be warned, however; every 15 or so years, nature lets the Indian Ocean islands know just how small they really are. A cyclonic storm comes tearing across the Indian Ocean, slamming into Mauritius and Réunion. The most recent cyclone of this nature was called "Hollander" and arrived in February 1994.

To avoid any threat of cyclones, or experiencing excessively high temperatures and humidity, visitors should consider July-September for their vacation. The Mauritius Tourist Board can supply interested visitors with climatic information. It is safe to say that visitors will find the island's coast warm all year, with a refreshing coolness in the highlands.

POPULATION

The population of Mauritius is large when compared to the size of the island. At present, there are an estimated 1,2 million people living on the island. Of these, close to 70% are of Indo-Mauritian origin. Minority groups comprise Creoles, of Euro-African extraction, Sino-Mauritians of Asian parentage and the small but exclusive group of Franco-Mauritians, who own most of the large agricultural estates and industry.

On the surface there appears to be a happy polyglot of groups living in harmony. But after just a few days of mixing with the locals, the differences and tensions become quite obvious. The smallest group, the Franco-Mauritians, living a life that has changed little since the days of colonial rule and slavery, have insulated themselves from the harsh reality of island existence in their luxurious surroundings. Most of their wealth is inherited, its origins based on human suffering and exploitation.

The largest ethnic group, the Indo-Mauritians, are the most vocal and politically powerful. Followers of the Hindu faith, their tolerance and assimilation of other life styles are typical of Indian culture. They are jovial, friendly and curious. Most of the contact you make will be with Indo-Mauritians and visitors will find them the most approachable and helpful of all the ethnic groups on Mauritius.

Most of the Sino-Mauritians are shop owners and tradesmen. Imported as indentured labour from China, they quickly grew to the stage where today they have their own suburbs in many of the larger towns. Their main areas of business are in tearooms, cafés, supermarkets and wholesaling. In Port Louis, a magnificent pagoda has been built for the local Buddhists. They keep to themselves, quietly acquiring wealth and property by their investments. The Sino-Mauritians are not as amiable as the Indo-Mauritians, but tourists can expect cordial, if stilted, assistance.

Euro-Mauritians are a rarity – apart from the small clutch of Franco-Mauritians – whom visitors will seldom see. A few English and German families do live on the island, involved mainly in tourism and farming. Of these the best known are the German Kux family at Cap Malheureux, renowned for their tourist accommodation and facilities, and the English Rowntree family in the south, famous for their exquisite colonial home and high grade sugar production.

There are not as many Creoles on Mauritius as there are on nearby Réunion. In the past, as it is today, there was very little cross-culture or cross-colour marriages. The relatively few Creoles occupy the lowest rung of Mauritian society. Their origins are shrouded in sadness, abuse and poverty. Most have French names, testimony to their French colonial and African slave ancestry. If you make an effort to meet and associate with the Mauritian Creoles you are in for a wonderful time. They are blithe and exuberant. Their food is as much French as African. Their all-night parties are legendary, their women beautiful and their hospitality endearing.

CULTURE

With its mixture of Indian, Chinese, African and European cultures, Mauritius has a fascinating blend of traditions, rituals and activities.

Topping the list of cultural activities, and something that every tourist is likely to see at least once, is the traditional sega dance. Many guides and agencies tout the dance as being Creole, but if you have ever seen Africans or Polynesians dancing, it is easy to dismiss any European influence. Certainly, some changes have been enforced over the centuries – mainly by the Christian churches who curbed the sensuality of the original slave dances.

The origins of the sega are vague. Obviously African in its beat and rhythm, there are other strange sequences that have not yet been traced. This can be seen in the Pacific-style hip movements, Southeast Asian hand actions and Middle Eastern shuffle. Whatever its roots, the sega is a feast of colour, sound, hot bodies and infectious handclapping. Normally the only opportunity visitors have of seeing sega dancing is at one of the tourist hotels. These shows are put on weekly, and even though you may not be a guest, it is easy to slip in and watch.

If possible, get someone from one of the secluded beach villages to take you to a sega dance on the beach. These usually occur on hot, humid weekend nights when there is a full moon and summer breezes. Under the palm trees, with drums and a lone guitar, you will see the real sega, memorable, exhausting, seductive and thoroughly intoxicating.

Not many tourists visit Mauritius with the intention of seeing the arts of the island. In some ways this is rather sad, as it not only provides an insight into the history, culture and tradition of the islanders, but also makes for wonderful entertainment. Away from the tourist locations there is a bewildering selection of the arts for the interested visitor.

On Nelson Mandela Place in the capital, you will find the Port Louis theatre. Productions are regularly staged by professional troupes and by talented local groups. Occasionally a foreign act arrives and visitors may then find it difficult to obtain seats. A larger but less ornate theatre complex is located in Rose Hill, south-east of Port Louis. This theatre is not as popular as that in Port Louis and there should be no problem getting tickets to a show.

Art and sculpture are in short supply, which is rather odd considering the visual extravaganza the island offers. Of note is Galerie H De Senneville, a small gallery in Belmont House, Port Louis. Original artworks are difficult to come by, but for the not so fastidious shopper there are numerous prints and lithographs on sale at tourist shops and larger markets. Sculptures are usually of monumental size and displayed in memorial gardens, churches and parks. One of the most attractive and artistically captivating pieces is the statue of the fictitious lovers Paul et Virginie, in the colourful flower garden of Curepipe's municipal building.

Literature has not been especially encouraged on Mauritius. By far the most famous and enduring work is the heart-wrenchingly sad tale of Paul et Virginie. Written by Frenchman Bernadin de St Pierre in 1788, the story is synonymous with Mauritius.

Cinemas are large, air-conditioned, always full and surprisingly comfortable. Movies are inevitably dubbed into French, sometimes Hindi. Although all the latest films can be seen, the Mauritians seem to have a penchant for soft-porn and violent movies.

You could be hard-pressed if you search for traditional music. Recorded cassettes of sega music can be bought at the tourist outlets such as hotels, tour operators and markets. Getting to hear Mauritian music inevitably means that you must get acquainted with locals. Between Pointe de Roches Noires and Pointe Lascars on the north-east coast are remote villages that have regular music gatherings during summer. Traditional instruments are used at these gatherings: rice-filled shakers, hide drums and stringed instruments.

ECONOMY

Mauritius has arguably the most successful economy of all the Indian Ocean islands. Although the economy is predominantly agriculture based, the last 15 years have seen a burgeoning of more diversified products and services. Under British rule, the economy was linked to the fortunes and failures of the British Empire. Today, an independent Mauritius has an inflation rate of less than 7%. Unemployment, too, remains low. Vagrants and beggars are a rarity. An increasing number of foreign companies are investing in Mauritius, notably from South Africa. With exports rapidly increasing, a low national debt and a hard-working population, it may not be long before Mauritius becomes the business powerhouse of the south-western Indian Ocean islands.

Sugar

Sugar has for decades been the island's major export and earner of foreign currency. Most of the land allocated to agriculture has been planted with sugar cane. Being a labour-intensive enterprise – the largest employer of all – has created certain problems for the sugar industry. With the growth of secondary and tertiary industries, people who would in the past have worked the land are now turning to less physically demanding jobs. This has however not deterred the planters, who have rapidly mechanised. Where once people burned, cut and loaded cane, now mechanical grabs hoist and pack bundles onto waiting trucks efficiently and quickly.

It is on the sugar estates that visitors will see the most beautiful houses of Mauritius. Sugar barons still hold deed to these plantation mansions, built during the gracious era of French and British colonisation. It is like stepping back into history when visiting these houses. Of particular beauty and interest are the plantation houses at Goodlands, Bel Air and St Aubin.

There are 20 sugar mills on Mauritius, many owned by the sugar estates. With a high quality sugar, but low total production, sugar production on Mauritius has always been subject to the vagaries of the world market. This uncertainty has led to the establishment of other, less fickle, agricultural undertakings.

Tea

It was the British who first decided to plant tea on Mauritius. They brought tea planters and labour from India, and it was not long before gardens were being planted in the cool, misty environment of the central highlands. Tea production did not stop with the departure of the British, and the Mauritian government has in fact encouraged it since independence. From its small beginnings, tea has become the island's major crop after sugar.

Although grown under conditions similar to those found in the tea-growing areas of southern India and Ceylon, Mauritian tea has never reached the high standards of northern Indian tea. It is however a brisk tea with a bright colour that suits its use as a blending tea. Visits to tea estates and tea factories can be arranged by contacting the Ministry of Agriculture's Tea Board, tel. 454-1091.

Other produce

Following sugar and tea production are a number of crops whose importance is gaining acknowledgement by Mauritian economists. Tobacco, potatoes, tomatoes, maize and fruit have for several years been competing with the traditional crops for export markets. Mauritian agricultural products are finding ready markets during the northern winter.

The infrastructure for these crops is still far behind that of sugar and tea, but a government drive to encourage production of these crops has led to a channelling of funds to this sector. Machinery, factories, sheds, tax incentives and subsidies for these crops may soon see sugar and tea replaced by more consistently profitable crops.

In its rush to reach First World status, Mauritius has made inviting offers to foreign companies to invest in the island. Knitwear, textile, footwear and beachwear light industries have proliferated with foreign investment. Visitors may be surprised to see some of the world's top brand names manufactured on Mauritius. European and South African firms find the low wages, hard-working people and incentive packages offered by the government a boon to their companies. Since the 1980s the clothing industry has surpassed the sugar industry as Mauritius's major export. Recently, Hong Kong and other Southeast Asian countries have begun ploughing millions into the Mauritian textile industry.

A rather strange irony is that although a tropical island, with sunshine, humidity and warm rain, Mauritius is the third largest producer of woollen knitwear in the world. It actually pays companies to import wool for knitwear manufacture. Sadly and inevitably, the increase in secondary and tertiary production has been followed by an obvious and devastating increase in pollution. Textile factories belch acrid black smoke into the once fragrant island air. Rivers that were edged by plants and filled with fish now run sick and empty. The Mauritian government seems to be unconcerned at this loss of natural beauty.

Tourism

Many influential Mauritians believe this will be the industry that saves their beautiful island from the ravages of factories, mills and intensive agriculture.

Tourism is Mauritius's fastest growing industry. A walk along any beach will have visitors at the door of some form of tourist accommodation. International hotel chains are investing in five-star hotels and inns all over the island. Hotel chains represented are the Beachcomber Group, Sun International and Maritim Hotels. It is not only accommodation that boosts the tourist industry. Restaurants, monuments, guided tours, happy, friendly people and an idyllic coastline have made Mauritius a favourite destination on world tourist routes.

Most tourists are from France. Special packages, the strong value of the franc against the rupee and long vacations allow French visitors to enjoy the beaches of Mauritius before crossing to the actively volcanic French island of Réunion. The second most numerous are South Africans. Banned from entering many countries for years, South Africans were forced to visit countries that turned a blind eye to their government's atrocious apartheid policies. Mauritius encouraged South Africans to visit. Even though South Africa's acceptance has now become universal, many South Africans still travel to this beautiful island. Italians, Britons and Germans make up the bulk of the remaining visitors.

Although the government goes out of its way to encourage tourism, the tourist office in Port Louis is not very helpful to, or interested in, tourists who arrive with backpacks. Air Mauritius is even worse, and it will be up to the traveller to find help elsewhere.

Tourism has had many spin-offs. In their enterprising way the Mauritians have exploited tourism's opportunities. Model ship building in particular has done well. With infinite patience and dedication craftsmen build delicate wooden replicas of famous vessels. These include such memorable vessels as the *Bounty*, *HMS Victory* and *Cutty Sark*. In addition, private taxis, buses, guides and touts all vie with one another for tourist dollars.

RELIGION, HOLIDAYS AND FESTIVALS

Without any indigenous people, it has been left to the immigrants to bring their own religions to Mauritius. Hinduism is the most widespread religion, but pagodas, churches, temples and mosques of other religions are also found on the island. There is religious tolerance, and the usual bickering and squabbling among faiths are virtually unheard of. No one seems quite sure why, but the strict discipline and codes of Hinduism, and especially Islam, are a great deal more relaxed on Mauritius than in India and the Arab world. The degrading and archaic caste system has long since been abandoned by the Indo-Mauritians and the demeaning chador of Islam has given way to exposed faces and headscarves.

Quietness and peace are hallmarks in the practice of beliefs. Even the mullah calling the faithful to prayer does so *sotto voce*. Hindu kirtans and bhajans are done with soft joy. Buddhist mantras are chanted with a relaxed and quiet tempo. Christians, too, have their Masses and services – also held in hushed tones.

Father Jacques Laval is the patron saint of Catholic Mauritians. His shrine can be visited at Ste Croix in Port Louis. For the Hindu population, Grand Bassin, dedicated to Lord Shiva, is the holiest place on the island.

With this mixture of the world's great religions, it is not surprising to find an abundance of public holidays and festivities throughout the year.

Hindu festivals are enlightening and certainly worth a visit. For detailed information on where and when the various Hindu and Tamil celebrations take place contact the Union Tamoule de Maurice, Royal Road, Belle Etoile, Coromandel, Beau Bassin, tel. 233-4412. The three main celebrations are:

Thaipoosam Cavadee – late January or early February

This is a public holiday and celebration of honour to the son of Lord Shiva, Subramanya. Commencing with a 10-day fast, devotees pierce themselves with skewers, pins and needles, before carrying a wooden arch decorated with flowers and palm leaves to their temple. It is a time for spiritual cleansing, when followers ask for forgiveness and purification of their souls. One of the requirements is that the milk, which has been placed on the wooden arch, must not have curdled by the time it is placed before the icon in the temple. Although the main cavadee takes place in late January or early February, many smaller cavadees occur at various temples throughout the year.

Maha Shivaratri – late February or early March

Lasting three days, Maha Shivaratri is the most important Hindu celebration held on Mauritius. In honour of Lord Shiva thousands of devotees make the pilgrimage to Grand Bassin lake in the highlands west of Bois Cheri. Here they wash themselves in the cold waters of the holy lake, which is in the crater of a long-extinct volcano. Most pilgrims dress in white and carry offerings on a wooden frame decorated with scented flowers. Known as a *kanvar*, this wooden frame is then presented to the gurus and Swamiji who are the custodians of the sacred lake. All-night vigils are held at temples throughout Mauritius during this time. Pilgrims who walk home from Grand Bassin are fed and honoured in all the villages they pass through. Even though many Western tourists may not understand the rituals and traditions, the commitment and dedication of the pilgrims are unmistakable. Getting transport up to Grand Bassin during this time can be difficult. Buses are full and taxis expensive. However, one can hitchhike to the lake. Hitchhiking from the towns of Vacoas and Curepipe is especially easy.

Teemeedee – late December or early January

This is the famous Hindu fire-walking ceremony. Commencing with a period of fasting, the fire walkers then have a ritual bath to purify themselves in anticipation of what is to come. At temples and ashramas a pit is filled with red-hot coals. Induced into a trance by inhaling incense, fasting and mantras, the devotees then walk slowly across the coals. There is no rush, signs of pain or discomfort. Protected by their faith, the fire walkers remain unburned even when they throw themselves onto the coals and roll about in a frenzy of spiritual ecstasy. No reasonable explanation exists for their immunity to the heat. Tourists can see the fire walking at the Hindu temples at Camp Diable, Vale and Quatre Bornes, where the ceremonies are especially well supported and festive.

Other celebrations

Diwali – the Hindu festival of light. This takes place annually in late October or early November and is marked by a public holiday. It is undoubtedly the most joyous of all Hindu celebrations. Lasting for five days, each day has a significance: day 1 is the start of the business year, day 2 is in honour of Krishna, day 3 honours Lord Shiva, day 4 recognises the lower world devil spirit of Bali. On the night of Diwali all electric lights are switched off and candles are placed in gardens and houses. This symbolises the lighting of the way for the return of Lord Rama from his imprisonment in Lanka. The festivities end with lavish meals that invariably include loads of traditional sweets. Travellers should get to the 100-year-old temple between Triolet and Trou aux Biches for this final night of Diwali. Meals are laid out in the temple grounds and all are welcome to partake and show their respects to the powerful deities.

The Chinese, Muslim and Christian faiths also have their respective festivals and holidays.

At the end of January, the Chinese hold their New Year. On this day the monks adjust the Chinese calendar so that there is a correlation between both solar and lunar days. Homes are scrubbed and decorated in red, the Chinese colour for joy and happiness. Fireworks are lit to ward off evil spirits, and the following day gifts of cakes made from rice flour and honey are exchanged. This is also a public holiday.

The Islamic month of dawn-to-dusk fasting, known as Ramadan, ends with a public holiday and the festival of Id-ul-Fitr. Exactly when this will occur is difficult to calculate because it coincides with the appearance of the new moon in the ninth lunar month of the Muslim calendar.

Christians celebrate Christmas, Easter, All Saints' Day and the Father Jacques Desire Laval Feast Day. Usually falling on 9 September, this ceremony sees Christians streaming to the shrine at Ste Croix, near Port Louis, dedicated to this missionary who not only converted many Mauritians, but was said to have miraculous healing powers.

There are 14 public holidays on Mauritius:
New Year – January 1 and 2
Independence Day – March 12
Labour Day – May 1
All Saints' Day – November 1
Christmas Day – December 25
Republic Day – December 30

Festivals and celebrations that are public holidays but whose dates vary are:
Thaipoosam Cavadee – January or February
Maha Shivaratri – February
Chinese New Year (Spring festival) – January or February
Ougadi – March
Id-ul-Fitr – May or June
Ganesh Chaturthi – September
Diwali – October or November

WILDLIFE

Mauritius is now sadly short of indigenous wildlife. The Dutch, who colonised the island from 1598-1710, are really to blame for the scarcity of land and airborne creatures. However, beneath the surface of the sea and in the realm of plants, visitors will be hard-pressed to find a more abundant and beautiful proliferation of natural splendour.

Flora

It is the plant life that will first grab the attention of visitors. There are well over 1 000 indigenous plant species on Mauritius. Of these 1 000 species, 300 are unique to the island. The most beautiful is the national flower of Mauritius, Boucle d'Oreille (*Trochetia boutoniana*). Among the family of Sterculiacea (trochetias) is the snow-white fragrant blossom of the *Trochetia triflora*. The most common, but no less attractive, member of the family is the black *Trochetia burniana*.

In the drier valleys, visitors will discover the *Hibiscus columnaris* tree with its flamboyant flowers and bright leaves. Another frequently seen family member is the colourful and delicate *Hibiscus boryanus*.

Despite the beauty of the coastal vegetation, it is in the rainforests that travellers will discover the floral treasures of Mauritius. At Pouce mountain and in the Macchabée Forest, you will encounter palms, vacoas, veloutiers and oil trees. No visit to Mauritius is complete without a tour of the world-famous Pamplemousses Gardens. There are over 80 species of palms, including the talipot palm, which flowers only once in 60 years and then dies. Another must is the Curepipe Botanical Gardens, which has the world's only surviving *Hyophorbe amaricaulis*. In the Curepipe Botanical Gardens and the garden reserves of Beau Bassin and Balfour Park, visitors can see rare black ebony trees (*Diospyros hemiteles* and *Pterocalyx*).

Adventurous visitors should, with the help of a guide, search the forests for the elusive and protected *Hibiscus fragilis*. Other species worth seeing are bois natte, makaks, colophane and tambalacoque. The tambalacoque especially should be seen as soon as possible: also known as the dodo tree, it is close to extinction. Legend has it that the seeds from the tree needed to first be digested by the dodo bird before they would germinate.

Filaos and eucalyptus trees are far more prolific than palm trees. Most of the beaches are lined with filaos (casuarina) trees. Occasionally a palm will poke its leafy branches out over a bay, but few grow in the wild. Indian banyans are very much in evidence. Their long roots hang like grey curtains, providing shade from the fierce tropical heat of the coastal regions. Bright red flamboyants compete with the plastic-like anthuriums. Flowers, blossoms and trees are as much part of the island as the reefs, lagoons and green hills.

Marine life

Although not as profuse as the marine life found around other Indian Ocean islands, life beneath the surface of the seas around Mauritius is definitely worth seeing. As spear-fishing is illegal, divers and snorkellers are able to get really close to fish that would otherwise have been killed off.

Created from a multitude of minuscule sea creatures, coral reefs surround most of Mauritius. Coral gardens are festooned with plant life and reef fishes. Multi-hued sponges, colourful anemones and fragile fan worms provide an amazing spectacle for those visitors who venture underwater. Technicolour parrotfish live in peaceful harmony with thick-lipped groupers and wrasse. Angelfish and squirrelfish lend grace to the drift currents, while box fish and trumpet fish are a puzzle to all with even the slightest interest in natural history. But be warned, along with comical clown fish and tiger fish, there are also dangerous species such as lion fish and stone fish in this undersea paradise.

Beyond the protective wall of coral, predatory sharks cruise the blue water in search of food. Blue, mako, hammerhead, black and white-tip sharks are common. Rarer, but far more impressive, is the lone great white shark. It is in the deep water that visitors will have the opportunity of seeing marlin and sailfish. These majestic creatures, the fastest in the oceans, are rapidly dwindling in numbers, victims of man's quest for dominance over everything.

An aquarium has been built within sight of the sea at Trou aux Biches. Stocked with over 200 fish species and operating on an open sea water principle, the aquarium is a must for visitors. Contact it for further details: Aquarium Centre, Coast Road, Trou aux Biches, Mauritius, tel. 261-6187.

Fauna

Visitors interested in getting detailed information about Mauritian wildlife, game guides and programmes should contact the Mauritius Wildlife Appeal Fund before arrival on the island: Mauritius Wildlife Appeal Fund, Royal Road, Black River, Mauritius, tel. 686-6331. Not only is this organisation responsible for captive breeding programmes of such endangered species as the Mauritian kestrel and echo parakeet, but it also plays the most significant role in the protection of the island's dwindling wildlife stocks.

Mauritius's defenceless wildlife has been decimated by a long line of settlers, visitors and introduced species. Arab seamen brought rats, Portuguese explorers introduced the mongoose, while the French were to bring an ornithologist's nightmare, cats, but it is at the feet of the Dutch colonisers that most of the blame must rest. They hunted the dodo and flightless parrot to extinction in an orgy of killing. Introducing Java deer and wild boar, the Dutch speeded up the destruction of this delicately balanced ecosystem.

Today, visitors may have considerable trouble even getting to see indigenous Mauritian wildlife. As an introduction, however, read Gerald Durrell's book, *Golden bats and pink pigeons* (Collins, 1977). Java deer and wild boar are hunted by the gentry on their private reserves from May to August. One private reserve that you may be able to visit outside the hunting season is that above Sans Souci falls. (The actual falls are no longer there. Now there is an Italian-built hydro-electric dam.)

Macaque monkeys will sometimes be heard chattering in the small clumps of forest that occur around remote places such as Grand Bassin and in the Macchabée Forest. Fifteen species of reptile inhabit Mauritius. They may be hard to find on your own, but with the assistance of a forestry service guide it becomes a lot easier. Entomologists are in for a treat on the island. Over 2 000 insect species live on Mauritius. Butterflies are the most beautiful living things on the island. Considered by many experts – including Gerald Durrell – to have the most beautiful butterflies in the whole Indian Ocean, Mauritius cannot be fully appreciated without at least one sighting of these little miracles. In the Macchabée Forest and on the forested sides of the Black river gorges, visitors will be able to find literally thousands of butterflies.

The only indigenous animal found on Mauritius is the Mauritius fruit bat (flying fox). This is also on the point of extinction and tourists should quickly try and see this secretive creature before it, too, is gone forever.

Many birds, apart from the endemic species, have proved hardy and wily enough to escape the ravages of hunting, habitat loss and the wildlife trade. At no stage of a Mauritian visit will you be far away from the sounds of birdsong. Ubiquitous Indian mynahs dominate the scene and fairy terns, weavers, paradise flycatchers, cock-of-the-woods and the shy merle cuisnier are all residents.

Mauritius has a human population which is growing at an alarming rate, and the pressure on wildlife preservation and natural habitats is increasing. National parks get smaller, poaching worsens and the small national parks department is hopelessly understaffed. Visitors are urged not to buy any wildlife products from private vendors. Having killed off the giant Mauritian tortoise, unscrupulous islanders have now taken to selling turtle shells to foreigners.

Nature reserves

Nature reserves are a relatively new phenomenon on Mauritius. Most try to survive on paltry subsidies and visitors' entrance fees and donations. Parks that should not be missed include:

Domaine des Grands Bois

Spread over 833 ha in the hills of the south-east coast, near Mahébourg, this is home to the endangered Mauritian kestrel.

Domaine les Pailles

Spread over almost 1 250 ha between Curepipe and Port Louis, this privately owned reserve must be visited. Forests, hills and superb tourist facilities including restaurants and accommodation make this Mauritius's best reserve. With guides, you will be able to see an abundance of birds, monkeys and exotic animals.

Le Val Nature Park

Tucked into the mountains of south-eastern Mauritius, near Cluny on the Plaine Wilhems, this seldom visited park has a plethora of natural wealth. Giant prawns are bred here, as are export grade anthuriums.

Black river gorges, Bel Ombre and Bassin Blanc forests

Southern Mauritius's first national reserve offers hikers and walkers thick tropical vegetation, extinct volcanic craters and a blissful absence of humanity. Scarce in animals, the reserve is beautifully situated.

Macchabée Forest

Between the Black river gorges and the holy Hindu lake at Grand Bassin lies the evergreen Macchabée Forest. Tourists must get permission from the Forestry Service at Curepipe before visiting this eerie reserve. Rare trees, including tambalacoque and black ebony, vie for attention with monkeys, birds, wild boars and occasional Java deer. Trails through the forest are well marked, and although not officially allowed, camping is possible.

Casela Bird Park

Just 10 ha in extent, this sugar estate-owned bird sanctuary insists on keeping the 2 500-odd bird species locked in cages for visitors to ogle at. A zoo has also now added to the sadness of the place.

North-east of the Mauritian mainland are the nature reserve islets of Îlot Bernache and Île d'Ambre. Lying about 550 km east of Mauritius, Rodrigues island has small but incredibly beautiful nature reserves at Anse Quitor and around the mountain peak of Grande Montagne. Still unspoiled by major tourist developers, this island remains wild and attractive. It was once home to hundreds of giant tortoises and another flightless bird, the solitaire, which is also now extinct. Some creatures managed to survive, notably the Rodrigues fody bird (unique to the island) and golden fruit bats which have small colonies around Mount Lubin, north of St Gabriel. Get in touch with the Ministry of Rodrigues for a guide and information on island nature trails: Ministry of Rodrigues, Public Relations Officer, Jenner Street, Port Mathurin, Rodrigues, tel. 831-1590, fax 00095 831-1815.

LANGUAGE

Although English and French are the official languages on Mauritius, visitors are far more likely to hear Creole, Hindi and Urdu spoken. Creole is almost impossible to learn in a short time. Even simple words come out all wrong. It has to do with getting the accent right – which is extremely difficult. An English-Creole phrase book is available at a few bookstores in Port Louis, but unless you are prepared to walk about showing people the sentences each time you need anything it is not a recommended purchase. English is spoken and understood in all tourist centres. Some knowledge of French is recommended for visitors who intend travelling to the more remote villages of the interior. Hindi is understood by over 80% of the population. English speakers should get themselves a French phrase book and it is recommended that you learn a few Hindi sentences as well.

Basic Hindi phrases

Hello	Namaste/Namashkar
Goodbye	Hari Om
Yes	Han
No	Nahin
Thank you	Shukriya
What is your name?	Apka shubh nam?
Where is accommodation?	Turist afis kahan hai?
How far is . . .?	. . . kitne dur hai?
How much?	Kitne paise?
How do I get to . . .?	. . . kojane ke liye kaise jana parega?
Medicine	Dawa
Fruit	Phal
Vegetables	Sabzi
Water	Pani
Tea	Chai
Milk	Dudh
Sugar	Chini
Rice	Chawal

4 FACTS FOR THE VISITOR

VISAS

All visitors must have valid passports when arriving in Mauritius. While visitors from certain countries are required to be in possession of a visa on disembarkation in Mauritius, these need not be purchased prior to arrival. At the customs booths, visitors will be granted a 30-day visa free. Travellers arriving by cruise ship or yacht will be issued a free visa by the customs officer who visits the vessel on berthing.

If you are not required to have a visa, an entry date will merely be stamped in your passport on arrival. Travellers, in particular back-packers, may have to show either an onward ticket or proof of sufficient funds to purchase an air ticket. This can be done by showing a credit card or a letter from your bank at home stating that there are enough funds available in your bank account.

Extensions are seldom necessary, but if visitors intend staying longer than 30 days, this will require a trip to the passport and immigration office. The office is located at police headquarters on Line Barracks Road, Port Louis, tel. 208-1212. Take along two passport-size photographs and your onward air ticket. A few people have been required to provide an affidavit giving reasons why they wish to stay longer on Mauritius. Visitors will then be given a temporary visa while their extension is being processed. Expect your papers returned within about four days.

Tourists arriving from the Comoros, Madagascar, Monaco, Portugal, San Marino and the Vatican are only issued a two-week visa by customs and passport control.

Should you prefer or need a stamped visa, and would rather get it prior to arrival, these can be obtained from Mauritian embassies and high commissions in foreign countries. Allow about 21 days for your visa to be granted.

Australia
Mauritius High Commission, 43 Hampton Circuit, Yarralumla ACT 2600, Canberra.
Tel. 281-1203, fax 282-3235

Belgium
Mauritius Embassy, 68 Rue des Bollandistes, Etterbrek, 1040, Brussels.
Tel. 733-9988, fax 734-4021

Egypt
Mauritius Embassy, 72 Abdel Moneim Riad Street, Agouza, Cairo.
Tel. 346-4659, fax 345-2425

France
Mauritius Embassy, 68 Boulevard de Courcelles, 75017, Paris.
Tel. 422-73019, fax 405-30291

India
Mauritius High Commission, 5 Kautilya Marg, Chanakyapuri, New
Delhi, 110021.
Tel. 301-1112, fax 301-9925

Madagascar
Mauritius Embassy, Ambatoroka, Lot No. VI 2113 (Bis), Antananarivo.
Tel. 32-157, fax 21-939

Malaysia
Mauritius High Commission, 14th Floor, Bangunan Angkasa Raya,
Jalan Ampang, 50450 Kuala Lumpur.
Tel. 243-1992, fax 241-5115

Pakistan
Mauritius Embassy, House No. 27, Street No. 26, Sector F6/2, Islamabad.
Tel. 82-3345, telex 54-362 Mau PK

United Kingdom
Mauritius High Commission, 32-33 Elvaston Place, London SW7.
Tel. 581-0294, fax 823-8437

United States of America
Mauritius Embassy, Suite 134, Van Ness Centre, 4301 Connecticut Avenue, N.W., Washington D.C. 20008.
Tel. 244-1491, fax 966-0983

EMBASSIES AND CONSULATES

The following countries' embassies, consulates and high commissions all have their offices in Rogers House at 5 President John F Kennedy Street in the capital, Port Louis:

Australian High Commission, tel. 208-1700
Austrian Consulate, tel. 208-6801
Embassy of Finland, tel. 208-1286
Italian Consulate, tel. 212-0891
Embassy of Norway, tel. 208-6801
Embassy of the USA, tel. 208-2347

Other diplomatic missions are:

Brazil
Consulate of Brazil, Harel Mallac Building, Port Louis.
Tel. 208-0861

Britain
British High Commission, King George V Avenue, Floreal.
Tel. 686-5795, fax 686-5792

Canada
Embassy of Canada, Blanche Birger and Co., Port Louis.
Tel. 208-0821

China
Embassy of the Peoples' Republic of China, 27 Royal Road, Tombeau Bay.
Tel. 247-2787

Denmark
Danish Embassy, 4 Edith Cavell Street, Port Louis.
Tel. 208-5051

Egypt
Embassy of Egypt, King George Avenue, Floreal.
Tel. 696-5012

France
Embassy of France, St George Street, Port Louis.
Tel. 208-3755

Germany
Honorary Consul of the Federal Republic of Germany, 32 Bis, St George Street, Port Louis.
Tel. 212-4100

India
High Commission of India, 14 Enniskillen Street, Port Louis.
Tel. 208-9896

Netherlands
Embassy of the Netherlands, New Quay Street, Port Louis.
Tel. 208-1241

New Zealand
New Zealand Consulate, Royal Road, Pailles.
Tel. 212-5579

Pakistan
High Commission of Pakistan, 24 Avenue des Hirondelles, Quatre Bornes.
Tel. 425-3740

Portugal
Embassy of Portugal, Harel Mallac Building, Port Louis.
Tel. 208-0861

Russia
Russian Embassy, Queen Mary Avenue, Floreal.
Tel. 696-1545

Seychelles
Seychelles Consulate, 3 Leoville L'Homme Street, Port Louis.
Tel. 208-4927

CUSTOMS

The importation of alcohol, tobacco and perfumes is only permitted for visitors over the age of 16. The quantities allowed are: 250 g of tobacco, 2 ℓ of beer, 2 ℓ of wine, 750 ml of spirits, 500 ml of eau de toilette and 100 ml of perfume.

Visitors are required to clear customs at either the airport or harbour. Yachtsmen must wait in the "roads" for a customs official to first visit the boat and clear her for entry to the international berthing port. Should you require a customs clearance for goods, go directly to the customs enquiries counter, with the goods, in the IKS Building, Farquhar Street, Port Louis, tel. 240-9702.

It is expressly forbidden for any foreigner to bring any plant or soil material into Mauritius without declaring it. This applies especially to sugar cane, any parts of which will immediately be confiscated and a hefty fine imposed. Other vegetation, such as bulbs, flowers, fruit and vegetables, must be accompanied by a permit from the Ministry of Agriculture, Fisheries and Natural Resources in Reduit. Write to the Ministry of Agriculture, Documentation Centre, Reduit, tel. 454-1018. Even with a permit, it is quite likely that the plant material will be taken for examination to the unit at Mer Rouge, Port Louis.

Pets and animals also need an import permit before being allowed entry to the country. This will not be issued without the owner first mailing a copy of an Export Health Certificate from his own country's Department of Agriculture. This export certificate will then need to be presented upon arrival in Mauritius. Unless you are immigrating to Mauritius, it is rather pointless taking your dog or cat along. The animal will immediately be removed and placed in quarantine for six months. If coming from Africa, expect a quarantine period of eight months.

Firearms and explosives are obviously not allowed, and will be confiscated by customs even if declared. If undeclared, the punishment for smuggling in a weapon is a 10 to 25 year prison sentence.

MONEY

Known as the Mauritian rupee (Rs), the currency is divided into 100 cents. There are notes in denominations of Rs1 000, Rs500, Rs200, Rs100, Rs50, Rs20, Rs10 and Rs5. Coins come in Rs5, Rs1, 50 cents, 25 cents, 20 cents, 10 cents and 5 cents.

Bank exchange rates are strictly controlled by the government, so that there are no differences between banks. Handling charges are a standard 10%. Cashing traveller's cheques or hard currency at hotels is however expensive. They usually have a lower exchange rate and a higher handling fee.

Credit cards are widely accepted at shops and tourist establishments. Many tourists pay all their accommodation and meal bills by credit card. Visitors venturing inland should note that it is almost impossible to use a credit card or cheque in the rural areas. Traveller's cheques have the highest return with the lowest charges, while personal cheques are the most expensive and difficult to cash. Eurocheques and Eurocard especially are not readily accepted.

Although visitors can bring in as much foreign currency as they like, no more than Rs700 cash may be brought in and not more than Rs350 taken out.

Not all credit cards are accepted on Mauritius. Diners Club, Mastercard, Visa and American Express are accepted. Visitors may draw cash with their credit cards.

Mastercard can be used at all branches of the Mauritius Commercial Bank. The most efficient branch is on Sir William Newton Street in Port Louis. Visa is accepted at Barclays Bank in the same street. At the main branch of the State Commercial Bank in the treasury building on Sir William Newton Street, travellers can draw cash with American Express and Diners Club cards. Some of the smaller State Commercial Bank branches are reluctant to give cash on a credit card.

There is a thriving black market for currency in downtown Port Louis around the market. It is illegal, although the penalties seem mild.

Crime is not a problem in Mauritius and it is quite safe to have merely a wallet in which to carry your money around, but if wandering through the bazaar in the capital, it is advisable that visitors keep their money in money-pouches or deep pockets.

COSTS

Mauritius is one of the cheapest places to visit in the Indian Ocean, but how long it will remain like this is uncertain. Making an accurate forecast of what it will cost to visit the island is difficult, as each traveller will have different needs. Some kind of budget should be prepared before leaving, though.

Most visitors arrive with tour groups and are bound by the hotels booked through the operator. It is far cheaper, not to mention more exciting, to find your own accommodation and meals. To keep costs down, travellers should visit the smaller villages along the coast and inland. Here you will find cheap accommodation with families, eat at local cafés and have the opportunity to buy curios a great deal cheaper than in towns.

Young, budget-conscious visitors should use the frequent and cheap public bus service that covers virtually the entire island. Eat at cafés and village restaurants, but do treat yourself to at least one lavish meal per week during your visit.

Those arriving from the other Indian Ocean islands, with the exception of Madagascar, will be pleasantly surprised by the low costs on Mauritius. If island-hopping, take advantage of these prices to replenish reserves and pamper yourself.

TIPPING

Once unheard of in Mauritius, tipping is becoming accepted practice. Despite a government surcharge of 10% on tourist bills, a tip of 15% of the bill is common. Salaries are abominable in Mauritius and each rupee is gratefully received. If staying at one hotel for a long period, it is amazing the personal attention visitors can get by judicious tipping on arrival. Porters are not normally tipped. Their knowledge of local affairs is staggering and tipping the porter will gain you a wealth of information.

Begging is not uncommon, particularly around Port Louis. To discourage such behaviour, visitors should refrain from giving money, and rather give an item of clothing or food. In the rural areas beggars are unknown, but with the population explosion it will not be long before this changes.

TOURIST INFORMATION

Getting accurate tourist information about Mauritius is difficult. Even at the main office of the Mauritius Government Tourist Office, in the Emmanuel Anquetil Building, Sir Seewoosagur Ramgoolam Street, Port Louis, tel. 201-1703, fax 212-5142, visitors will be disappointed. The staff are unhelpful and often rude and unless you are part of a well-heeled tour, do not expect much in the way of brochures, maps or pamphlets. Instead of writing directly to the headquarters, get information from overseas branches. There are several of these; they are usually helpful and prepared to send prospective travellers detailed information.

Australia
Mauritius Tourist Information Bureau, 313 Abernathy Road, Belmont 6104, Perth.
Tel. 479-4283, fax 479-4322.

France
Bureau d'information de l'Île Maurice, 41 Rue Ybry, 92200 Neuilly
Cedex, Paris.
Tel. 464-03747, fax 464-01123.

Germany
Mauritius Informationsburo, Goethestrasse 22, 6000 Frankfurt/M1.
Tel. 28-4348, fax 29-3362.

Switzerland
Mauritius Tourist Information Service, Kirchenweg 5, CH-8032 Zurich.
Tel. 383-8788, fax 383-5124.

United Kingdom
Mauritius Government Tourist Office, 32-33 Elvaston Place, London
SW7 5NW.
Tel. 584-3666, fax 225-1135.

United States of America
Mauritius Tourist Information Service, 15 Penn Plaza, 415 7th Avenue,
New York, NY 10001.
Tel. 239-8367, fax 695-3018.

Apart from these tourist offices, visitors can also obtain a wealth of
information by contacting local tour operators or travel agents. Those
in Germany, Italy, South Africa and Great Britain are especially helpful.
If not living in one of these countries, visitors are advised to write for
information to either Beachcomber Tours, PO Box 1633, Bedfordview,
2008, South Africa, tel. (011) 455-1018, fax (011) 455-2818, or Club
Med, La Pointe aux Canonniers, Grand Baie, Mauritius, tel. (230) 263-
8610, fax (230) 263-8617.

Air Mauritius occasionally puts out a booklet that includes small maps
of Mauritius, Port Louis, Curepipe and Grand Baie, entitled *What's on
in Mauritius,* but do not expect staff to send you a copy. You can pick
up a free issue from its enquiries counter: Air Mauritius, Rogers House,
5 President John F Kennedy Street, Port Louis.

POST OFFICE

Virtually every settlement has a post office. Visitors will find the Mauritian postal service efficient, reliable and fast. Counters are always well
staffed by helpful and friendly personnel. Dependable poste restante

mail can be received at any of the urban centres. The poste restante at the main post office along Quay Street, in Port Louis, tel. 208-2851, has a good reputation among travellers and can be recommended. Here, letters are filed, according to the first letter of the surname, where they are held for about 27 days before being returned to the sender.

All post offices have the same working hours: Monday to Friday 8h00-11h15 and 12h00-16h00; Saturday 8h00-11h45.

One of the great attractions of the Mauritian postal service is its ability to design the most spectacular and sometimes faulty stamps. One of the most sought-after and valuable stamps in the world is the 1848 Mauritian Blue Pence. Emblazoned with a bust of Queen Victoria, the stamp is printed with the inscription, "Post Office" instead of "Post Paid". Colourful stamps depict Mauritian wildlife, notably birds.

TELECOMMUNICATION

The international dialling code for Mauritius is 230, which must be preceded by your own country's access code.

Mauritius's telecommunications system is quite simply exasperating. Although an automatic network has been built, it is still prone to numerous "tugs" (could this be "bugs"?), as explained to me by the company's PRO. Still, once connected, the lines are clear and tariffs cheap. If you want to make an international call at a village post office, reserve a line to your destination. In Port Louis, linkups are instantaneous anywhere in the world. When the cyclone season arrives it is impossible to make calls other than from a large urban centre such as Grand Baie. Both local and international calls from Mauritius have the cheapest rates in the south-western Indian Ocean.

Cellular phones are reaching Mauritius. At top-class hotels such as the Royal Palm and Meridien Paradis, visitors will soon be able to use satellite communications from the concierge's desk.

To send a telegram or telex, you will need to go to the offices of the Overseas Telecommunication Services (OTS). There are three branches, with one 24-hour service:

Rogers House, President John F Kennedy Street, Port Louis, tel. 208-1036

PCL Building, 43 Sir William Newton Street, Port Louis, tel. 208-0221

24-hour Overseas Telecommunication Service, Cassis, tel. 208-0221

TIME

Mauritius is four hours ahead of Greenwich Mean Time. It is two hours ahead of South African time, while most European arrivals must add three hours.

ELECTRICITY

With a 220 volt electrical grid, Mauritius could prove problematic for some American and European visitors. Take along a small multi-voltage AC adaptor, plus a three- and two-pin double adaptor.

Most larger settlements have street lights, but once into the remote areas of southern Mauritius, travellers who wander about at night must have a torch. On moonless nights it can be difficult finding your way back to the hotel.

BUSINESS HOURS

Government offices
Monday to Friday 9h00-16h00 (except in Port Louis where administrative offices close at 17h00); Saturday 9h00-12h00

Commercial offices
Monday to Friday 8h30-16h30; Saturday 9h00-12h00

Banking institutions
Monday to Friday 9h30-14h30; Saturday 9h30-11h30

Shops
Monday to Wednesday, Friday and Saturday 9h00-18h00; Thursday and Sunday 9h00-12h00

Informal sector and markets
Monday to Saturday 6h00-18h00; Sunday 6h00-12h00

MEDIA

Mauritius's media cater well for the population, which has a high rate of literacy. The *Mauritian Times* is published once a week in English. The two dailies, although printed mainly in French, do include several news items in English. *L'Express* is sold in the morning, from about 7h00, and *Le Mauricien* from 16h00.

Visitors interested in politics and controversial subjects should buy a copy of the weekly tabloid, *Le Defi*. This is full of satire, debates and pointed arguments designed to make readers think and question the policies of their government. It is in French, with the odd advert or snippet in English.

Local magazines are in short supply. The two worth getting, provided your French is fluent enough, are *Le Nouveau* and *Les Gazette des Îles*. These magazines are costly and not really of any great interest to holiday-makers.

Foreign magazines are in plentiful supply, especially those from South Africa, France and Australia. International newspapers, such as the *Sunday Times*, are delivered in the week of publication.

Visual media are in the hands of the state-controlled Mauritian Broadcasting Corporation. The number of television channels is limited, as are programmes. News, however, is accurate and up to date. Television signals from Réunion can easily be picked up by Mauritian viewers. Réunion television – RFO – is in French, with a broad spectrum of programmes and current events.

Radio is the media of the masses on Mauritius. Even the poorest of families has a radio, which is faithfully tuned to news programmes. Most of the radio programmes are in French, English and Hindi. They include religious topics, sports, some light music and detailed news reports.

ACCOMMODATION

Although catering primarily for tour groups and tourists to luxury hotels, Mauritius does offer budget travellers a fairly good selection of cheap accommodation. From the grace of the Royal Palm Hotel, through the friendly ambience of the PLM Azure, to the functional rooms at Kuxville, visitors will find a bewildering array of accommodation. And these are just the registered establishments. By enquiring at cafés, for example, you will be able to locate either an apartment for rent or lodgings with a local family.

In top-class hotels, visitors must expect to pay high prices. Even for a single room, rates seldom drop below Rs1 000. Service is however exceptional. Guests' every whim is catered to, meals are lavish and so many activities are offered that residents seldom need to leave the grounds of the hotel. These activities include water sports. There is a huge difference in price between high and middle-class accommodation, the range in which most visitors to Mauritius stay. In budget and family accommodation, tourists are offered no entertainment and recreation facilities, and usually also have to provide their own food. This keeps overall costs down and gives visitors the opportunity of eating in local canteens and cafés.

With its balmy warm weather, Mauritius does not have high and low seasons. Accommodation establishments are busy throughout the year, and visitors are advised to book with most places at least 30 days in advance. In its information guide booklet, the Mauritian government tourist office has a list of what it considers suitable accommodation at hotels, plus the contact telephone numbers. The sections are divided into hotels on the beach and in town. In the Air Mauritius *What's on in Mauritius* there is also a short list of tourist-class accommodation in hotels with more than 30 rooms. Travellers to Mauritius should be aware that a 10% government tax is added to all tourist accommodation and restaurant bills.

Hotels and other accommodation located on the beaches are the most expensive, but the best. Away from the beach, prices start to drop progressively, with the cheapest hotels in towns like Curepipe and Quatre Borne. There is no need to worry if you cannot find or afford a beach hotel, non-residents are allowed to use the beaches of even the most expensive and exclusive hotels.

Reasonably priced accommodation can usually be found in the larger urban areas such as Port Louis, Grand Baie, Mahébourg, Quatre Bornes and Curepipe. Those planning to stay longer than 30 days should consider renting an apartment. These are always cheaper than hotels and apart from being furnished, have cooking facilities. Numerous families also offer a room to visitors. Trying to find these can be frustrating. Travellers should contact the local café or speak to hotel staff – cleaning staff are most likely to be helpful in this regard.

Travellers used to visiting and camping are going to be disappointed on Mauritius. There are no designated campsites, so you will have to make your own arrangements. Beaches are open to everyone and make for unique pitches. Inland, approach an estate house and ask the manager for permission to camp somewhere on the grounds. Most of the planters are friendly and will often invite you in for a meal and to wash.

Examples of accommodation for each grade of traveller, depending on budget, and offering excellent service and facilities, are listed below. (For addresses and telephone or fax numbers look under the relevant sections in this book.)

Top: Royal Palm, St Géran, Meridien Paradis and Maritim
Middle: PLM Azur, Club Med, Belle Mare Plage, Meridien Brabant
Bottom: Kuxville, Gold Crest and Continental

If you want to hire an apartment for your stay, contact either of the two agencies listed below at least 60 days before arrival:

Express Estate Agency, 44 St Paul Avenue, Vacoas, tel. 686-6653
Beprim Ltee, 32 Bis, St George Street, Port Louis, tel. 212-7333

The Association des Hôteliers et Restaurateurs Île Maurice publishes a detailed annual listing of tourist hotels on Mauritius. You can obtain a copy prior to arrival by contacting the association at Royal Road, Grand Baie, Mauritius, tel. 263-8971, fax 263-7907.

FOOD AND PLACES TO EAT

With a population mostly of Indian origin, it is hardly surprising that curry features prominently. So does fish – from the island's bounteous natural larder, the sea. Tourist restaurants can be found at all hotels. Grand Baie in particular has a good selection.

In urban centres, restaurants are usually owned by Chinese or Arab traders. The menus always have at least one curry and Creole dish. European cooking is a favourite at hotel restaurants, and guests will have to go out for traditional food.

To really experience Mauritian Creole meals, visitors should head for the inland villages and the backstreet cafés. Here you will find the food eaten in the homes of locals: sticky rice, curried vegetables and fish. Of course, they add their own spices of chili, tumeric and masala. The meals are filling, cheap and very tasty.

Dinner and breakfast are usually included in hotel rates. They are both normally a buffet, with a staggering selection of English choices for breakfast. Lunch is a light affair, with the locals eating snacks, which are sold on the streets. Even the smallest rural village will have at least one snack vendor. The samosas are delicious, and a roti filled with spicy vegetables makes for a wonderful snack as you wander about exploring.

American-style fast-food outlets are springing up at an alarming rate. Hamburgers, hotdogs and fried chicken are a regular feature at beachside takeaways. Prices are high and the food not that good when compared with Creole-style cooking. Kentucky Fried Chicken is popular and is at present scouting locations for several new branches around the island.

Vegetarians will enjoy Mauritius. Because of the predominance of Hinduism, the eating of meat in general, and beef in particular, is frowned upon. Mauritius has a subtropical to tropical climate, and farmers produce excellent crops. Fruit is plentiful. All settlements have a fresh produce market. The largest is located in Port Louis, and should not be missed. Prices vary from market to market, and as few visitors are used to bargaining, get a local to help you negotiate the price.

DRINK

Although you will be told that it is safe to drink the water on Mauritius, foreigners may experience stomach problems if they do. Bottled water is available at all cafés and is a safer choice. You will get thirsty on Mauritius. High temperatures and humidity mean that tourists usually perspire considerably more than they normally do. Drink lots of fluid, especially when walking about in the midday heat.

Cold drinks, while quenching the thirst, only do so for a short while. If you must drink a fizzy liquid, try ice-cold soda water. Fruit juice is popular. Local and imported brands are sold. As the majority of hotel rooms and guesthouses have a fridge, it is worthwhile stocking up with your own drinks. Not only is this much cheaper, but it also offers you a wider selection.

Tea and coffee are grown on Mauritius. You will see the coffee estates around Chamarel and the Seven Coloured Earths. Coffee is cheaper than tea and of a high export quality. The central highlands of the island are used for growing tea of Chinese origin. The tea is not of high quality, but the flavoured teas are tasty. Vanilla tea is refreshing and unusual to most Western palates. You can buy tea from the factories or any of the supermarkets around Mauritius. The supermarket at the Salaffa shopping centre in Curepipe has a wide selection.

Mauritius is famed for its rum. Green Island rum is exported all over the world and has won numerous awards at international fairs. It can be bought in food shops, supermarkets and the duty-free shops of Port Louis and the airport. Home-brewed rum can also be found. Along the northwest and southern coasts, the sugar plantation workers make a potent brew to their own traditional recipe. It is strong: around 84% proof.

Beer made in Mauritius is tasty and refreshing. Phoenix is the most popular brand. Other brands, several imported, are available at hotels and restaurants. Guinness is made on the island under licence.

At top-class hotels visitors will find the usual range of cocktails, spirits and wines. Imported spirits are expensive, but South Africa wines are relatively cheap.

BOOKS

Large-format books about Mauritius are a delight. *Mauritius from the air* by Guido Alberto Rossi is a must.

Scuba divers should consider the following books: *Underwater Mauritius* (AJ Venter, available at bookshops on the island); *Smiths' sea fishes* (Margaret Smith, Southern, South Africa); *Underwater guide to the coral fishes of the Indian Ocean* (Brent Addison, Southern, South Africa). The last book is out of print but may be available in bookshops on the island.

If venturing the 563 km north-east to the island of Rodrigues, make certain you get hold of *The island of Rodrigues* (Alfred North-Coombes, Mauritian Advertising Bureau, Port Louis, Mauritius, 1971).

The most famous novel about the south-western Indian Ocean is the story of two lovers. *Paul et Virginie,* first published in French by Bernardin de St Pierre in 1788, is based loosely on the tragic events during the sinking of the *St Géran* off Île d'Ambre in 1744. The novel, whose characters are featured in sculptures, paintings, on liqueur bottles and menus, has now been translated into English and can be bought from the airport shop and bookshops in Port Louis or Curepipe.

Try the bookshops at:

Librairie Allot Limitee, Arcades Currimjee, Curepipe, tel. 676-1253
Librairie le Chandelier, Royal Road, Curepipe, tel. 676-1338
Librairie du Trefle, 5 Royal Street, Port Louis, tel. 212-1106
Librairie Bourbon, 28 Bourbon Street, Port Louis, tel. 212-1467

MAPS

Mauritius has a confusing number of roads. A map is therefore essential for visitors who plan to travel about the island. Numerous small maps are presented in brochures given to visitors, but are also full of errors. Of these free maps, the one offered by the Belle Mare Plage Hotel is the most accurate. It does not, however, include district roads or points of interest. If you are keeping to the main roads around the island then this is possibly the most suitable map. You can get a copy by asking at the hotel's reception desk – you need not be a guest.

The Tourist Road Map of Mauritius is not too bad. It can be bought from any Store 2 000 and a few petrol stations. At the Mauritius Government Tourist Office, visitors will find a booklet containing a map of Mauritius that indicates all major tourist hotels and has a detailed insert of Port Louis. Air Mauritius puts out maps of Curepipe, Grand Baie, Port Louis and Mauritius.

Topographical maps are hard to find, but I was able to obtain one by contacting the Ministry of Housing, Lands and Town and Country Planning: Lands and Planning Division, SILWF Building, Edith Cavell Street, Port Louis, tel. 208-2831. The Ministry of Agriculture, Fisheries and Natural Resources apparently also has a supply of detailed maps that may be photocopied at Government House in Port Louis, tel. 201-1552.

Mauritius is a small island. Finding your way again after getting lost is seldom a problem. Bus drivers are friendly and helpful. Villagers will go out of their way to assist you in finding the route back to your accommodation or some local point of interest. There is no need for expert guides. Armed with a few phrases and a fairly accurate map, visitors will discover that Mauritius is well planned and easy to get around on.

THINGS TO BUY

Mauritius is a shopper's paradise. Prices are usually low, there is an amazing selection and quality is high. In the tourist resorts visitors will find boutiques, which although normally duty free, sell goods that are extremely overpriced. Rather browse through the markets and arcades that are located in all urban areas.

In the busy market of Port Louis, the bazaar is divided into specific sections, making it easy to find your choice. Avoid shopping at boutiques in Grand Baie or around Mahébourg. Wait until you have gone into the interior or along the remote coastal areas. In the villages of southern Mauritius, travellers will find locals crafting baskets, handmade quilts and exquisite furniture.

Clothing and textiles are big business on Mauritius. Some international designers and fabric corporations have factories on Mauritius, as labour is cheap and costs low. This has kept prices down as well. Shoppers can find excellent quality T-shirts, lengths of hand-woven fabric and Indian-print dresses. The markets usually sell designer-labelled clothing. Bargaining is expected, except on Port Louis' famed La Corderie Street, the 5th Avenue of Port Louis.

Flowers have been grown for decades in the mild climate of Mauritius. Anthuriums are the most popular, and you will see them in displays at all hotels. The government has set up flower farms for the production of export quality flowers. Departing visitors will receive their flowers at the airport, complete with an export and health clearance certificate. Smuggling seeds or plants out of the country is forbidden.

Pottery and leatherwork are prolific. Using imported leather, craftsmen design, cut and tool stylish shoes, jackets and accessories. Potters, using local clay, create beautiful ceramic works of art and practical items. These are on sale at weekly village markets.

Two things that create attention are shells and model ships. There are an estimated 1 212 shelled species in the seas around Mauritius. The colours range from bright pink and luminous green through a rainbow of shades and hues to pastel blue and snow white. With the government's passing of environmental laws, shells are now protected. Visitors can still buy them with clearance certificates, but it is illegal to just pick shells up off the beach and sneak them home. The largest collection of shells for sale is at L'Argonaute Souvenir Shop at 3 Sir William Newton Street, Port Louis, tel. 208-6597.

For anyone who has dreamed of pirates, tall ships and adventure, there is the chance to buy a model of a famous sailing vessel, built by hand in wood. Mauritius has, undoubtedly, the best model-ship builders in the world. Prices seem high, but when compared with the amount of work that goes into even the smallest of vessels, they are reasonable. The fragile model will be carefully packed for transportation, or if you prefer, the shops willingly arrange to pack and post the model. Make an effort to see at least one workshop while on Mauritius. Working only from plans, with no pre-cut kits, the modellers work for months on one project. You can arrange for the manager of Les Maquettes P Bauwens to take you to the factory: Les Galeries P Bauwens, Pointe aux Canonniers, tel. 263-8117.

The most comprehensive selection of curios under one roof can be found at La Maison Creole Eureka on Montagne Ory in Moka settlement. It has a museum and handicraft centre that sells most Mauritian items. Prices are fixed, but well below those demanded in Port Louis, Curepipe or Mahébourg boutiques. It is not always open and should be contacted, to find out the next few days' schedule, on tel. 433-4951.

Other good selections can be found at: Quatre Cocos Handicraft Centre, Quatre Cocos; Women Self Help Boutique, Royal Road, Curepipe; Mauritius Alliance of Women, St Jean Road, Quatre Bornes, and Handicraft Boutique, Company Gardens, Port Louis.

THINGS TO DO

The majority of tourists to Mauritius go for a beach holiday. However, hotels do arrange sightseeing tours and shopping visits for guests. They put on discos and galas and offer a variety of water sports. Non-motorised water sports are usually free to guests. Hotels that do not provide water sports normally arrange for their guests to use the nearest facilities.

Water sports enthusiasts are catered for by windsurfers (some hotels supply free tuition), Laser dinghies, pedalos, Hobie-cats and canoes. Waterskiing is also offered gratis by certain hotels, e.g. the PLM Azur and Club Med. Snorkelling equipment is available, and usually requires a refundable deposit from the user.

Motorised water activities include scuba diving, parasailing and deep-sea fishing. An estimated 17 diving schools are located on Mauritius. They run courses from beginner to divemaster, and visit exciting scuba locations. The most professional and experienced diving centres are: Islandive, Veranda Bungalow Village, Grand Baie, tel. 263-8015; Sinbad Diving, Kuxville, Cap Malheureux, tel. 262-8836; Maritim Diving Centre, Maritim Hotel, Balaclava, tel. 261-5600, fax 261-5670.

Parasailing is great fun. There is no guarantee that you will not get addicted and spend your days suspended above the translucent waters of the Mauritian seascape. The larger hotels offer this expensive activity. Paragliding lessons (over land) can be taken at Vieux Grand Port, tel. 631-9261.

Game fishing is popular. Boats, rods and tackle can be hired by visitors. Majestic blue marlin, sleek sharks, beautiful yellow-fin tuna and graceful sailfish all swim in the warm waters around Mauritius. Each year, international fishing competitions have people flocking to cast their deadly lures into the sea. October to March sees the arrival of fishermen in search of marlin, while March to May sees the yellow-fin tuna running. A halfhearted attempt to enforce a "tag-n-release" programme is now left to the discretion of the skipper, as slowly but steadily, the large fish, once so copious here, dwindle. Fishing boats can be chartered through most big hotels, which charge a handling fee. Tourists may contact Big Game Fishing, Grand Baie, tel. 423-9627, fax 208-8103, who provide all food and beverages for a minimum six hour charter, or Beachcomber Fishing Club, Le Morne, tel. 683-6775, fax 683-6786.

Trekking and surfing have great potential. Trekking is best in the highlands of south-central Mauritius. Using Vacoas as a centre, trekkers can walk through deep canyons and river valleys to the mountains of the Black River gorges or wander among the ancient trees in the Macchabée Forest and up to the holy Hindu lake on the heights of Grand Bassin. Kanaka crater beckons travellers who are willing to walk up the thickly vegetated sides for a view down into prehistory.

Surfing is fairly new still. South Africans and Australians are gradually finding the best surfing spots, which occur where there is a break in the reef. The best rideable waves are off Baie du Tamarin. Continuing along the southern coastline, surfers will find "barrels" off Pointe Sud Ouest, and an excellent "point-break" off Pointe aux Roches. Carrying your surfboard may present a problem. To overcome this, many families at St Felix and Baie du Cap will look after your board while you spend a day or two scouting out locations or going to one of the urban centres.

Golf is another major attraction. Top of the list of courses is that at Le Paradis Golf Club, on Le Morne peninsula. It has 18 holes of challenging fairways, plus a practice green, driving range and clubhouse. The club is affiliated to the Meridien Paradis and Brabant hotels. The course, designed by David Dutton, is 5 800 m long with a 72 par rating. It must surely rate as one of the most beautiful golf courses in the world. You need not be a resident of the hotel to play and temporary membership is easily arranged. Contact Le Paradis Golf Club, Case Noyale, Le Morne, tel. 683-6775, fax 683-6786 or the Beachcomber Group, PO Box 1633, Bedfordview, 2008, South Africa, tel. (011) 455-1018, fax (011) 455-2818.

Other activities available to visitors include horse riding at all Beachcomber hotels, tennis at most tourist-class hotels and cycling tours, plus the usual array of discotheques, nightclubs and casinos. A Chinese casino is located at Amicale de Port on Royal Street in Port Louis. Other casinos include those at the Meridien Paradis and St Géran Hotels. The most festive discos, and certainly worth a visit, are: Club Climax on Grand Baie, tel. 263-8737; Palladium in Quatre Bornes, tel. 454-6168 and Le Capricorne along Baie du Tombeau, tel. 247-2533.

5 GETTING THERE

AIR

This is the way that most tourists travel to Mauritius. The international airport, Plaisance, is about 3 km from Mahébourg, on the south-east coast, and 43 km east of the capital, Port Louis. All foreigners over two years old leaving Mauritius from Plaisance airport must pay airport tax. You must have an onward or return ticket upon arrival in Mauritius. This is unlikely to be verified if you come in with a tour group, but is certain to be checked if travelling independently.

International flights connect Mauritius with Antananarivo, Bombay, Dar es Salaam, Durban, Frankfurt, Geneva, Harare, Hong Kong, Jeddah, Johannesburg, Kuala Lumpur, London (Gatwick and Heathrow), Moroni (Comoros), Munich, Nairobi, Nice, Paris (Charles de Gaulle and Orly), Perth, Réunion, Rome, Seychelles, Singapore, Taipei and Zurich.

The airlines servicing these routes are listed below, with their addresses in Port Louis and telephone numbers on Mauritius. For their latest flight schedules and fares, contact a travel agent or these airlines' representative in your own country.

Air France, Rogers Travel, Rogers House, 5 President John F Kennedy Street, tel. 208-6801

Air Mauritius, Rogers House, 5 President John F Kennedy Street, tel. 208-6878

Air Tanzania, Fon Sing Building, Edith Cavell Street, tel. 212-2563

Air Zimbabwe, Sunset Aviation, Fon Sing Building, Edith Cavell Street, tel. 208-3446

British Airways, Ireland Blyth, Chaussee Street, tel. 208-1039

Kenya Airways, Airworld, Blendax House, Dumat Street, tel. 208-4935

Singapore Airlines, Currimjee Jeewanjee and Co. Ltd, 5 Duke of Edinburgh Avenue, tel. 208-7695

South African Airways, Rogers Travel Ltd, Rogers House, 5 President John F Kennedy Street, tel. 208-1281

Most tourists are on organised tours which include the cost of an airfare. Getting to Mauritius independently is expensive. The usual "bucket-shop" tickets do not seem to be easily available for Mauritian flights. As tours include accommodation, meals, sightseeing, transport and flights, visitors on a tight schedule should seriously consider this option. World Leisure Holidays can be contacted for its fully inclusive fares to Mauritius. World Leisure Holidays, PO Box 1474, Randburg 2125, South Africa, tel. (011) 886-9710, fax (011) 886-9709.

A round-the-world air ticket is useful if you are planning to visit other Indian Ocean islands or other countries. This ticket may initially seem costly, but the more you travel over the 12 month period, the better value it becomes. If coming from North or South America, it makes more sense to first fly to South Africa, Australia or Singapore, and from there take a flight to Mauritius. There are also weekly flights from Mauritius to Réunion. Many of the larger hotel groups, such as Club Med, arrange day excursions to Réunion, which include the return flight and a tour of specific points of interest. You do not need to be a guest at Club Med to take its tour. Contact it at least five days ahead: Club Med Excursions Manager, La Pointe aux Canonniers, Grand Baie, Mauritius, tel. 263-8610, fax 263-7511.

Remember to confirm your flight and reservation at least 72 hours before you are due to leave. This can be done either telephonically (the telephone number will be on your ticket), or through the reception desk at the hotel where you are staying.

SEA

This is undoubtedly the most pleasant way of reaching Mauritius. Budget travellers might consider asking around for a berth on one of the many cargo ships that ply the sea lanes to Mauritius. In South Africa, try asking at the offices of the Mediterranean Shipping Company (MSC) in the port city of Durban. A few container ships leave Australia from Perth every two months or so. In Europe, spend time around the docks of Marseilles or Naples. It can be extremely difficult getting a trip on a commercial vessel, and many visitors have found it easier looking for a place on a yacht instead. From about mid-June to the end of November, yachts frequently leave from South Africa, Australia and Southeast Asia to cruise the Indian Ocean Islands. In South Africa, check the notices pinned on the boards in the Point Yacht Club and Royal Natal Yacht Club in Durban. In Southeast Asia, visit the Singapore Yacht Club and ask to speak to the club manager. He has numerous contacts with cruising skippers. Australians seldom cruise this far west, but it may be worth trying the deep-water yacht moles at Exmouth, Dongara and Perth.

Getting transport from Mauritius by ship or boat is difficult unless you have a pre-booked passage on a cruise liner. Talking to a few travellers in Port Louis, it seems as though a voyage can be made – if space is available – aboard one of the vessels of Ireland Blyth Limited. Contact the shipping division and ask to speak to one of the three managers. These gentlemen are helpful, full of useful information and humorous anecdotes. They will go out of their way to assist you with a berth on board a vessel leaving Mauritius. Ireland Blyth Shipping Division, 10 Dr Ferriere Street, tel. 208-3241, fax 208-8931.

6 GETTING AROUND

Travelling around Mauritius is easy. Whether by public transport, hired car, helicopter or boat, the experience is thoroughly enjoyable. There are organised tours, private transport operators and, of course, ubiquitous Air Mauritius flights.

AIR

Air Mauritius runs six weekly flights from Plaisance international airport on Mauritius to the island of Rodrigues 564 km to the east. Monday to Saturday the little 46-seater aircraft buzz their passengers across the Indian Ocean to Rodrigues. These flights all depart Mauritius at 9h30 and return the same day, leaving Rodrigues at 13h15. Over the festive season these daily flights are always booked out well in advance, especially as discounted fares are offered if you stay longer than 12 days on Rodrigues. Book at least 30 days before. Contact Air Mauritius, 5 Rogers House, President John F Kennedy Street, Port Louis, Mauritius, tel. 208-6878.

For a truly spectacular view of Mauritius, consider a flight with Air Mauritius Helicopter Services. While it is possible to book a helicopter flight through the tour organiser at your hotel, prices are somewhat lower when reservations are made directly with Air Mauritius Helicopter Services. Its airborne tours include:

- The full round-the-island tour, which lasts about 60 minutes. This flight is a must for those who can afford the very high price. It commences by lifting you over Port Louis, up to Pieter Both mountain. From there the flight crosses the highlands to the tea gardens of Curepipe, hovers above Trou aux Cerfs crater and then turns west. Edging past the gloomy mountain of Le Morne, the helicopter then crosses the Seven Coloured Earths to hover above the impressive Chamarel waterfall. Keeping to the south of the island, you swoop over the holy Hindu lake at Grand Bassin, and on over Kanaka crater to the east coast. Whirling up the coast the flight passes Île aux Cerfs and lands at Grand Baie. This is only one example, as the pilots will fetch and drop passengers from anywhere on the island.

- A tour lasting about 30 minutes to Pieter Both mountain. Starting from Grand Baie, the flight swoops down the west coast over Port Louis and on to the Black River gorges. Turning north you then fly through the jumble of mountains to hover above Pieter Both mountain and the spectacular views of Port Louis, before returning to Grand Baie along the east coast.

- A tour lasting 30 minutes to cascades and craters. Starting at the heliport at Le Morne, passengers are flown over the Seven Coloured Earths to the waterfall at Chamarel, before crossing the lake at Grand Bassin. From here the course changes to include Mare aux Vacoas and the volcanic crater at Trou aux Cerfs. Returning to the west coast, the flight skirts Flic en Flac before landing once again at Le Morne.

These are the most popular routes chosen by tourists. You may, however, prefer planning your own route, to which the pilots gladly acquiesce. Every effort should be made by visitors to take at least one helicopter flight while on Mauritius. Be certain to make reservations a minimum of two days in advance. Air Mauritius Helicopter Services, tel. 637-3420, ext. 1419.

BUS

This is the most exciting and adventurous way of touring Mauritius. It will require some ingenuity and perseverance, but the rewards of travelling by public transport are unsurpassed, particularly if you want to meet the locals. Buses cover virtually every destination on the island, provide cheap transport and run on a regular basis. Their timetables are not always adhered to, but with the island being so small, it hardly matters. Most bus services start their first journey at about 5h30 and stop at 20h00. In the very remote regions, around southern Mauritius or between Beau Rivage and Eau Coulee – in what are called the rural areas – the buses commence services at around 6h30 and continue until 18h30. Linking the main urban centre of Port Louis with Curepipe, Quatre Borne and Mahébourg (including the international airport), buses continue travelling along the main road until about midnight. The major drawback to travelling about by bus is that there are no long-distance buses. For example, there is no bus that travels from Grand Baie to Souillac. There are however buses that cover the route from Centre de Flacq to Port Louis and back, and buses from Port Louis to Mahébourg. Normally, visitors must make several changes to reach a distant stop. Bus drivers are friendly and will oblige foreigners who ask for assistance.

Taking a bus from the airport first involves a bit of a walk. Leave the terminal building and walk south-west along the tarred road for about 1 km. Just beyond the entrance to the airport is the bus shelter. Buses serving this route usually go as far as Quatre Borne, from where you can change buses for Port Louis or other destinations. There are bus depots in all large urban settlements. The biggest is in Port Louis, on Labourdonnais Square, near New Quay Street. Visitors arriving by sea should ignore the expensive taxis and walk about 200 m into town to the bus depot along Quay Street. Quatre Borne also has a busy bus depot, near the market and the Gold Crest Hotel. In Centre de Flacq, buses serving the east coast and Port Louis line up next to the fire station.

Six companies operate buses on Mauritius. If planning to travel by bus, contact the various operators and ask for their current timetable. They usually send a representative to your hotel with the information, but remember to use this only as a guide.

Mauritius Bus Transport, tel. 245-2539
National Transport Corporation, tel. 426-2938
Operateurs Individeuls, tel. 212-3758
Rose Hill Transport, tel. 464-1221
Triolet Bus Service, tel. 261-6516
United Bus Service, tel. 212-2028

You can also collect a brief schedule of bus times from the Mauritius Government Tourist Office in the Emmanuel Anquetil Building, near the town hall in Port Louis.

A far more enjoyable alternative, if you have the time and patience, is simply to wait for the bus along with other islanders. Budget travellers should even consider a mixture of modes of travel. Using buses, bicycles, hitchhiking and walking, you will be able to reach places that few tourists ever see, exploring those parts of Mauritius that tourists who prefer the beaches miss, the authentic Mauritius in the villages and hamlets away from the coast.

TAXI

The "madmen" of Mauritius, was the way one British visitor described the taxi drivers of the island. After one ride with them, you will probably agree. On arrival at the airport or harbour, visitors will be approached by taxi drivers offering transport and charging in foreign currency, most likely US dollars. Beware. They believe that you are probably on your first trip and do not have any idea of prices, are insecure and in a hurry to reach your accommodation. The price, at the time of writing, was US $25 for about a 10 km trip. This is ridiculous. Do not accept their first offer and bargain hard. After a few days on Mauritius travellers will realise that touring by taxi is very expensive and hardly worth the cost. Also note that you will be charged for a two-way trip. The driver will include the charge for his return journey, whether you are travelling with him or not.

The reception desk at all hotels has a list of taxis and will call one on request. There are always lines of them outside the larger hotels. To avoid an argument over the price, ask the receptionists to arrange it before setting off. They have a much better idea of what should be charged. If, however, you are travelling from rural places like Goodlands, Quartier Militaire or Bois Cheri, visitors will find reasonable prices, old cars and talkative drivers. Still, the charges are high compared with those asked for on buses. You will recognise a taxi by its number plate, white with black letters, and the driver hooting as he passes. Do not expect tariff meters. A price will simply be quoted and you will be expected to agree or negotiate. Do this before setting off, and make certain that the price includes the carrying of your luggage.

BOAT

The boat operators of Mauritius are also cashing in on tourism. Prices are high, but they usually give good value. Sailing about exploring the offshore islets is a wonderful way of seeing unspoilt Mauritius. Most trips go north, to the islets and islands of Coin de Mire, Île Plate, Îlot Gabriel and Île Ronde. If you have some sailing experience, speak to the activities manager at your hotel and ask if you can take a sailing dingy offshore, but do not venture beyond the reef in an open sailing boat.

Alternatively, contact any of the five yacht charter companies that operate cruises around Mauritius. Three of these have luxurious catamarans that are literally floating palaces. They are: Croiseres Turquoises Ltd, Riche en Eau SE, tel. 631-9835, fax 631-9379; Croisere Emeraude Ltd, Cap Malheureux, tel. 263-8974, fax 263-7009; Aquacat Co. Ltd, Bain Boeuf, Cap Malheureux, tel. 263-8974, fax 263-7009. If you want to experience the thrill of sailing the way the pirates and island traders of ages past did, try a trip aboard the schooner owned and operated by Yacht Charters, Royal Road, Grand Baie, tel. 263-8395, fax 263-

7814. A small company that offers guests a personalised service, including snorkelling, meals and drinks, is Sinuhe Yacht Charters, Grand Baie, tel. 263-7037. It goes off the usual routes and even ventures further east to visit Île d'Ambre and lands you for a swim on Anse la Raie.

Most of the yachts leave their berths at about 9h30 and return by 17h30.

Cheaper, yet more exciting, trips offshore can be had by speaking to any of the fishermen who land their boats along the more secluded beaches. Get to these sites by about 5h00 and ask around. If your price is right – and it will require considerable bargaining – you will be given a boat with a skipper for the day. You decide the route or tell him what you would like to see, and the skipper does the rest. The best places to try and get a fisherman to help you are: Poudre d'Or (these men will also tell you the legend of the enormous pirate treasure buried somewhere around the Rivière du Rempart), Grande Rivière Sud-Est, Ferney, Baie du Cap and along Petite Rivière Bay.

You can reach the famous Île aux Cerfs and Île de L'Est islands off the east coast by catching the small ferry that leaves from outside the Pointe Maurice restaurant.

If the weather and season are right, the owner of Kuxville Beach Cottages, Nico Kux, will agree to charter his yacht and act as skipper for a week-long voyage to the island of Rodrigues. He includes all meals and drinks. You will need to book this trip at least 60 days in advance. Nico Kux, Kuxville-Serendip-Sinbad, PO Cap Malheureux, Royal Road, Mauritius, tel. 262-8836, fax 262-7407.

CAR RENTAL

This is the ideal way for visitors with limited time to get around Mauritius. As the island is only 58 km long and 46 km wide, it is easy to drive around it in a day. Foreigners must be in possession of a valid driver's licence – there is no need for an international driving permit. You will see many tourists shooting about the island in Mini Mokes, Suzuki Samurais or Daihatsus. Affluent foreigners can hire closed cars and travel in air-conditioned luxury. Between these extremes, visitors have a choice of Uno, Daihatsu or Renault. Mauritius is the cheapest of all the Indian Ocean islands for car hire. When collecting the car check that tools and a spare tyre are indeed in the vehicle. Check that indicators, lights and hooter work and make a note of any body damage to the car.

Because Mauritius is so small, operators will bring the car to you and collect it from any point on the island – obviously, an extra charge is made for this. Several international rental companies have offices on Mauritius. Their head offices are in the larger centres, but through local tour agents, they are represented at almost every tourist hotel. If their fleet is hired out, they will find an independent operator from whom to hire a car for you.

Avis, M1 Motorway, Port Louis West, tel. 208-1624
Budget, Mer Rouge, Link Road, Roche Bois, tel. 242-0341
Europcar, M2 Motorway, Pailles, tel. 208-9258
Hertz, Froberville Lane, Curepipe Road, tel. 675-1453

Numerous small independent operators offer a vehicle or two for hire. Some are excellent, others suspect. Their prices are always lower than the big multinational firms, and some sort of deal regarding collection and deposit can be arranged. Ascertain exactly what you are to get, and read the contract carefully. Among the more popular and reputable of these are:

Kevtrav, 6 Orchidees Avenue, Quatre Bornes, tel. 454-5760
Beach Car, Royal Road, Grand Baie, tel. 263-8759
Fone-A-Car, 20 Thompson Street, Vacoas, tel. 686-5502

BICYCLE

After public transport, this is the best alternative for budget travellers. Bicycles can be hired at most tourist resorts, or you can ask a local for assistance. Rates are either per hour if less than half-day, or else per day. Most guesthouses keep a few cycles, and while these may not be in top condition they are usually 50% cheaper than hiring through hotels. Visitors wanting to get away from the beach and into the remote rural areas will need to either walk or take a bicycle. Hills may present a slight problem in the highlands, but are nothing like as difficult as on Réunion or Anjouan.

As with car hire, make certain that you thoroughly check the bike before accepting it. Ask to have a lock and chain included as well. Also ask for some basic tools, so that any breakages do not leave you stranded.

Get hold of a map of Mauritius, strap on a day-pack and head off. Start early and leave the main coastal road as soon as possible. There are countless gravel roads that have yet to see a tourist. Even if you hate cycling, put aside your prejudice and try taking a bike along the flat coastal routes. Good places for cycling are along the rugged south coast, north-central highlands and west of Vacoas, in the wilderness of the Black River gorges. The latter is mountainous, and challenging even for experienced mountain-bikers.

HITCHHIKING

You are unlikely to see foreigners hitchhiking around Mauritius, despite the fact that hitchhiking here is both easy and enjoyable. Lifts are frequent, and the opportunity for mixing with Mauritians should not be missed. Seldom do travellers have to wait longer than 10 minutes before someone stops. Do not expect to be picked up by tourists. Virtually all rides will be with locals, very few of whom hitch. If at all possible, avoid hitchhiking on a Friday or Saturday evening, when alcohol flows freely and drivers may get reckless. Hitchhikers are also advised that nearly every bus that passes will stop and offer you a ride.

Hitchhiking along the main routes is a pleasure. However, once off the tarred roads, you are unlikely to get lifts as few cars venture onto the gravel. The one advantage is that any vehicle that does pass will stop for you. Recommended places from which to try hitchhiking are from Port Louis north to Grand Baie; Port Louis south to Black River; St Pierre for rides east to Centre de Flacq; Curepipe east to Mahébourg and west to Port Louis; Grand Gaube south to Rivière du Rempart and Plaine Magnien south through Souillac to Bel Ombre.

TOURS

Tourists wishing to join a tour can do so by contacting the company representative desks at all top-class hotels. White Sand Travel has the highest profile among the tour groups and offers several tours that take in the nature parks, city lights and plantations. White Sand Travel, La Chaussee, M1 Motorway, Port Louis West, tel. 212-3712.

Mauritours, 5 Venkatasananda Street, Rose Hill, tel. 454-1666, has guided and self-drive tours that explore most of the sights worth visiting on Mauritius.

Beachcomber Tours is the most experienced international tour operator to Mauritius. Its clientele encompasses all categories of visitors and its tours are individually tailored. From August to November it runs special package trips to Mauritius. These include both seven and 10 night visits. Tourists have a choice of accommodation from among the five top hotels on the island. Included in the price is the air fare, airport transfers, cocktails, free land and water sports, plus discounts on car hire and scenic tours of the country. You should contact it at least 60 days ahead of your intended departure. Beachcomber Tours, PO Box 1633, Bedfordview 2008, South Africa, tel. (011) 455-1018, fax (011) 455-2818.

Another recommended group is World Leisure Holidays. Its packages are structured to include the best sightseeing tours available on Mauritius. World Leisure Holidays, PO Box 1474, Randburg 2125, South Africa, tel. (011) 886-9710, fax (011) 886-9709.

Club Med, however, steals the show as far as island tours go. At its resort on La Pointe aux Canonniers, it has a department devoted entirely to organising and assisting guests with sightseeing visits. Non-residents are also catered for. Club Med's personalised tours to the last unspoilt regions left on Mauritius are well worth taking, especially the one to Le Domaine du Chasseur. If a guest, you can book yourself onto a tour on arrival, but non-residents must make reservations at least three days in advance and pay a small handling fee. Club Med, La Pointe aux Canonniers, Grand Baie, Mauritius, tel. 263-8610, fax 263-7511.

7 PORT LOUIS

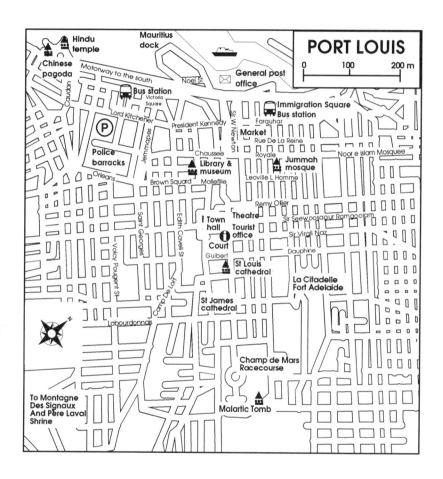

Known to early Dutch sailors as Noordt Wester Haven, Port Louis did not begin to flourish until the arrival in 1736 of that most famous of Indian Ocean Frenchmen, Mahé de Labourdonnais, governor of all French territories in the Indian Ocean. Through the years of French rule, British colonialism and finally independence, Port Louis has remained the capital of Mauritius. During the heyday of its sugar industry, over 120 tall ships could berth in the harbour. Along the shore, taverns, hotels and brothels proliferated in answer to the seamen's needs. Then the slump came, fewer ships arrived on the long passage from Europe, and many islanders turned their attention to other ways of making a living.

Today, Port Louis is growing at an alarming rate. Housing estates and squatters compete for space against an awesome backdrop of towering mountains, edged on three sides by the deep azure of the Indian Ocean. Port Louis is a kaleidoscope of colours, sights, sounds and smells. Almost 15% of the population live in or around Port Louis. Many tourists will initially be appalled by the filthy streets, but there is still an enchantment to wandering through alleys and visiting markets, museums and the old harbour. No visitor should miss a trip to this typically colonial island capital.

GETTING THERE

Tourists who arrive by ship or boat dock in Port Louis. Cruise ships berth on the north side of the harbour, about 300 m from town. You can either take a penny-ferry from the ship to New Quay Street (payment in dollars), or have the more enjoyable option of walking into town. Once clear of the harbour security area, visitors will be faced with hoards of taxi drivers, hoping for fares and all demanding payment in dollars. Rather forego taking one of these taxis. They are very expensive and will also charge for baggage and their own return journey to Port Louis. Instead, turn right outside the main gate and go down Marine Road (keep Trou Fanfaron to your right) to where it joins Quay Street. Turn right again and within 100 m you will arrive at the bus depot on Immigration Square, where all buses covering northern Mauritius arrive and depart. If you are wanting to go south, continue along Quay Street past the post office. The bus depot for buses serving southern Mauritius is about 200 m south, on Victoria Square.

To reach Port Louis from the airport involves two choices. Both initially involve a short walk from the airport terminal. Walk out through the main airport security gate and follow the road south. Less than 100 m from the gate is the bus stop. The choices are either a direct bus that stops at Curepipe and Moka before reaching Port Louis or a series of hops. The former takes about one and a half hours. The latter, while more demanding, is much more fun. It gives visitors an immediate introduction to the country and people. On local buses it will take about three hours to reach Port Louis.

Many new arrivals reject public transport in favour of quickly getting to the capital or their hotel in an expensive taxi. Mauritian taxi drivers are supposed to have a tariff card that must be shown to all passengers. This only occurs in theory and unless you ask, the card will not be offered. Make certain you do see the rates, and then, armed with that knowledge, discard it and negotiate a price to Port Louis. Check that the charge includes carrying your luggage, and find out where you will be dropped in the bustling capital.

GETTING AROUND

There is no need to worry about transport around Port Louis. The city has been laid out in a grid pattern and is wedged onto a narrow piece of land between mountains and sea. You can simply walk about visiting the sights. Of course you may want to hire a taxi to take you up to the Citadel or out to the Champ de Mars racecourse. Visitors wishing to take a taxi around town or back to their hotel will find them congregating along Dumas Street, at the western end of Edith Cavell Street, next to the bus depot on Victoria Square.

The best way to get orientated in Port Louis is to locate Sir William Newton Street. From Victoria Square bus depot go east on Dumas Street, turn left into President John F Kennedy Street. The seventh street on the right is Sir William Newton. From the Immigration Square bus stop, go south on Farquhar Street. The third street on the left, after Louis Pasteur Street, is Sir William Newton. East of Sir Seewoosagur Ramgoolam Street, Sir William Newton becomes Church Street and goes out to the Champ de Mars racecourse. Within a few blocks of Sir William Newton Street visitors will find most sights and any required administrative offices. Get a copy of the Air Mauritius booklet *What's on in Mauritius* from its offices in Rogers House, 5 President John F Kennedy Street. It has a detailed map of Port Louis that includes points of interest to tourists.

The city limits are marked by Monseigneur Leen Avenue in the south, Port Louis harbour to the west, Magon Street to the north and Military Road to the east. Within this area visitors will have an amazing diversity of cultures, sights and routes to explore.

TOURIST INFORMATION

Tourist information can be found at either Air Mauritius or the Mauritius Government Tourist Office. Neither is particularly helpful though, and many tourists receive better assistance at the National Museum on the corner of Chaussee and Intendance Streets.

Air Mauritius is at Rogers House, 5 President John F Kennedy Street, tel. 208-3739, fax 208-8331. The Mauritius Government Tourist Office is in the Emmanuel Anquetil Building, on the corner of Sir Seewoosagur Ramgoolam and Church Streets. This office is open from 9h00-16h00 on weekdays and 9h00-12h00 on Saturdays.

Home to the head offices of all the banks on the island, Port Louis is the ideal place in which to change money and carry out any other business affairs. Most of the banks are grouped together in the financial district along Sir William Newton Street. Their operating times are Monday to Friday 9h30-14h30 and Saturday 9h30-11h30.

Barclays Bank, on the corner of Rue de la Reine, tel. 212-1817

Bank of Baroda, tel. 208-1505

Banque Nationale de Paris Intercontinental (BNPI), near the post office and motorway, tel. 208-8142

Hong Kong Bank, Place d' Armes, corner of Chaussee Street, tel. 208-1801

Mauritius Commercial Bank, corner of Rue de la Reine, tel. 208-2801

State Commercial Bank, Intendance Street, in the treasury building, tel. 208-5301

International Union Bank, tel. 208-8080

Visitors arriving independently may want to arrange a tour of Mauritius or reconfirm their flight. This can be done through any of the numerous travel agents and tour operators who have offices in Port Louis.

Budget Travel and Tours, Labama House, 35 Sir William Newton Street, tel. 212-4700, fax 212-5162

Oceania Travel Agents Ltd, 44 Jummah Mosque Street (the fourth street north of Sir William Newton Street), tel. 208-1230, fax 208-8868

Tropic Tours Ltd, Fon Sing Building, Chevreau Street (south of the Company Gardens and across Edith Cavell Street), tel. 208-8332, fax 208-8579

The main post office is to the harbour side of Quay Street, opposite the T-junction with Sir William Newton Street. This is arguably the most efficient post office on the island. Tourists are strongly advised to make use of the facilities. You can also have poste restante mail sent here. Ask at the postmaster's office for poste restante assistance. It is open for service Monday to Friday 8h00-11h15 and 12h00-16h00 and Saturday 8h00-11h45.

If you are looking for books on local history, customs and culture, the best place to try is Port Louis. Visitors will find bookshops with extensive stocks of non-fiction and fiction titles from international publishing firms. Travel guides and tourist maps are also available at these "librairies".

Librairie Amicale, 43 Royal Street, tel. 242-3707

Librairie Bonanza, corner of Sir Virgil Naz and Bourbon Streets, tel. 208-5179

Librairie Desforges, Sir Seewoosagur Ramgoolam Street, tel. 241-6179

EOI Book Centre, 30 Joseph Rivière Street, tel. 242-3738, fax 464-3445

Should you need film, batteries or basic repairs carried out on your camera equipment, there are only two recommended places on Mauritius.

ERA Photo Cine House Ltd, 6 Edith Cavell Street, tel. 212-0171
Scott Photoproducts, 4 Edith Cavell Street, tel. 208-5051

The medical services on Mauritius are excellent. Both state and private facilities are available to foreign visitors. If you consult a private doctor, you will be required to pay the fee, and then claim from your medical aid or medical insurance policy. Visitors must ask for a receipt from the medical clerk on duty. State-controlled clinics and hospitals provide free medical service to all who arrive. Tourists must pay for medicine bought from a pharmacy, but not if it is a prescription drug. Naturally, hospitals are open 24 hours, and hotels have a schedule of local doctors on call. Embassies also keep a comprehensive list of suitable medical personnel, who are used by their staff.

Mauritius offers visitors treatment with Chinese Ayuvedic medicine. The consultation includes treatment, usually with homeopathic remedies.

The hospital which serves Port Louis is Dr AG Jeetoo Hospital, on Volcy Pougnet Street, tel. 212-3201. You can contact a 24-hour ambulance service by dialling 999. City Clinic, tel. 241-2951, is a private clinic on Sir Edgar Laurent Street. Its charges are high but the personalised attention is unsurpassed.

The National Library is in the National Institute museum building, on Chaussee Street. Its archives are interesting and informative. Journalists may be required to fill in a questionnaire for the relevant material to be sourced. A large research department has been set up for the study of the Mascarene archipelago.

While only Air Mauritius and Air Tanzania have offices in Port Louis, all the other airlines serving the island have representatives in travel agencies. Remember that return flights must be confirmed at least 72 hours before departure. Onward tickets can be booked via these agencies, and discounts are the norm for trips to Réunion, Madagascar and the Seychelles.

British Airways, Ireland Blyth Ltd, Chaussee Street, tel. 208-1039

Air France, Rogers Travel Ltd, Rogers House, 5 President John F Kennedy Street, tel. 208-6801

Kenya Airways, Airworld Ltd, Blendax House, Dumat Street, tel. 208-4935

Air Mauritius, Rogers House, 5 President John F Kennedy Street, tel. 208-6878

Singapore Airlines, Currimjee Jeewanjee and Co. Ltd, 5 Duke of Edinburgh Avenue, tel. 208-7695

South African Airways, Rogers Travel Ltd, Rogers House, 5 President John F Kennedy Street, tel. 208-1281

Air Tanzania, Fon Sing Building, Edith Cavell Street, tel. 212-2563

Air Zimbabwe, Sunset Aviation, Fon Sing Building, Edith Cavell Street, tel. 208-3446

THINGS TO DO

The best place to start a walking tour of Port Louis is from the post office on Quay Street, at the harbour. Go east along Sir William Newton Street to Rue de la Reine (Queen Street). Turn left to the central market.

The market is a jumble of stalls selling everything from fresh produce to curios. The left side is devoted to food, fruit, vegetables and spices. To the right are mainly textiles and curios. Bargain hard for purchases and get vendors to compete for your custom. The market is open Monday to Friday 5h30-18h00; Saturday 5h00-12h00.

Continue north on Queen Street. Turn right into Anquetil Street and walk east for one block to L'Amicale de Port Louis Chinese Casino. Turn right into Royale and return south to the impressive mosque on the corner of Jummah Mosque Street. Painted brilliant white and towering over the Chinese quarter, Jummah Mosque is open for visits every day from 9h00-12h00 except Friday (the Muslim holy day). Visitors must take off their shoes and enter through the intricately crafted wooden doors on Royale Street.

Stay on Royale Street, heading south, to Queen Elizabeth Street and the statue of the queen below Government House. Where Queen Elizabeth Street forms a T-junction with the motorway, there is a statue of Mahé de Labourdonnais at the end of a long line of palm trees. Further along Chaussee Street visitors will find the Company Gardens and National Institute Museum and National Library. The Company Gardens are the lungs of Port Louis. Trees, benches and birds now fill the place that was the vegetable and fruit gardens of the French East India Company. It is quiet here, and at lunch time, office workers flock to the park for a bit of relaxation. Alongside the gardens is the Mauritius National Institute, which houses a museum and library. Established in 1880, the museum is rather disappointing for an island with such a colourful history. Its biggest attraction is the skeleton and stuffed replica of the dodo bird, which became extinct in about 1693. The museum itself is historic. Once the offices of the East India Company, it now includes shabby displays of Mauritian wildlife. The saddest piece is a magnificent blue marlin (*Makaira nigricans)*. Peeling and faded, it but hints at the true beauty that so many people come to hunt in the deep sea. Obviously uncared for, the museum may leave many visitors depressed. Open Monday, Tuesday, Thursday and Friday 9h00-16h00, and Saturday, Sunday 9h00-12h00. Entrance is free and visitors are given a guide booklet to the specimens.

Leaving the institute, walk east on Intendance Street, alongside the 18th century Government House to the Port Louis theatre on Nelson Mandela Place. Opposite is the Mauritius Government Tourist office in the modern Emmanuel Anquetil Building. Intendance Street becomes Jules Koenig Street further east.

Turn left into Dauphine Street and then first right up Church Street to the Roman Catholic cathedral of St Louis. East of the cathedral take a right turn into Lislet Geoffroy and then left up Poudriere Street. This narrow road goes past the gothic Anglican cathedral of St James. Follow Poudriere Street to Labourdonnais Street and turn left (north). At Pope Hennessy Street go right and stay on this road, which becomes Duke of York and ends at the Champ de Mars horse-racing track. The citizens of Port Louis know the racecourse as the Hippodrome, and if you have been to Rome it will be easy to see the similarity. The racecourse was completed in 1812, and is considered one of the oldest in the world. There is a statue of Edward VII at one end and the Malartic Tomb, an obelisk, at the other. Horse racing starts in May and continues through to the end of November. The major event on the racing calendar is the Maiden Cup, which takes place at the end of August.

To reach Fort Adelaide (the Citadel), return along Duke of York Street and then go right into D'Estang Street and around the corner down Dr Eugene Laurent Street. At Dauphine Street go north to Jummah Mosque Street. At the Empire Video Club go uphill along the cobbled pavements of Jummah Mosque Street, to the woodwork shop where the road becomes an alley. There are steps going up the side of the hill and visitors should take these to the fort overlooking the city. Built for the British garrison at the end of the 18th century by William IV, Fort Adelaide is the only one of the four around Port Louis that is still fairly intact. In ruins, Forts Victoria, William and George are closed to tourists.

There is a legend that all four forts are linked by a complex system of tunnels and doors. The tunnel leading off the armoury in Fort Adelaide is certainly worth investigating more. There seem to be no firm opening times and visitors regularly complain of walking up to the citadel and finding it closed. Check with the tourist office before going up.

The views from the fort are awe-inspiring. Below, Port Louis looks miniscule, the ships in the port mere toys. To the east, the ranges of mountains and vegetation appear like protective walls. Goats and children hang about the fort site, woefully eyeing the tourists who rush up to the fort in taxis. It can be a little eerie wandering around the guardrooms and storehouses of the old fort. There are rumours around the local bars that the citadel is soon to be torn down, to make way for the ever-increasing tourism industry. A rumour has it that a Malayasian multinational company is hoping to build a five-storey hotel where the citadel now stands.

Heading west, back towards town, walk downhill to Joseph Rivière Street and through the area of warehouses and Chinese food shops before exiting on Farquhar Street, at Immigration Square bus depot. If you continue along Farquhar Street to Louis Pasteur Street, and there turn right, you will be back on Quay Street.

To reach the Chinese pagoda, Hindu temple and Signal Hill south of Port Louis' CBD, either prepare for a long walk or take a taxi. If walking, go along the trunk road south to the circle junction. Take the Maupin road east and then D'Entrecasteaux Street, which exits behind the police barracks. At the juncture of streets continue east along Raoul Rivet Street. Stay on this road until just past Harris Street, where the road branches off to the summit of Signal Hill.

Many Roman Catholic visitors are eager to see the shrine of St Père Laval. This is at Ste Croix a few kilometres out of the city. You can take a taxi from Dumas Street or the Père Laval bus from Immigration Square. The bus stops outside the chapel and you must walk to the nearby shrine, which is open to visitors daily from 6h00-18h00. A number of stalls have been set up around the shrine. They sell the usual assortment of Christian memorabilia and candles for devotees.

THINGS TO BUY

Shopping in Port Louis is an experience. You will be approached by people selling the most bizarre items; anyone for a pet dove, cannabis or rubber-tyre sandals? Poncini Boutique is the official duty-free tourist shop in Port Louis. Located at 2 Jules Koenig Street, it has a staggering amount of curios for sale. Its diamonds and jewellery are world famous, but the prices can be prohibitive. All major credit cards are accepted. Pearls are gaining in popularity and you might want to visit the showrooms of Mikado Ltd at 6 Sir William Newton Street. If you are stuck for a traditional Mauritian curio, go to the Argonaute Souvenir Shop, 3 Sir William Newton Street.

The market is a wonderland for shoppers. Check prices before starting to negotiate with the shrewd tradesmen. Of particular interest are the beautiful hand-made tablecloths and settings. Depicting island life, they are a great deal cheaper here than anywhere else on Mauritius. Green Island rum is another useful buy. As you leave the market, shady-looking hawkers will try to sell you fake Rolexes, replica Nikons and genuine leather belts.

The Handicraft Boutique in the Company Gardens is another good place to hunt down curios. A lot of the work comes from the remote villages in the highlands and north-central parts of the country. The subtle blending of art forms in cloth, wood and pottery is a delight. Expect to pay handsomely for these goods, which are nevertheless very good value. In the Ocean Queen on Queen Street, and Arc-en-Ciel Boutique along Farquhar Street, visitors will find the usual array of shells, coral, T-shirts and trinkets associated with tourism.

ACCOMMODATION

It seems pointless staying in the urban confusion of Port Louis when within a few kilometres you can relax in indolent luxury at any number of beach hotels. Still, businessmen must occasionally stay over in the capital. Hotels in Port Louis are never full, and although you may be quizzed about a reservation on arrival, there have not been any reports of tourists being turned away. Budget travellers will find it exceedingly difficult finding cheap accommodation in Port Louis. The only possibility is to ask around the warehouses in the Chinese quarter. A room with a bed and access to washing facilities, at a small charge, will be found for you.

There are no luxury hotels in Port Louis. These are only to be found along the beaches away from the chaos of the city. Top of the available accommodation is the *City Hotel* (medium tariff), in the Ambassador Building on Sir Seewoosagur Ramgoolam Street, tel. 212-0466. It is never full and therefore reservations are unnecessary. Beware, the additional 10% government tax is not added to your bill until it comes time to check out.

Other hotels, used almost exclusively by travelling salesmen and businessmen are:

Bourbon Tourist Hotel (medium tariff), 36 Jummah Mosque Street, tel. 240-4407

Le Grand Carnot Hotel (low tariff), 17 Edouard Laurent Street, tel. 240-3054

Le Rossignol Hotel (medium tariff), 36 Pope Hennessy Street, tel. 212-1983

Palais d'Or Tourist Hotel (medium tariff), 26 Jummah Mosque Street, tel. 242-5231

PLACES TO EAT

Port Louis has an abundance of places to eat. From fast foods, takeaways and snacks to five-star restaurants and bistros, there is something for every pocket and taste.

A well-known takeaway spot in Port Louis is *Pizza Paradis*, in the Fon Sing Arcade, 12 Edith Cavell Street, offering over 20 pizza toppings. It will be almost impossible to come away unsatisfied. For other snacks and takeaways visit the area around the two bus depots on Immigration Square and Victoria Square. Samosas and chili-bites are very popular with street vendors, while Chinese meals can be bought from any number of cafés around Anquetil and David Streets. Excellent American and Mauritian style takeaways and light meals can be eaten at *Le Gazebo Fast Foods* near the Port Louis theatre. Another place worth trying, especially for its highly spiced Indian snacks, is *Marmite d'Or Snacks and Takeaways* at 3 Farquhar Street. For a coffee break, with cake or sandwich, visit *DSL Coffee House,* 21 Lislet Geoffroy Street, near St Louis cathedral.

Reasonably priced sit-down Indian and Creole lunches are available from *Bonne Marmite,* 18 Sir William Newton Street. On the corner of Labourdonnais and Pope Hennessy Streets is the cosy Chinese restaurant *Foon Teng. Kwang Chow,* on the corner of Anquetil and Rue de la Reine (Queen) Streets, is well known among travellers for its enormous servings, spicy food and low prices. Offering a good selection of Creole and Indian meals is the *Underground Diner* on Bourbon Street.

Port Louis' top restaurant is the *Carri Poule* in Duke of Edinburgh Avenue. It serves lunch daily, and dinner on Friday and Saturday evenings. Prices reflect the well-heeled clientele. Menus are typically Indian with a variety of European offerings. Reservations must be made at least three days ahead, tel. 212-1295. Vying for top honours is the Chinese restaurant *Lai Min.* Very popular despite the high prices, this restaurant is frequently included on organised tours of Port Louis. It is open only in the evenings and diners must book five days before arrival, tel. 242-0042. A fairly extensive menu is offered in the dining room of the *Palais d'Or Hotel* on Jummah Mosque Street. There is no need to make reservations, but there is an extra service charge for non-residents.

8 NORTHERN AND EASTERN MAURITIUS

It is to the northern and eastern regions of the country that most visitors to Mauritius will go. This is where you will find the best beaches, top hotels, numerous restaurants, budget accommodation and most water sport activities. Do not, however, make the mistake of spending all your time lying in the sun. Mauritius has a multitude of things to both interest and fascinate those who travel to other districts around the "Green Island".

Two provinces make up most of the northern region of the island, Pamplemousses and Rivière du Rempart. Flacq and a portion of Grand Port comprise the eastern section described.

TOMBEAU BAY

Taking the national highway north from Port Louis, visitors will cross the Rivière du Tombeau. West of this river is Tombeau Bay. Named for the many ships that have foundered here and entombed their passengers, the bay is also where Pieter Both drowned. A prominent member of the Dutch East India Company, Both's vessel was caught in a fierce storm here in 1615 and sank, losing most of her crew to the wild sea. The beaches are long, safe and surprisingly empty.

No buses serve this location and visitors must either hire a taxi from Port Louis or walk from Bois Marchaud Esperance on the main road. The walk takes less than 10 minutes to the cliff-protected bay.

Medium tariff accommodation is available at the 25-roomed Arc-en-Ciel Hotel on Royal Road. Its bay-view restaurant is expensive but offers excellent meals from a Chinese, European and Creole menu. Arc-en-Ciel Hotel, Royal Road, Tombeau Bay, Mauritius, tel. 247-2616, fax 247-2772. In the same price range is the small and cosy Le Capritel, tel. 247-1071, further south on Royal Road. Its biggest attraction is the lively disco that takes place on Friday and Saturday nights. Budget accommodation is difficult to find, reservations impossible to make. Just walk south along Royal Road and ask at the houses that display *pension* signs on their gates.

BALACLAVA (TURTLE BAY)

Across the river is the district of Balaclava (Turtle Bay). A road winds from the tiny settlement of **Arsenal** west to the sea. With remote beaches surrounded by sugar cane fields and some interesting historical ruins, Balaclava is likely soon to be inundated with new hotels. At the moment, however, it remains relatively unvisited by most tourists. It is also here that the only marine national reserve in Mauritius is found. Surrounded by reefs and shallow water, the site is ideal for those who snorkel or scuba dive. Qualified scuba instructors and guides are available at the local resort hotel.

Taxis can be hired to take you to Arsenal from either Port Louis or places south of the area. Make sure you fix the price before setting off.

Maritim Hotel (high tariff)

This is the only place to stay. The Maritim's secluded beaches were one of the sites used during the filming of the successful television series Tropical Heat. The Tropical Heat Bar provides guests with drinks while they soak up the sun or relax in the warm, crystal clear sea. This top-class, German-owned hotel has 180 sea-facing rooms, all with bathroom en suite, television (including 24-hour Reuters print news) and mini-bar. The hotel was only completed in 1990. Many of the guests return again and again, often booking up to 12 months in advance. Just 12 minutes from Port Louis by car, the hotel provides free water sports and one of the best locations for watching those spectacular Mauritian sunsets. Its meals, too, are worth trying. You do not have to be a guest, but should reserve a table. Regular theme nights feature buffets of Italian, German, Creole or French food. The breakfasts are considered among the best on the island. On Creole theme nights clients are also able to see sega dancing on the beach, accompanied by a beach grill of seafood. All major credit cards, traveller's cheques and foreign currency are accepted as payment. Maritim Hotel, Balaclava, Terre Rouge, Mauritius, tel. 261-5600, fax 261-5670.

The biggest drawcard in the area is the hotel's 25 ha, 18th century historical estate. Non-residents are allowed in to explore the site, but ask the desk-manager at the hotel for permission first. The estate itself is late 18th century, but many of the ruined buildings were built by the French in the early 1700s. To reach the crumbling buildings, turn right as you enter the main hotel gate. Follow the path to the stables and then go left down the hill to the ruins. For some odd reason the hotel also keeps a few tortoises in a stone-walled pen near the kiln. A flour mill, storerooms, arsenal and living quarters can all be explored.

The area around the historical site is worth a visit. There are thick mangroves, head-high grass and cascades of red bougainvillaea along the trails through the bush along the shallow Citron river. The Maritim offers guided nature walks of both the wilder parts of its estate and its garden, which has won the Best Garden of the Year award.

Travelling north, visitors pass the settlement of **Solitude** with its sugar mill and textile industries before arriving at the largest village in Mauritius, Triolet. Buses from Port Louis and north-west Mauritius serve this village. The bus stop is in the middle of town near the Esso garage. Remember that a 50 km/h speed limit is applied in the CBD.

TRIOLET

Triolet is 3 km long by 3 km wide, with several restaurants, banks and a post office. The small, fresh-produce market is near the Anand cinema, which shows Hindi movies on Wednesday, Friday and Saturday nights from 20h00. There is not a great deal to see, but if you have any banking or postal matters to sort out, rather do them in Triolet than pay the high handling charges at beach resorts.

Opposite Triolet Cold-Store is a branch of the BNP (Banque Nationale de Paris). The State Commercial Bank is near Brijmohun Photo Studios, on the road through town. The post office and Mauritius Telecom are also on the main road. Visitors needing medical attention may call, without an appointment, at the rooms of Dr S Ramdass, opposite the Esso fuel station. A dentist has a small surgery next to Mauritius Telecom. Items worth buying in Triolet are limited to fashionware. Prices are much lower than in hotel boutiques or Port Louis. Along the main road, try Triolet Fashion and Art and Stylish Knits.

Triolet has a wonderful range of places to eat. From local food in shanty cafés to French dishes in restaurants, there is something to suit nearly everyone. The Moonflower Restaurant, near the market, has a good menu of fish and chicken dishes at reasonable prices. Blue Marlin Snacks on Shrimati Indira Gandhi Road has a fast-food counter with typical American offerings. Self-catering visitors will find a selection of food, both local and imported, at the Free Look Food Centre, which also sells takeaways. And, of course, there is a large assortment of fruit and vegetables at the market.

From Triolet, turn left into Shivala Road. This road takes you past the Shree Sanatan Sarvoday Ashram – where foreigners are allowed three-day Hindu retreats – and on to the 104 year old Maheswarnath Shiv Mandir built in 1891. There are seven temples within the site.

Opposite the temple is the Triolet bus service compound, where travellers will find the service's latest bus schedules. West of this is the tourist area of Trou aux Biches.

TROU AUX BICHES

Reaching Trou aux Biches from Port Louis is simple. Public transport travels the route between Grand Baie and Port Louis or Triolet throughout the day. There are several bus stops along Route Royale and taxis wait outside most of the hotels.

There is a Banque Nationale de Paris (BNP), next to Mosquito T-Shirts. Traveller's cheques or foreign currency can be changed at any of the top-class hotels in the area, but hunt around for the lowest handling fee, there can be big differences between hotels. You can usually buy stamps and deposit mail at hotel reception desks.

Things to do

Apart from the water sports offered by the hotels, visitors can also hire bicycles through the PLM Azur Hotel, or take part in a guided tour of the area. For a real treat, get to the beach in front of the aquarium before 5h00 and arrange to go out fishing with the locals. Often no payment is expected, but this should be ascertained before sailing.

The aquarium is worth a visit for those who don't go snorkelling or scuba diving.

It is suggested that you hire a bicycle, get a packed lunch, and take the flat road south to the interesting little village of **Pointe aux Piments**. In the stone-walled lanes and between free-roaming pigs, visitors will find friendly locals who are quite likely to invite you into their small, clean homes. Mark Twain wrote that here were the most beautiful beaches on Mauritius, and it is hard to refute that observation of the shimmering sand, whispering casuarina trees and achingly blue sea.

There are no private beaches on Mauritius. No matter that hotels have extended grounds down to the water, they remain public property. The problem of course comes in trying to cross a causeway or bridge that belongs to the hotel. The best method of getting to a good beach is simply to walk in through the hotel reception area. There are usually so many guests coming and going that no-one is likely to notice you. In this part of Mauritius, the most protected and beautiful beach is in front of the PLM Azur.

Accommodation

Accommodation in Trou aux Biches is expensive. Unless prepared to doss down with a local family, most people are forced to stay at the hotels which line the beautiful beach.

Hotel PLM Azur (medium-high tariff)

This hotel is highly recommended and very popular with foreigners and islanders alike. Part of the French group ACCOR, it is definitely a family hotel. Many of the guests are on package tours from France, Italy and Germany. The value for money offered by this hotel is unrivalled on Mauritius. It offers free water and land sports, as well as scuba diving and excursions. Game fishing can also be arranged. The sales manager has an amazing knowledge of this area of Mauritius and is able to offer suggestions for independent outings and nightlife activities.

There are 88 air-conditioned rooms, all with bathroom en suite, television, mini-bar, telephone and private balcony. Three restaurants, two bars and a conference centre complete the amenities. Even free baby-sitting is provided. Here visitors will see the most professional sega dance groups on Mauritius performing on Saturday night after the Mauritian Creole buffet supper. Credit cards are accepted, traveller's cheques and hard currency can be changed at the hotel and a postal service is available.

In the restaurants and dining room you may choose from an à la carte menu or from the long buffet tables. The meals are enormous and the prices low. Non-residents are advised to reserve a table for evening meals. The Wahoo beach-restaurant is a favourite at lunch time. It serves fresh fish and crispy green salads. Theme evenings are usually held in Le Barachois restaurant, with dancing around the pool.

Bookings need to be made at least 90 days in advance. Hotel PLM Azur (Mont Choisy), Route Royale, Trou aux Biches, Mauritius, tel. 261-6070, fax 261-6749.

More expensive accommodation is available at the 52-roomed *Casuarina Hotel*. Family accommodation is offered in 15 apartments with two bedrooms each. These are aimed at visitors wanting to do self-catering. Each has a small, well-equipped kitchen. The hotel also offers water sports and can arrange tours of the island. Trou aux Biches, Mauritius, tel. 261-6552, fax 261-6111.

The most expensive, but by no means the best for service or quality, is *Trou aux Biches Village Hotel*. It falls under the management of the Beachcomber Hotels group. Prices are high for what is offered. Trou aux Biches Village Hotel, Royal Road, Trou aux Biches, c/o PO Triolet, Mauritius, tel. 261-6562, fax 261-6611.

Budget accommodation is scarce in Trou aux Biches. The best chance you have of finding cheap accommodation is to ask at the Trou aux Biches police station, near the casino, or speak to the assistant at the Mexico store. Alternatively, walk south on Route Royale until reaching Stephanie Super Marche. In the lanes around the supermarket are numerous small, family-run *pensions*. Suggested places are the *Villa C'Est Ici* and *La Felicita*, both near Trou aux Biches Chez Popo store. There is also cheap accommodation at *La Rose Snack and Takeaways*, near La Sirène Bar and Restaurant.

If you've brought along a tent, then camping is possible under the casuarina trees in the park south of Villas Pointe aux Biches Protea Hotel. Ablution facilities are available in the park. Campers can do their grocery shopping and eat light meals at the Crystal restaurant near the Shiva shrine. Close by are the remains of a British outpost and legends tell of pirates who frequently landed on this stretch of beach to get food, water and wood.

Places to eat

Meals can be eaten at any of the hotels. For authentic local dishes visit *L'Exotique* restaurant for a meal or takeaway. Its late-night snacks are cheap and tasty and the beer is ice-cold. *La Sirène* bar and restaurant has a daily special, plus an à la carte menu. Its Indian and Creole specialities are delicious, but service tends to be slow and prices high. Low to medium tariff accommodation can also be arranged with the management of La Sirène.

Things to buy

Most hotels have their own curio boutiques, but the prices are inevitably ludicrious. Rather try L'Argonaute souvenir shop, south of the aquarium. Marine Antiques is also nearby. Its range of model ships is small but they are of exceptionally high quality.

North of Trou aux Biches is **Pointe aux Canonniers**, the location of the best-known holiday resort on the island, Club Med. To reach the hotel, take the Port Louis to Grand Baie bus and ask the driver to drop you off at the circle for Grand Baie and Pointe aux Canonniers.

Club Med (medium-high tariff)

All activities, excluding excursions, are included in the rate. It has standard rooms with accommodation for nearly 420 people. Meals can be taken in one of two restaurants. One restaurant is open for late breakfast and à la carte meals, while the other offers meals from a lavish buffet.

No money is used by guests staying at Club Med. Instead, tokens are used in exchange for use of the many facilities. Sailing, windsurfing, archery and tennis lessons are provided and both waterskiing and parasailing are offered. There is a six-hole "pitch and putt" golf green and a magnificent garden. Details of daily sports tournaments are placed each morning on the notice board in five languages. Extensive entertainment programmes are run each night of the week, and attending at least one of these is a must. There is dancing in the nightclub every night.

Although the Mauritian staff are sometimes rude, the foreign staff are professionals. Their attention to detail and the wellbeing of guests has many visitors returning regularly. Even if you are not a guest, you can make use of the excursion office for tours around the island. The people who work here have spent years perfecting tours of Mauritius. Non-residents are able to join an excursion and merely pay in the required fee. Specialised tours are run to see the flora and fauna of the island, handicraft workshops, the sugar industry (both past and present aspects), plus tours across to Réunion.

A highlight of any stay at Club Med must be sitting on the beach at sunset listening to the classical music which is played through enormous speakers. Dress is always informal, and even à la carte dinners may be taken while wearing shorts or a sarong. A quirk of the main restaurant is that each table seats eight people. The reason originated in the early days of the club. As European train compartments always accommodated eight people, it was decided that tourists, who usually travelled by train then, would inevitably arrive in groups of eight. It has never changed.

Casual visitors may reserve themselves a seat for dinner. This includes access to the nightly show and dancing afterwards.

Club Med, Pointe aux Canonniers, c/o Grand Baie, Mauritius, tel. 263-8610, fax 263-7511.

An interesting walking or cycling tour can be taken from Club Med east towards Grand Baie, via the suburbs. Whatever you do, avoid hiring one of the dilapidated bicycles from outside Club Med. Rather walk if you have to; chances are that you would've ended up pushing the bicycle anyway. Turn right past Hotel Canonnier and take the coastal road. There is a small, empty beach suitable for swimming near Chez Vijay Tailleur. Where a gap between the houses opens up, past Filaos village, there is another beach with good views across Grand Baie. Next door is *Villa La Caleche*, which offers low to medium-priced rooms for rent. It is seldom full and claims that reservations are never necessary. The Anais souvenir store, which has a fair selection of curios, is situated where a side road joins the main road between Grand Baie and Pointe aux Canonniers.

The only other hotel here is *Hotel Canonnier*. Graded as high tariff, this 173-room hotel offers much less than Club Med, at a higher price. Hotel Canonnier, Pointe aux Canonniers, Grand Baie, Mauritius, tel. 263-7999, fax 263-7864.

GRAND BAIE

Grand Baie is indisputably Mauritius's major holiday destination. Here, visitors will encounter the entire range of travellers, from the world's elite at the Royal Palm, through package tourists at the Merville Beach Hotel to budget travellers staying in local homes. Catering exclusively for the tourist industry, Grand Baie lacks the Mauritian flavour associated with other parts of the island. This is not to say that you will not see sega dancing or be unable to eat Creole food. If tourism requires it, then it is available at Grand Baie.

Getting there

Getting to Grand Baie via the north-west coast can be done by bus or taxi. Every 30 minutes buses leave from Port Louis, going to Grand Baie and on to Cap Malheureux before returning the way they came. The first bus north leaves at about 6h00, and the last starts its return to the capital at around 18h00. Taxis are always available. Taking a taxi from or to Grand Baie always results in lengthy negotiation over the price.

Tourist information

The post office and Mauritius Telecom are next to Mauricienne Snacks in the main road through the town of Grand Baie. Tourists are able to change their traveller's cheques and foreign currency at any of the graded hotels on the bay. Commissions are often high though, and whenever possible banks should be used. The BNP and Hong Kong Bank have offices in Grand Baie. They are near one another between the Model Ship Gallery and Grand Bay Store, on Royal Road. The Mauritius Commercial Bank is next to Eurocar Rental. Barclays Bank has a branch close to the Caltex fuel station on Royal Road. The State Bank is near the Cyclone Refugee Centre in town.

Five-star hotels all have a doctor or nurse on call. If you need a doctor, contact Dr Wong at his surgery, tel. 263-8577, all hours. He is willing to make house calls, but requires that you pay and then claim from your medical insurance. Pharmacie Lo, near Sunshine Tours, has a good range of medicines and the chemist is able to make minor diagnoses and recommendations.

Self-catering and budget travellers, if not using their accommodation's service, can do clothes washing at Lavamatic, on the western side of town.

Travel agents and tour operators come and go, but some of those that have remained are worth contacting should you want to go scuba diving, game fishing, yachting or on an excursion to other parts of the island. Yacht Charters, tel. 263-8395, is an established firm that offers sunset cruises, diving and trips to the outer islands, plus long-distance sailing to Rodrigues or even further. The office is between Fitwell Tailored Garments and Residence Peramal on Route Royale. An operator recommended by the Mauritian Tourist Board is Sunshine Tours, tel. 263-8519. It is located near the Papyrus Stationery Shop.

Things to do

As the beaches are the main attraction, few visitors ever stray too far from their hotels. There are, however, a few things worth doing in and around Grand Baie. A small Hindu temple is located near Lennard's Super Marche. Always open, the temple is for the daily use of the local community. Henry Koombes' Art Gallery, next to Grand Bay Leather, is an interesting place to spend an afternoon. A small mosque, close to the Tropic Gallery, is open every day except Friday and Sunday. Wash your feet, head and hands at the taps in the courtyard before going inside. Visitors can arrange for glass-bottomed boat excursions of the bay and surrounding reefs with Bateau Tour Operator, tel. 263-6231. Tourists interested in scuba diving, whether to do a course or dives, should contact Paradise Diving, tel. 263-7220. Its sales office is near the Tee-Shirterie on Royal Road. Islandive is the premier dive centre on Mauritius. It offers over 35 different dive locations and can train visitors in beginner to advanced courses. It specialises in night dives and wreck dives. Very popular, the dives should be booked before arriving on Mauritius. Islandive, Pappy and Jeni Bordie, c/o Veranda Bungalow Village, Grand Baie, Mauritius, tel. 263-8015, fax 263-7369. The Centre Nautique, tel. 263-8017, also offers scuba trips and boat excursions. You can get a boat to take you out to snorkel off Coin de Mire island, or further, to the bird sanctuary on Île aux Serpents.

Although many of the hotels have nightclubs, rather try the one patronised by the Creoles of Grande Baie, the Number 1 Disco, on Royal Road. Doors open at 22h30 on Friday and Saturday, and you can expect to be there until well after 2h30.

A little east of the Cyclone Refugee Centre is the Shiv Kalyan Nath Mandir. During Hindu religious festivals many of the pilgrimages start here. These offer excellent photo opportunities, but first ask the pundit for permission to take photographs.

The small slipway where fish are landed provides interest if you can get there as the boats come in at about 7h00. There is much loud, good-natured haggling between the fishermen and Grand Baie's housewives.

Things to buy

Shoppers are in for a treat. Whatever Mauritius has to offer in the way of curios and crafts is available at Grand Baie. Prices are considerably higher than if you tracked the pieces down in remote villages, but the selection is huge. Mauritian and foreign-style art works can be chosen at *Henry Koombes' Gallery* on Royal Road. Leather belts, handbags, shoes and accessories are sold at *Grand Bay Leather*, while nearby is *Koko Beach Wear*. The latest styles in costumes, wraps and casual clothing are offered in a wide variety of international and local brand names. *Island Curios* is the ideal place at which to buy gifts and trinkets. At the *Tee-Shirterie*, an amazing number of silk-screened shirts are on sale. Prices are fair, but the quality of workmanship tends to be low. Check the stitching before making a purchase. Beautiful but fragile models of wooden ships can be chosen from a large selection at the *Model Ship*

Gallery near the BNP. Ask the manager to take you out to where the crafters work. You could easily find yourself passing hours watching the dexterity of the model builders.

Accommodation

Most visitors to the area will readily find suitable accommodation. At the large hotels it is necessary to book in advance, but at many of the self-catering lodges and *pensions* you can usually just turn up and find a room. One of the top hotels in the world is the Royal Palm.

Royal Palm Hotel (high tariff)

If you must spoil yourself, even for just one night, then the Royal Palm is the place at which to do it. Part of the Beachcomber group of hotels, the Royal Palm Hotel is the choice of kings and queens, tycoons and the jet set, who usually transfer by helicopter from the airport. The hotel's limousine will gladly collect you, if necessary.

Photographs of some of the more famous guests can be seen in the passage behind the jewellery shop. Attention to detail, from the manager's welcome to each guest's preference in fruit juice, has made this one of the leading hotels in the world.

The tropical garden alone is an enchanting walk through Eden, made more beautiful by the shy smiles of the gardeners in their colourful saris and wide-brimmed straw hats.

There are no group tours here. Each of the several island excursions it offers is arranged with a personal guide and transport. Even water sport lessons are on a one-on-one basis. The mood is serene and relaxing; 72 luxury suites with lounge, 24-hour room service and television lull guests into a frame of mind that should last way beyond the holiday. Game fishing, windsurfing, sailing, snorkelling and pedalos are all available. There are also sauna and massage facilities and a hairdresser. The boutique is stocked with the finest apparel from the top fashion houses of the world, and a jeweller sells exquisite watches, fine necklaces and delicately crafted rings.

Tourists in search of thrills on the open sea should take a fast ride on the powerful Royal Palm "cigarette-boat". More sedate trimaran cruises with drinks and light snacks are available.

Two of the most delightful restaurants on Mauritius are found here. La Goelette juts out over the sea, offering breathtaking views and a splendid menu for breakfast, lunch, supper and late dinner. At the romantic and tranquil Le Surcouf restaurant, diners may choose from daily specialities or an à la carte menu. Make certain to book at least 24 hours in advance if not a resident.

Once a week, traditional Mauritian dancing and short theatre productions are performed for guests.

Guests must book well in advance. All major credit cards are accepted and traveller's cheques may be cashed at reception.

Royal Palm Hotel, Grand Baie, Mauritius, tel. 263-8353, fax 263-8455.

Merville Beach Hotel (medium tariff)

The Merville Beach Hotel is situated east of the Royal Palm. Catering for many tour groups, the Merville offers comfortable accommodation and the usual range of water sports. Its main restaurant has reasonably priced set menus, but seats must be reserved by non-residents at least 48 hours ahead. Most accommodation is pre-booked through an agent, but direct reservations cut out the agent's commission. This value-for-money hotel is well situated along the coast and can arrange for a number of local excursions.

Merville Beach Hotel, c/o PO Grand Baie, Mauritius, tel. 263-8621, fax 263-8146.

Low tariff

Low cost accommodation is best found with local families. Few of them ever advertise and travellers will need to ask around. Good recommendations can be obtained by speaking to the owner of the Mola Boutique (which actually sells fruit and legumes), and the waitresses at Le Grillion Cocktail Bar. *Residence Peramal* has reasonably priced rooms for rent, tel. 263-8109. The management is jovial and friendly, often inviting guests to join in for a drink or a trip to the local disco over the weekend.

Places to eat

No one will go hungry while staying in Grand Baie. On virtually every block there is a restaurant, snack bar or fresh produce counter. For long, slow dinners there is little to compete with the *Sakura* Japanese restaurant, next to the Model Ship Gallery. For light meals try *Don Enrico Pizza* parlour near Island Curios. *Chez Lindsay* offers popular fast foods.

If self-catering, then choose your supplies from the well-stocked shelves of *Store 2 000* at the eastern end of town. Midday meals and coffee can be enjoyed at *Le Café de Paris*, near Store 2 000. Quick snacks can be bought from *Flammarion Snack*, between Papyrus Stationery Shop and the Tropic Gallery.

PERÉYBÈRE

North-east of Grand Baie is the settlement of Peréybère. The buses which run through Grand Baie stop at Peréybère on the way to or from Port Louis. The bus stop is near the plantation of casuarina trees along the beach. Expect one to pass by in either direction every 30 minutes from about 6h45 until 17h15.

Things to do

Visitors will find the BNP bank in the Max Plaza and the Mauritius Commercial Bank near the pizzeria. Miracle Travel Tours, on Beach Lane, is the only local tour operator, tel. 263-7443. It does wonders for travellers with small budgets and even throws in specials when a prospective client is obviously backpacking in Mauritius.

Paradise Diving also has a representative here. You will find its office near the Hibiscus Bar and Restaurant. The shallow reefs off Pointe d'Azur offer some of the most fascinating snorkelling sites on the island. Gawtam Dive Centre takes dive trips out to the offshore islands and offers speciality dives at night, tel. 263-7273. It also hires out snorkel equipment for the day. You may be required to leave a deposit.

For those so inclined, there is the Amway Private Massage Parlour, open from 9h00-13h00 daily. The Hindu style of massage is highly recommended after a day of cycling or scuba diving. You must call for an appointment at least 12 hours in advance, tel. 212-2480. Tourists should take the side road next to Chez Bala shop to visit Exotica nursery. This is a veritable park. Down at Pointe d'Azur, visitors can arrange a day's fishing excursion with local fishermen. They may seem a little surprised, as it is seldom that a foreigner asks to accompany them on their demanding jobs.

Things to buy

Few tourists ever bother shopping in Peréybère. The biggest attraction of shopping here is the difference in prices compared to Grand Baie. *Anyway Curio Shop* has an interesting range of local curios and casual clothing, and the *Peréybère Boutique*, near La Côte d'Azur Bungalows, has a selection of silk-screened clothing, curios and Mauritian works of art.

Accommodation

Peréybère is packed with low-medium tariff accommodation. Whether you want to camp, rent an apartment, do self-catering or stay at an hotel, it is all available here. *L'Escale*, tel. 263-7379, hires out studios to visitors wanting to stay for longer than three days. In the same price range is the clean and comfortable *La Côte d'Azur Bungalows,* tel. 263-8320. Campers and budget travellers would do well to find accommodation at *La Sirena Camping and Rooms.* For tourists wanting to stay longer than a week, the most reasonable accommodation is found at *Domarjana*, tel. 454-2292, near the Epicure Bar and Restaurant. At *Binos Villas* there are facilities for camping, and room hire, tel. 262-7072. Campers are permitted to use the small park on the sea-front for free. There are toilet facilities, and if you only plan to stay for one night, the management at the nearby Binos Villas will allow you to use its washing amenities.

Should these rooms still be too expensive, then go a block back from the main road. In the lanes there are a seemingly endless number of family *pensions* and private rooms for hire. Prices are negotiable.

Places to eat

Restaurants are not as profuse as they are in Grand Baie, but those available are well worth the visit. Prices are lower than in Grand Baie and the menus just as good. The *Hibiscus Bar and Restaurant* has a fairly comprehensive menu for lunch and dinner. Try its fresh line fish in a light lemon sauce with steamed vegetables and short-grain rice. Fast food can be bought from *Mississippi Fried Chicken*, which is little more than a lower class Kentucky Fried Chicken. *Espresso Fast Foods* does a range of American-style food that includes hamburgers, pizza and hot-dogs. For snacks, try any of the street vendors. They sell spicy samosas, rotis and chili-bites from little glass boxes. The *Bounty Restaurant* has snacks and a tasty midday meal menu. The restaurant itself is rather special. It is built in the shape of a schooner's bow and is a popular location with tourists. *Epicure Bar and Restaurant* is always full, but prices are high and the service needs attention. *La Fontaine Snack Bar* is popular and a good place to meet local youths. Visitors staying on a self-catering basis will find a selection of foods at *Mont Oreb Supermarket*. Less well stocked is *La Sirena Supermarket*.

CAP MALHEUREUX

East of Peréybère is Cap Malheureux, the northern tip of the Mauritian mainland. Buses can be taken from Port Louis and Grand Gaube to Cap Malheureux. Those from Port Louis do not always travel through the settlement itself, but will drop you outside the Sir Seewoosagur Ramgoolam Government School on Royal Road. From there it is a less than five minute walk into Cap Malheureux. From Grand Gaube, the buses travelling west all pass Cap Malheureux.

There is a small post office near the Paille en Queue Shop. There are no banks and visitors will have to go to Peréybère or Grand Baie. Emergency medical treatment can be had at the Percy Selwyn Health Centre, close to the government school. Treatment is free and the staff are pleasant.

Things to do

There is not a great deal to do in Cap Malheureux. The red-roofed church, Notre Dame Auxilia Trice, is quaint. You cannot always go inside, but can peer in through the lattice doors. Fishermen land their daily catches to the west of the church. From the church there are good views to the northern islands. A trip out around the closer islands can be arranged with the local fishermen at the Mauritius Fishermen's Co-op, opposite the camping ground. The area is still relatively undeveloped and travellers can explore the inland regions from here, either by hiring a bicycle from Kuxville Cottages or a moped at Nicol Moped Services.

The best place to go for water sports is Sinbad. Owned by an ex-commercial diver, who worked on North Sea oil rigs, and under the direction of a qualified guide, Sinbad offers a diversity of aquatic options. Top of the list is scuba diving. It arranges scuba gear and dives off both local reefs and around islands further north. No instruction is provided and people hoping to dive must arrive with their qualification cards, current medical certificates and dive insurance. Sailing charters are also offered, and guests may enjoy sunset cruises or trips to Coin de Mire for snorkelling, or to the unspoilt islands of Île Plate and Île

Ronde. You can make use of the canoes and windsurfers for a small fee. Again no instruction is offered. There is also a general purpose boat for fishing and for taking divers out to the reefs.

Accommodation

Suitable accommodation at Cap Malheureux is limited to Kuxville Cottages and Serendip Bungalows.

Kuxville Cottages/Serendip bungalows (medium tariff)

These are owned by the same people and both are self-catering. The atmosphere can best be described as casual. No one stands on ceremony and visitors are left to their own devices. Two small secluded beaches are accessible from Kuxville.

Few guests do their own cooking, and you can arrange for a local woman to come in at breakfast and dinner time to prepare your food. You can also give her money and she will do your shopping. Food deliveries are made daily; just give the management your order the day before.

Serendip has five bungalows, each with four beds. Kuxville has 13 rooms. These are located on the beach in bedsitters, apartments and studios. Serendip is the newer, but has no sea view and is across the road from the beach. A few houses are also offered for rent if you want to stay longer than 10 days. All accommodation has ablution facilities and fully equipped kitchens. Topless bathing is forbidden in deference to the mostly Muslim staff.

Make sure to book a room at least 60 days in advance. Almost all the guests have been there before and it is easiest to find room during June and July. Kuxville/Serendip, Cap Malheureux, Mauritius, tel. 262-8836, fax 262-7407.

Places to eat

Basic meals can be eaten at *Le Coin de Mire Restaurant and Bar*. There is not a big selection and most people simply buy a few supplies at the Minishop and prepare food at their accommodation. Out past the Young Eagles Soccer Club is the local eatery, *Pazanimalaye Restaurant and Bar*. This is arguably one of the best places in Mauritius to get authentic

Creole cuisine. Its curries are pungent, tasty and cheap. Just before Petit Raffray village is the *Bubbles Restaurant and Takeaways* which offers a selection of fried fast foods.

GRAND GAUBE

This village, on the north-east tip of Mauritius, has seen a decrease in tourism over recent years. The poor beaches and lack of suitable tourist facilities have prompted visitors to go further west to Grand Baie or the north-west coast. Still, it is a pleasant little place.

You can reach Grand Gaube from the west and east coasts. The bus that leaves Cap Malheureux for Flacq stops here, as does the bus from Goodlands (take the Ste-Antoine bus to reach Goodlands from Grand Gaube). The buses for Flacq and Port Louis leave from the bus depot in front of Au Barachois shop at the western side of town. The first departs for Goodlands and Flacq from 6h45 and the last runs at about 17h15. The first bus to Port Louis leaves at 6h00, the last returning to Grand Gaube at around 17h30.

There is a post office at the south-western entrance to town. Banking amenities are non-existent, and those wanting to cash traveller's cheques or exchange currency will have to do so at local tourist-class hotels. An alternative is to travel into the nearby town of Goodlands and do your financial transactions at one of the many banks there.

Fishing, swimming, snorkelling and scuba diving are popular tourist pursuits in Grand Gaube. You will need to arrange all this through Le Grand Gaube Hotel. Cheaper fishing trips can be organised by speaking to the fishermen who hang about on the public beach, or with the manager of the Au Barachois shop. By hiring a bicycle or moped from one of the hotels, it is possible to spend hours discovering the many villages, estates and colonial ruins that dot the region.

At **Melville** village you may be fortunate enough to get a fisherman to take you across to the little island of Île d'Ambre, with its empty white beaches. The public beach at Grand Gaube is attractive, clean and popular with locals over weekends. There is also a protected beach at Le Grand Gaube Hotel. For a small fee it is possible to make use of the hotel's water sport facilities.

Two places with tourist accommodation are *Le Grand Gaube Hotel* and the cheaper *Island View Club Hotel*. Le Grand Gaube is the more established and well known of the two, graded as high tariff. With 119 rooms, all with en suite bathrooms and sea views, the hotel has become popular with affluent visitors to Mauritius. There is a restaurant and two bars, four tennis courts and a seldom-used conference centre. Reservations are expected 30 days in advance. Le Grand Gaube Hotel, c/o PO Grand Gaube, Mauritius, tel. 283-9350, fax 283-9420.

At the Island View Club Hotel on Royal Road, guests are accommodated in comfortable rooms with splendid views. Classed as a medium-high tariff hotel, the attention to detail and casual ambience are rare in this part of Mauritius. Excursions on land or sea are available from the hotel and the staff can provide detailed information for independent tours in the vicinity. Book well in advance. Island View Club Hotel, Grand Gaube, Mauritius, tel. 283-9544.

Groceries and snacks are obtainable at *Marie and Sons Mini-Market*. Delicious meals from an extensive menu can be enjoyed at the *Nomad Restaurant*, near the public beach. À la carte dishes, buffets and theme-meal evenings are offered by both hotels.

GOODLANDS

Sitting deep in a sea of green sugar cane, Goodlands seems to have remained in the colonial era of Mauritius. It is virtually impossible finding a place to stay in Goodlands, but a visit is a must. It is a busy rural centre with sites worth visiting.

You can get to Goodlands from Flacq or, with a long detour, from Port Louis. The quickest way is to take the Port Louis to Grand Gaube bus, change in Grand Gaube and take the Flacq bus which stops in Goodlands. It should not take you more than an hour to reach Goodlands from Port Louis. At the bus depot on the south-eastern side of Goodlands, you will find buses covering the entire northern region of Mauritius. It closes after 17h30 and no buses are found until the next morning at 5h30. There are taxis, but if you are stuck for transport, go to the police station, near the Total fuel station. A policeman will quickly find you a taxi or a relative to drive you to your destination.

There are several banks in Goodlands. The Union International Bank is next to the Commercial Centre, in the busy main road. BNP is near Alliance Française, while the Mauritius Commercial bank is close to Royal Trading. The State Commercial Bank is in town, not far from Historic Marine Model Ship Factory.

The post office is in the central business district. Sun Island Tours, also in the CBD, can arrange a guided tour of the local sugar mill and of some of the plantation mansions. Medical attention can be had from Dr BS Cavssy, near Alliance Française. On the main road is a European-trained dentist, Dr A Mangou. Goodlands Pharmacy, opposite Royal Trading, has a wide range of prescription and unscheduled drugs.

Every visitor to Goodlands should visit the plantation house south of the sugar mill and Eglise Ste Claire Mission. Sitting in a manicured tropical garden, the mansion evokes a bygone era. The gracious rattan furniture, roof-high slatted doorways and cool scented breezes will transport visitors to the age of colonial living. Very few of the plantation houses are open to the public, but a request to visit is hardly ever refused. The estate owners and managers who live in these houses appreciate the interest and will spend hours telling you the history of the plantation, local legends and the folklore of Mauritius.

The sugar mill can also be visited, provided you have made arrangements at least 12 hours before with the plant manager. Cathay Garment Manufacturers, near the youth centre, is one of the few factories that allow visitors to see its work in progress. Eglise Ste Claire Mission, at the south of town, is also worth a visit. The volunteers are amiable and talkative. Unless you manage to arrange accommodation at one of the sugar estates or through the people at the mission, there is no place to stay in Goodlands. If you are French, the Alliance Française may arrange a room with one of its staff. Those who do not mind sleeping rough are gladly offered a corner in the youth centre. There are spartan washing facilities on site.

Snacks and light meals are available from the many street vendors who line the main road through town. *Bonne Bouche Snacks* has a selection of fast foods, but can provide meals if you give them about three hours' notice.

Good places at which to do shopping are *Network Leather*, close to Cathay Garment Manufacturers, and *Tolaram Tulsidas* duty-free curio shop, opposite the Total fuel station. They both offer a good range of items although Tolaram Tulsidas is rather expensive, despite selling duty-free goods. Take along your passport and air ticket if buying at this shop. Goodlands' greatest attraction is the *Historic Marine Model Ship Factory* on the road south. This is one of the workshops where visitors can watch the model makers at work. In comparison to other locales, the prices are reasonable, and the factory will arrange posting of the item you buy. There is no need to worry about its reliability, as over 42% of all purchases are sent via the postal service.

POUDRE D'OR

Poudre d'Or village, south-east of Goodlands, is the centre for the search for pirate treasure on Mauritius. Tourists have not yet discovered this quiet little village in the sugar cane fields, but for years, treasure hunters have visited the area to gather clues in their search for the hidden millions of La Buse (Olivier le Vasseur) and Butin Nageon de L'Estang.

To start any search for treasure, one must cross the river and inspect the church of Ste-Philomène. Built in 1847, this striking Gothic church will be opened for you by the curator. Palms and wild flowers surround the church. There is a small statue to Father Pierre Laval and scenes from the life of Christ on the walls. In the St Augustine cemetery are tombstones that date back to 1845.

Legend has it that if you walk about 260 m north-east from the altar in Ste-Philomène you will find a sinkhole in the river. It is said that this is where pirate treasure lies hidden. The stories started when L'Estang established his base in the north-east of Île de France (Mauritius) in 1797. In letters to a nephew in 1800, he speaks of pirate markings in the north-east of Mauritius, pits in the river and gives directions on a map of northern Mauritius. In his book *The treasure seeker's treasury*, Roy Norville devotes an entire chapter to the search for this elusive treasure.

Only three buses per day stop at Poudre d'Or. The first arrives from Flacq at about 7h30, the second at midday and the last bus enters the village at around 16h45 on its way from Grande Gaube to Flacq.

The monument to the vessel *St Géran* is on the coast east of the village. It was the sinking of the *St Géran* in 1744 that inspired the writing of the famous love story by Frenchman Bernardin de St Pierre, *Paul et Virginie*. Most of the artifacts brought to the surface in 1966 from the wreck can be seen in the Naval Museum in Mahébourg.

Snacks can be bought from *Mon Reve Snacks* and light meals eaten at *Restaurant Coin du Nord*, which also does a nice line in traditional Creole takeaways, and sells cold sodas.

PAMPLEMOUSSES

One of the highlights of any visit to Mauritius is a tour of the world famous Royal Botanical gardens of Pamplemousses. A small town has developed around the gardens and has a number of things which might interest travellers. You can reach Pamplemousses from Port Louis by taking the Rivière du Rempart or Centre de Flacq bus. From Grand Gaube catch the Flacq bus.

The Mauritius Central Bank is across the Atard river bridge, built in 1868. A community health centre offers basic treatment of minor ailments free of charge. Light midday meals are available from *Master's Snacks* on the main road through the settlement. Two places which sell model ships are *Galerie Fur* and *Art of Historic Naval Models*. At *Moussa Boutik,* those searching for island wear will find a colourful range that includes silk saris.

Tabagie Supermarket, which bakes the most delicious bread rolls, has shelves full of South African products at inflated prices.

To reach the Pamplemousses gardens, cross the Fropier river bridge and turn right through the big wrought-iron gates – donated by Frenchman Lienard de la Mirois. Founded in 1735 by Mahé de Labourdonnais, and intensively cultivated by the father of Indian Ocean spices, Pierre Poivre, the gardens were later abandoned. In 1850 the English botanist, James Duncan, restarted them. Today the famous gardens are home to a bewildering variety of plants that include such rarities as the giant Victoria regia water lilies and the talipot palm (*Corypha umbraculifera*), which flowers but once before dying.

Palms are a feature of Pamplemousses. You will see royal palms, bottle palms, *Birmarkia,* raffia and fan palms. One of the oldest trees in the park is the 205-year-old Buddha tree. Ask the gardeners for directions to it. There are also majestic stands of mahogany and ebony trees. Visitors may view neat plantings of spices such as nutmeg, cinnamon and allspice.

Start your tour by wandering along royal palm (*Roystunea regia*)-lined Avenue Poivre. Turn left into Avenue Cossigny and proceed to the monument to Lienard de la Mirois. On the corner, in a small area to the right, are talipot palms. Turn right into Avenue Labourdonnais and follow it past the water lily pond until it becomes Avenue James P Koenig and skirts the tranquil and beautiful lotus pond. On Avenue Sir John Pope Hennessy, turn right again, walking down to the T-junction on Avenue Her Royal Highness Princess Margaret. The Château Mon Plaisir, in which Governor Mahé de Labourdonnais is supposed to have once lived, is on the square here. This magnificent house is now part of the gardens' administrative centre. Where Avenue Shrimati Indira Gandhi enters the same square, there is a collection of tortoise pens that contain specimens of the endangered Giant Aldabra tortoise – feeding time is 10h00. To the right of Indira Gandhi Avenue is the reconstruction of a French sugar mill. Going right into Avenue Mon Plaisir, visitors pass two large, well-stocked fish ponds. Where this avenue meets Avenue Paul et Virginie is a monument to the two lovers. Avenue Cere will take you back to the main gate.

It is advisable to purchase one of the informative pamphlets on sale at the kiosk before starting your tour. Most of the plants are in bloom between late November and early April. The gardens become a world of bright colours, tantalising scents and gentle beauty. Guides can be hired from the many who will approach you on arrival, but their fees are high and the well-planned park is easy to explore alone.

The gardens are open every day from 6h00-18h00. Cyclones continue to wreak occasional havoc on the site and when this happens the grounds are closed until cleaning up has finished.

CENTRE DE FLACQ

This bustling market and transport depot town on the east coast has somehow managed to escape getting caught up in the tourism industry. True, there are curio shops, taxis and touts, but the main populace is engaged in the production of sugar cane, fresh produce and poultry farming, plus a little illicit alcohol distilling.

Buses from Port Louis, the north, central and south-eastern regions of Mauritius congregate here. The main bus depot is next to the fire station, east of the CBD. Numerous taxis gather opposite the bus station, to take people to the surrounding villages or to the hotels along the coast to the east.

There are branches of BNP, Union International and Barclays banks in town. An efficient post office keeps poste restante mail for 21 days before returning it to Port Louis.

There is not a great deal to see or do in the town itself, but by hiring a bicycle from one of the hotels, trips can be made to the surrounding area. At **Bon Accueil** there are two architecturally exquisite Hindu temples (Gayanath Mandir).

To the west is a road that turns south from the tiny settlement of Pont Bon Dieu. This road will take you down to the small La Nicoliere Nature Reserve and lake. Visitors are a rarity at this nature reserve and the staff are very helpful. Visitors may see one of the rarest creatures on earth, *Pteropus niger*, the blonde bat. They take to flight as evening falls, the sunlight turning their dull brown fur to blonde and gold.

To the north-east, banana plantations, conifers and swamps hide the Mauritius radio telescope deep in the woods. Although the site is off limits to the general public, you are allowed to visit with permission from the university or Mauritius Telecom. University of Mauritius, Science Faculty, Port Louis, tel. 454-1041. Mauritius Telecom, Corporate Office, Port Louis, tel. 208-7000, fax 208-8881.

The areas around the town are full of ruined sugar mills, lime kilns and sugar burners' huts. A sparkling white Hindu temple is at the end of a long causeway leading out into the ocean at the north point of Belle Mare beach. Visitors who are interested may visit from about 6h00-7h30 and then again at sunset.

The old Christian church, St Julien, built in 1854, is near Poste de Flacq to the north-east of Centre de Flacq. The Constance Sugar company provides tours of its estates to watch the day to day running of the sugar plantation and sugar mill. Call them at least 24 hours in advance, tel. 413-2543. Between Bonne Mere and Camp de Masque is the FUEL (Flacq Union of Estates Ltd) sugar mill, one of the largest on the island. Visitors are permitted to enter and watch the production of molasses and "hard" sugar from the raw cane.

The beaches at Belle Mare are long, white and accessible to the public via the coastal road. St Géran Hotel has the best location on the north point of the beach, but the Belle Mare Plage also has reefed lagoons and a long white beach lined with casuarina trees. On the trip from Poste de Flacq to Belle Mare you will pass a privately-owned deer reserve on the left. Visitors cannot actually visit the reserve, but the deer are tame and graze near the fence.

Accommodation

Two of the island's top hotels are located on the coast east of Centre de Flacq, St Géran and Belle Mare Plage. Getting to them can be difficult. Buses no longer make the trip from Centre de Flacq, through Poste de Flacq and on to Belle Mare. You must walk from Poste de Flacq, or take a taxi from Centre de Flacq.

St Géran (high tariff)

Vogue magazine described St Géran as "a pearl of rare perfection". Owned by Sun International, St Géran was opened by the first prime minister of Mauritius, Sir Seewoosagur Ramgoolam, in October 1975. Since then the hotel has come to be considered among the best holiday resort hotels in the world. It may not be quite the same standard as the Royal Palm, but the differences are so small as to go unnoticed by most vacationers.

There are 175 luxurious rooms. Each room has a European-styled bathroom, air-conditioner and a small safe. Two top international interior decorators, Oscar Llinas and Robert Bilkey, have created a hotel of subtle shades, relaxing tones and vibrant hues.

Seafood is a speciality at the Paul et Virginie restaurant. Meals are also served on La Terrasse and in the elegant Les Cascades restaurant. There are seven internationally renowned chefs working at St Géran, reason enough to stop and have a meal here. Non-residents may reserve a table for dinner, but it is advisable to book at least three days ahead.

At night, the hotel explodes into life, with a casino and open-air dancing around the water-filled canals that edge the building. Free water sports, guided island excursions, sailing, tennis and golf on a nine-hole course – lined by over 4 000 palm trees – complete the outdoor activities offered to guests. The hotel is popular with French and South African tourists alike. It is vital that you book at least 90 days in advance. St Géran Hotel, Poste de Flacq, Belle Mare, Mauritius, tel. 415-1825, fax 415-1983.

Belle Mare Plage (medium-high tariff)

Also on Belle Mare is the luxurious Belle Mare Plage Hotel and Golf Resort. Renowned for its ambience and good service, the Belle Mare Plage is one of the gems of Mauritian hotels. Its excursions are considered among the best on the island. Two of the more popular tours are to Île aux Cerfs and the waterfall at Grand Rivière Sud-Est, and sailing cruises to the site of the famous English and French naval battle of Grand Port. Other activities organised by the hotel are scuba diving and game fishing.

The hotel has 178 rooms, decorated in various tropical designs. It also has a health centre and casino piano-bar. The casino is of international standard, with roulette, blackjack and slot machines. The hotel's conference room is able to accommodate over 80 people. The swimming pool extends all around the buildings and grounds.

An 18-hole golf course surrounds the hotel in a profusion of trees, lawns and flowers. Free water sports are offered: windsurfing, sailing, snorkelling, waterskiing and pedalos. Among the more unusual activities available at the hotel are daily yoga classes in the tropical garden and a giant chess game in the park-like grounds.

Three restaurants and two bars add to the comprehensive list of amenities. Residents on half board have breakfast and dinner in the main restaurant overlooking the beach. In the à la carte restaurant, near the sea, diners may choose from a menu that includes Creole and Continental dishes. During the day, snacks and lunch are available from the Beach restaurant around the swimming pool.

This is the only hotel on Mauritius that provides guests with a detailed map of the island when they check in. This map is detailed enough to include streets in Port Louis and roads around the island. The hotel is popular with package tours and you should make your reservations 60 days ahead, and restaurant bookings no later than 24 hours ahead. Belle Mare Plage Hotel and Resort, Poste de Flacq, Mauritius, tel. 413-2083, fax 413-2082.

Places to eat

Unless you enjoy eating Creole meals, there is not much to select from in and around town, other than the restaurants at St Géran and Belle Mare Plage, which have expensive but excellent menus and daily specialities.

There are several snack bars and cafés in Centre de Flacq. The street vendors offer the more traditional snacks of samosas and chili-bites. *Kentucky Fried Chicken* has a successful outlet in the CBD. *Café Monaco* has tasty seafood and rice dishes at low prices. The best place for a reasonably priced meal is *Le Pekinois* restaurant, across the road from the bus depot. In Poste de Flacq, light traditional meals may be eaten at *Bijouterie*.

Fresh-produce sellers set up their stalls every day in Centre de Flacq, and on Saturday and Sunday, lots of rural people also bring in their wares. The market spills out all over the town, offering vegetarians and budget travellers a wonderful array of goods from which to choose.

ÎLE AUX CERFS

Lying off the east coast of Mauritius, this island, with its northern neighbour L'Îlot Mangenie (Île de L'Est), is arguably the most visited island off Mauritius. St Géran offers guest exchanges with its other hotel, Le Touessrok Sun, on the mainland a few hundred metres from Île aux Cerfs. The island itself belongs to the Sun Group, but non-residents are permitted to visit.

Frequent ferries ply the short stretch of water between the island and the mainland every 30 or so minutes. The ferry leaves from Pointe Maurice, where you purchase tickets if not on an organised tour. Depending on the tide and weather conditions, the trip usually takes about 20 minutes. Water sports equipment may be rented from the boathouse but prices are higher than on the mainland. One of the two restaurants on Île aux Cerfs is the Paul et Virginie. It is costly, overcrowded at lunch time and offers a rather disappointing menu. Budget travellers should consider taking along a packed lunch from their hotel. People on organised tours are all provided with lunch or taken to the Paul et Virginie for a light meal. The second restaurant is just as expensive and has an even smaller menu.

Curio shops have been built at strategically placed sites around the island, and, if you laze about on the eastern beaches, sellers will bring you their wares for inspection. Bargaining is expected and few of the vendors actually expect to receive their first asking price. A good starting point is about 50% less than they ask. Count on a long, mirthful tussle until reaching the proverbial, "Okay, last price."

To reach Îlot Mangenie requires some ingenuity. You could always try to sail across on one of the dinghies from Le Touessrok. Some knowledge of currents and winds is advisable though. Alternatively, speak to the fishermen who land their daily catches on the beach. They are usually in by 7h00 and, for a negotiable fee, will take you across. There are excellent places for snorkelling off this island but beware of the spiny sea urchins that litter the shallower reefs. Belle Mare Plage Hotel runs boat excursions to and around these islands. Its prices are fair and worth considering, especially if you also want to see the majestic waterfall of Grand Rivière Sud-Est, on the coast.

Guests at the high tariff, luxury, 162-room Le Touessrok Sun Hotel must book well in advance if they hope to get accommodation. La Passerelle restaurant presents enormous Mauritian buffets and the Pergola caters for those who want Italian dishes. The hotel frequently hosts traditional sega dancing. Le Touessrok Sun Hotel, c/o Trou d'Eau Douce, Mauritius, tel. 419-2451, fax 419-2025.

9 SOUTHERN AND WESTERN MAURITIUS

The southern portion of Grand Port province, all of Savanne and Rivière Noire, plus most of Plaines Wilhems province, make up this part of Mauritius.

This is the least developed part of the island. It has areas of striking beauty and the island's last wilderness regions. Southern and western Mauritius is quiet, sedate and sparsely populated and many of the beaches are relatively empty. From the blowhole at Le Souffleur, to the holy lake at Grand Bassin, on through the forests of the Macchabée Nature Reserve and down into the valleys of the Black River gorges before ending at the brooding bulk of Le Morne, the natural beauty of this area is astounding.

A journey through southern and western Mauritius inevitably starts from the town of Mahébourg on the east coast. (The town itself is dealt with in chapter 10.) Proceed south along the Souillac road. There are signs in the settlement of L'Escalier pointing the way to Le Souffleur blowhole on the coast. Buses travelling from Mahébourg to Souillac also pass through the village. From the sugar mill it is about 2 km to the site. To reach Le Souffleur proper, visitors have to get a permit from the reception office at the sugar mill. Located near the point, Le Souffleur is awe-inspiring. At high tide or during storms it can get quite frightening standing near the edge of the hole, especially when it's overcast and the angry ocean crashes against the headland, causing the earth beneath you to tremble. Tourists are only allowed to visit the site from Monday to Friday and Saturday morning, but there are no gates and no-one seems to mind your wandering down on a Saturday afternoon or Sunday.

In the village of **Britannia**, west of L'Escalier, is the beautiful Tookay Hindu temple. You can reach Britannia by taking the bus from Mahébourg bound for Rivière des Anguilles. At Rivière des Anguilles get off and wait for the bus that travels north to Rose Belle via Britannia.

Between Tyack and St Aubin is the village of **Rivière des Anguilles** and the turning for La Vanille Crocodile Park. The park, which breeds Nile crocodiles imported from Madagascar, may trouble sensitive visitors. Breeding crocodiles just for their skin is rather disturbing to some. The walks through the thick forest are, however, enjoyable and worth doing. The boutique sells an assortment of crocodile skin handbags, belts, a few pairs of shoes and other expensive accessories.

The settlement of Rivière des Anguilles was built in 1914, and a second section added in 1968. Accommodation is difficult to find in the area and those who need a place to stay should ask at Newton College in Tyack or at the Shri Krishna Ashrama in Union. The district around Rivière des Anguilles is full of indigenous forests, gorges and wide rivers, as well as numerous little waterfalls and deep pools to swim in. The small Combo Nature Reserve is located to the west, on the outskirts of town. There is not a great deal to see, but the solitude and tranquillity are very pleasant.

You can reach Rivière des Anguilles by taking a bus from Mahébourg, on the east coast, or via a scenic trip down from the large urban centre of Curepipe, in the centre of the island.

A few kilometres east of Souillac is the mysterious "Rock that Cries" (La Roche qui Pleure), so named because of the striking similarity between the shape of a man crying and the rock formation over the sea. The site is far off the tourist trail, but definitely worth the detour. A pleasant stroll can be made along the coastal cliffs from Gris Gris to La Roche qui Pleure. It should not take more than 30 minutes of unhurried walking.

Before reaching Souillac, there is a turn-off to the intriguingly named Gris Gris. Pronounced "Gree Gree", the site has a small beach and fascinating black rock sculptures created by aeons of ocean and wind erosion. Few visitors make the trip down to the beach, but those who do are rewarded by the wild, eerie atmosphere of the place. The name means "witch" or "spirit", but its origins are lost in Mauritian legend. No buses make the journey to Gris Gris and you will have to walk from the turning on the main road. A taxi from Souillac can take you to the top of the hill, from where it is a short walk down a steep path to the isolated shoreline.

SOUILLAC

Situated on a sheltered bay where the Patates and Savanne rivers spill into the sea, Souillac is named after a former island administrator. Viscount de Souillac governed Mauritius for almost nine years, from 1779-1787, until sent east to sort out the problems of the French companies operating out of India and Indo-China. Apart from the forests and spectacular coastal cliffs, the other attractions of Souillac are the Robert-Edward Hart Museum and Dr Charles Telfair Gardens.

There are regular buses between Souillac, Mahébourg and Curepipe throughout the day. The first bus leaves from Curepipe at 7h00, and from Mahébourg at 6h30. The journey can take up to two hours, depending on whether you catch an express or the local bus. It is far more interesting taking the local bus which makes a scenic detour through several small villages.

There is a post office in Souillac and two Mauritian diners serving traditional seafood meals and drinks. The inhabitants are not used to seeing tourists drifting about the streets of their town and are very friendly.

Overlooking the sea, the Telfair Gardens is a place of quiet and fragrant flowers. There are no official guides to the gardens, but the gardener speaks good English and enjoys taking visitors on a tour of the grounds. The views from the garden are impressive, especially of the cliffs above the sea, and across to the lonely graveyard where the famed poet Robert-Edward Hart is buried.

No visit to Souillac is complete without a tour of the Robert-Edward Hart Museum. Not clearly marked, the house lies about 1 km east of Souillac on the coast. Robert-Edward Hart was a Mauritian-born poet who wrote in French. You can find a few copies of his works, in English and French, at the larger bookshops in Port Louis. The house where he spent the last years of his life has been turned into a museum by the Ministry of Culture and Education. Named Le Nef, the house, made of crushed coral and local rock, has changed little since his death in 1954. The Mauritius Institute has arranged the display of his writings inside.

About 4 km north of Souillac, on the Patates river, is Rochester Falls. No public transport goes directly to the falls and taxis are difficult to find in Souillac. The walk from town to the falls is pleasant and winds through sugar cane fields. Just past the church in Souillac, take the gravel road signposted to Rochester Falls and Pepiniere de Terracine. Follow the road through sugar cane and palm groves until it crosses a small bridge. Continue up the hill and keep left for the falls. Proceed alongside the litchi and mango orchards, and, at the banana plantation, take the road which goes downhill to the left. The falls – both sets – are at the bottom of this gravel road.

The best swimming beach in the area is near Villas Pointe aux Roches. Once across the bridge at the settlement of **Surinam**, turn south at the Père Laval shrine. Medium tariff accommodation and the beach are about 5 km away. To reach the beach you must either walk, have your own transport or hire a taxi. *Villas Pointe aux Roches* is situated on a beautiful long beach and provides accommodation in fully equipped bungalows. Its restaurant has tasty seafood dishes and daily specials, all at reasonable prices. Villas Pointe aux Roches, Coastal road, Chemin Grenier, Mauritius, tel. 625-5112, fax 626-2507.

Cheaper accommodation, in the low tariff category, is available in Surinam at the *Eldorado Hotel*. The small hotel is located between the Shell fuel station and Southern Tour Agency. The rooms are clean and the staff friendly. No reservations are necessary. Campers may find a suitable pitch by speaking to the Mother Superior at St André Convent, near Mauri Garments Ltd, near Chemin Grenier.

Excellent meals are available at the *Eldorado Hotel* and *Villas Pointe aux Roches*, and snacks are available at *John Snack* in Surinam and the *Bobby Snack Bar* in Chemin Grenier. The *Souillac Store* in Souillac and *Las Vegas Mini-Market* in Chemin Grenier have a few shelves with groceries.

There are branches of Barclays Bank, MCCB and the State Commercial Bank in **Chemin Grenier**.

Between Bel Ombre sugar estates and Chemin Grenier is Rivière des Galets public beach. Over weekends, this is where local families come to enjoy themselves. The large bay creates some rideable waves as the sea rushes in through a break in the reef. Surfers in search of Mauritian "tubes" are advised to try this spot – or anywhere along the southern coast for that matter.

The Bel Ombre sugar mill allows visits between 8h30 and 16h00 Monday-Friday. West of **Bel Ombre** is a small monument surrounded by casuarina trees, dedicated to the seamen who died after the SS *Trevessa* sank 4 June 1923. Their vessel went down 2 590 km from Bel Ombre. Travelling aboard a raft, completely at the mercy of the sea, they drifted ashore here on 29 June 1923. Only 16 remained alive. Eight had died at sea, and another died soon after making landfall.

La Prairie public beach, further west, is also a popular destination over weekends.

Le Morne mountain rises like a gloomy thundercloud off the south-western tip of Mauritius. Miles of deserted white beaches and forests of casuarinas surround the mountain, but few people swim on the eastern side or stroll through the woods. A village crowds the north-eastern hills of the promontory. There are scattered islets in the sheltered bays. Îlot Fourneau can be reached at low tide. Narratives of buccaneers abound in the area, but little has been done to verify them.

LE MORNE

You can reach Le Morne from Port Louis on the west coast, Quatre Bornes in the highlands, or from Souillac to the east. Frequent buses run down from Port Louis and Quatre Bornes, but only two buses per day make the journey from Souillac.

Basic supplies can be bought from *Sydney Tabagie* and information on local accommodation can be had from Le Morne community centre.

There is a deer park to the north-west of the village. It is private and visitors are not welcome. However, it is fairly easy to sneak in from the road and wander about in the thick forest looking for the elusive Java deer. The more energetic should walk through the reserve and make the strenuous walk to the summit of the hills in the centre of the deer park. Just before reaching the turn-off for the Le Morne hotels, there is a ruined watchtower near the private hunting reserve. You can reach the top of the tower, though the climb is difficult. From the top magnificent views stretch in all directions.

Numerous sad stories surround Le Morne mountain, the most tragic of which involves slaves. In the 1800s a band of slaves escaped their cruel masters and struggled to the summit of the mountain. A few weeks later they saw a file of soldiers climbing the cliffs. Unbeknown to them, slavery had been abolished and the soldiers were hoping to reach them and give them this news. Desperate, near starvation, but still determined not to be captured, they flung themselves from the cliffs in a suicide pact.

Accommodation

At Le Morne, there are only two hotels of any repute. Belonging to the Beachcomber group, they are expensive, luxurious and very popular. Their site has the reputation of being the largest beach resort in the Indian Ocean. Despite the tariff, they are both highly recommended by international travel agencies.

Paradis and Brabant Hotels, Golf Club, Fishing Club and Casino (high tariff)

With 150 ha of land surrounding the hotels, and the best golf course on the island, Paradis-Brabant has become a popular destination. The beachfront alone extends for almost 7 km around the peninsula.

The Paradis has 176 rooms, of which 104 are sea facing. The equally sumptuous Brabant has 87 rooms, of which 76 are sea facing. All rooms have air-conditioning, bathroom en suite and a terrace. Three restaurants offer lavish meals of Continental and Mauritian delicacies. Guests and even non-residents should try to eat at least one dinner in the elegant and romantic Blue Marlin restaurant, which specialises in seafood dishes. Three bars provide refreshments during the day and into the early hours of the morning.

A band provides nightly entertainment and on certain nights there are sega dancing, theme evenings and short plays. The casino is open each night from 21h00, and has the usual gaming tables and computerised machines. During the day, visitors may try horse riding, tennis or mountain biking. Free water sports facilities include windsurfers, sailing boats, pedalos and kayaks. Expensive game fishing can be arranged on one of the nine Challenger boats. Scuba diving is another popular pursuit and both instruction and equipment are available.

The complex has facilities for carrying out financial transactions, exclusive boutiques, a hairdresser, and for parents, baby-sitters and a mini-club. Three sparkling swimming pools have been built to complement the glorious sea and carefully tended tropical gardens.

The hotels' biggest outdoor attraction – apart from the long white beach and crystal clear sea – is the challenging 18-hole golf course designed by David Dutton. The course hosts regular competitions. The Beachcomber group has even employed a golf pro to coach novices and those eager to improve their game.

Reservations must be made at least 60 days in advance. Paradis and Brabant, Case Noyale, Le Morne, Mauritius, tel. 683-6775, fax 683-6786.

Proceeding north, visitors arrive at the village of **La Gaulette** with its interesting Ventricosa Sea Shell Shop along the main road.

CHAMAREL

At Case Noyale, turn east at Mater Dolorosa church for Chamarel. The road climbs steeply from the coast into thick rainforests – among the few left on Mauritius. Pass the Chamarel restaurant on the summit and continue straight on for the coloured earths. A little east of Chamarel Lumiere store is the entrance to the geological site. An entrance fee must be paid if you are driving into the area – walkers are allowed in free – and a permit received (Permis d'Acces aux Terres de Couleurs de Chamarel).

It is virtually impossible getting public transport to Chamarel. You can take the Port Louis-Le Morne bus and get off at Chamarel, then hitchhike up, but there is little traffic and the walk up the hills is exhausting. Those vehicles that do pass, provided they are not other tourists or tour buses, usually stop and offer lifts. Taxis are available at Le Morne in the south and Tamarin to the north.

The gravel road to the coloured earths skirts a plantation of Arabica coffee before twisting alongside palm trees, bananas and sugar cane. Then, unexpectedly, you are there. Located deep in an indigenous forest, the little exposed hills cover a small area. There are about seven different colours of soil here. Entwined layers of rock create an imaginative kaleidoscope of browns, yellows, grey and red bands. Get there early if you are to avoid waiting in a queue for a peek.

Do not miss seeing the Cascade Chamarel on the way out. Situated near the entrance gate, this high waterfall is quite breathtaking. A number of paths lead into the forest and down to the pool at the bottom of the waterfall, but the walk is dangerous and you will be plagued by clouds of mosquitoes near the bottom. Instead, follow one of the paths that parallels the waterfall and exits at a view-point about a third of the way down.

MACCHABÉE NATURE RESERVE

By driving east, visitors can cross Piton St Denis and then turn north, below Piton Grand Bassin, to reach the Macchabée Nature Reserve. There are several hiking trails around the park, and visitors interested in walking some of them should contact the Forestry Service head-quarters in Curepipe for a permit. Its offices are on Botanical Gardens Street, Curepipe, tel. 675-4966.

Two buses per day run past the Macchabée Forest and Grand Bassin before returning to the national road near Rose Belle. The one leaves at 7h30 from Quatre Bornes and the other departs Vacoas at around 13h00. There is talk of increasing this to four buses per day. Details of public transport to and around the area are best obtained by enquiring from the National Transport Authority, Domun Building, 14 Barracks Street, Port Louis, tel. 212-1448.

The hikes are graded to last from between 15 minutes to two hours. Visitors can view a variety of indigenous and exotic trees and may get a glimpse of blonde bats, shrews and deer. From the eastern and southern sides of the Macchabée Forest there are wide vistas across the imposing Gorges de la Rivière Noire (Black River gorges). You can see some of the steep hills and folded valleys from Plaine Champagne, or travel further south to the viewpoint near the entrance to Macchabée Forest. To really appreciate them you should shoulder a pack, hire a guide and make the journey into the forested gorges yourself. It is also possible to walk through the forests and thick vegetation to the summit of Piton de la Rivière Noire. At 828 m, it is Mauritius's highest peak.

From Macchabée Forest it is a short trip east to Grand Bassin. Known to the locals as Ganga Talao, this holy Hindu lake is reputed to have unique curative and spiritual powers. There are a number of temples on the lake shore. Surrounded by fragrant pine forests, the water-filled crater – which is one of only two natural lakes on Mauritius – is the site of yearly Hindu pilgrimages during late February and early March.

The next site of interest is Kanaka crater. Proceed east through the forest, until entering the tea gardens. Across the Ruisseau Marron bridge, visitors will arrive at the Rivière des Anguilles, where a delightful set of cascades is located downstream. At the Hindu shrine follow the signs for Kanaka crater through sugar cane and tea estates. Where the tea gardens are fringed by thick natural scrub, take the gravel road left. This brings visitors to the base of the crater. Push your way up through the bush to the eroded rim, for a view down into the extinct caldera. If you have no transport, take the bus from Vacoas or Curepipe that stops at **Bois Cheri**, then walk from the village to the crater. It is about 3 km to the base of the hill.

TAMARIN

Famous for its salt pans and surfing, Tamarin is one of the cheaper tourist areas of the country.

Buses run from Port Louis and Quatre Bornes to Tamarin. The first bus leaves the capital at 6h30, the last returns at 17h00. From Quatre Borne, travellers must catch the local bus that goes through Vacoas and then to the coast. The trip itself lasts about two hours. Take the early bus that departs at about 7h00, bound for Baie du Cap.

Tamarin has a post office in the main street and the MCCB bank has an office not far from the steel Tamarin bridge.

Surfers will find the waves off Tamarin good. A local surf crowd hangs out on the beach. They are a friendly bunch of youngsters, who enjoy chatting to visitors. Tamarin beach is safe for swimming, and usually has a good shore-break for body surfing.

Things to do

Three sites worth seeing around Tamarin are the salt pans, Tamarind Falls and Tourelle du Tamarin. The salt pans are located between the Apostrophe Bookshop and the Catholic church. You can hardly miss them alongside the road. Visitors are not actively encouraged, but permission to enter will be granted by the site manager. Lying in thick layers over concrete beds, the oddly yellowish salt is turned, dried and then packed in the warehouse behind the pans.

Just getting to Tamarind Falls is an accomplishment. At the T-junction, follow the signs for Yemen and Magenta. The gravel road continues through sugar estates for 1 km before reaching a small sign on the left, pointing the way to the falls. Where the road reaches the river, near the Electrical Services Division, turn up-stream to reach the small falls, overhung with trees and lush vegetation. There have been several reports of visitors being turned back by estate managers. According to the Ministry of Environment and Quality of Life, no official regulation exists to limit visitors to the falls. If you have any problems, contact the Director, Department of the Environment, 9th Floor, Ken Lee Tower, corner St George and Barracks Streets, Port Louis. Alternatively, phone to find out the latest on negotiations between the sugar barons and the government, tel. 212-6080.

A walk to the top of Tourelle du Tamarin is best started from the Apostrophe Bookshop in Tamarin. A number of paths lead to the summit. The one that follows the fence alongside the salt pans is the most popular. The relatively easy journey to the top should take about an hour. Remember to pack something to drink on the hike. The high humidity and heat have often taken their toll on unwary walkers.

Accommodation

The *Tamarin Hotel* is well situated on the beach, but tends to increase rates substantially during the Christmas festive season. With Le Morne and highland towns being so close, it is preferable to seek tourist accommodation there. However, if you would rather stay at Tamarin, then make your hotel reservation no later than 20 days in advance. Tamarin Hotel, c/o PO Tamarin Bay, Mauritius, tel. 683-6583.

You could always find medium-high tariff accommodation at **Flic en Flac**, less than 10 km away to the north. There is tourist accommodation at:

Le Pearle Beach Hotel, 60 rooms, restaurant and pool. Wolmar, Flic en Flac, Mauritius, tel. 453-8428, fax 453-8405

Villas Caroline Hotel-Bungalows, 34 double rooms, 12 self-catering bungalows, free water sports. Flic en Flac, Mauritius, tel. 453-8411, fax 453-8144

Klondike Village Vacances, 20 self-contained studios, restaurant, swimming pool and nightly entertainment. c/o PO Flic en Flac, Mauritius, tel. 453-8333, fax 453-8337

Budget travellers may find lodgings with local families. Try asking at the police station or among the salt workers. Overnight accommodation is also available at the WWF Wildlife Supporters Club, along the main road near the salt warehouse.

Tasty meals are available at *Jardin des Îles Restaurant*, near the Caltex fuel depot. It has a wide range of Creole dishes. The seafood, however, is its forte. The fresh line-fish is especially delicious.

Tourists looking for authentic Mauritian shells should not miss the opportunity of visiting the largest shell outlet on the island, Shellorama. Both a shop and museum, the building has an unbelievable selection of seashells. Prices are much lower than in Port Louis or in the northern areas, but the sheer quantity may trouble environmentally sensitive visitors. You tend to wonder if there is anything left in the surrounding sea.

The Casela Bird Park is less than 3 km south of Bambous. Crouching below 780 m high Mt du Rempart, this 8 ha park contains about 3 000 birds of over 140 species. The birds have been captured all over the world and sit together in cramped aviaries. One of the rarest birds on earth, the pink pigeon, is also kept in captivity here. Equally disheartening to see are the caged tigers and monkeys. Open from 9h00-18h00, between 1 October and 31 March, and 9h00-17h00, between 1 April and 30 September, Casela Bird Park is an unsettling place. You will find many tour groups arriving here, and guides can be hired at the payment counter.

VACOAS

Spreading south of the national road between Port Louis and Mahébourg, Vacoas encompasses the villages of Floreal and Réunion. As Quatre Bornes continues to grow in its unplanned way, it will not be long before Quatre Bornes and Vacoas become one. The town is famous for growing colourful and delicately scented flowers. The people of Vacoas pride themselves on their gardens, and a stroll around town looking at the flowers is recommended.

There is plentiful public transport serving Vacoas. Nearly all the Quatre Bornes buses travelling the southern parts of Mauritius stop at different places in Vacoas. The main bus depot is near Blendax Knitwear. Look for the National Transport Corporation sign. To reach Vacoas from the north, take a bus for Quatre Bornes or Curepipe. Buses which stop in Vacoas leave from the bus station in both towns every 45 minutes.

The post office is next to Sunshine store on the main road through town. The State Bank and MCCB bank have representation here. The State Bank is near Victoria hospital, while MCCB is between the mosque and Klodinot T-Shirts.

There is no tourist accommodation in Vacoas. Budget travellers who want an overnight room should ask at Restaurant U-Bees or, if desperate, the swami at the Kali Mata Mandir (Hindu temple), to the side of GG House. A limited range of foodstuffs is sold at the Sunshine store. Street vendors offer spicy snacks and a cheap, filling plate of vegetable curry and rice.

In and around Vacoas visitors can find several things of interest. In town, the Kali Mata Mandir is a colourful temple. The World Spiritual University is also situated in Vacoas.

Out south, at the little settlement of La Marie, visitors are taken on guided walks through the vast anthurium nurseries. Further south, in an area of conifers and mist, is Marie aux Vacoas Lake. With permission from the Department of Forestry in Curepipe, campers may pitch their tent along the lake shore for up to three days, free of charge. The old foresters' houses are deep in the woods above the lake, and make for cosy, if eerie, accommodation.

10 CENTRAL MAURITIUS

Central Mauritius is the most cosmopolitan region of the island. Commencing at Pointe aux Sables in Rivière Noire province, through the large towns of Quatre Borne and Curepipe on the northern edge of Plaines Wilhems district, and on to Mahébourg in the province of Grand Port, central Mauritius offers a change from beach resorts, casuarina trees and curio vendors. Here, you will discover cool, mist-laden tea gardens, towering mountains, affectionate locals and a distinctly European flavour to daily life.

POINTE AUX SABLES

Less than 5 km south-west of Port Louis, Pointe aux Sables is a favourite weekend destination of families from the capital. It also has the reputation of being the most rowdy area on the island. The entertainment is, however, not aimed at tourists, but rather at city businessmen and their clients. Take care when indulging in the delights – this is also the island's centre for petty crime, the occasional punch-up and even robbery.

Getting there

You can reach Pointe aux Sables from Port Louis on a 20 minute bus ride through the capital's southern suburbs. Take a bus going specifically to Pointe aux Sables, or one of the buses serving the southern provinces. The buses leave from Victoria Square bus station every 60 minutes. During the Hindu holiday season this is increased to one every 30 minutes. The last bus leaves Port Louis for Pointe aux Sables at about 18h30. Visitors on a tour of the nightlife at Pointe aux Sables will need to take a taxi from Port Louis.

Things to do

At night, Pointe aux Sables is transformed from a lazy, sun-baked village into a vibrant, swirling mass of music, dancers, prostitutes, drug-peddlers and nightclubs. Younger visitors are sure to find the pace and vitality exciting, and should make every effort to spend a few entertaining hours at the Golden Moon Nightclub.

Apart from swimming at the safe beach off the point, there is not a great deal of interest for families at Pointe aux Sables. There are plans to spruce up the area and turn it into another major tourist destination, but as yet nothing has been done.

Accommodation

The biggest drawback to changing the area will be the sharp increase in accommodation rates. Catering mainly for the islanders, prices are still low enough to be attractive to budget travellers. Bear in mind also that the Mauritian holidaymaker is not that concerned with the appearance or cleanliness of the room. Take along plastic sandals for wearing in the shower, and include some form of insect repellent in your luggage.

Low-medium tariff accommodation, suitable for foreign tourists, can be found at the somewhat run down *Venus Hotel*, near the beach on Royal Road. Its restaurant does a good range of cheap meals, and the hotel is well situated for night-time excursions to the Golden Moon Nightclub, or for drinks at the Beach Hotel Bar (which is exactly that, a bar with rooms for hire by the hour). In the same price range are the *bungalows* belonging to Sir Harroon Hossenally. These clean chalets are set in a small garden south-west of the Venus Hotel. They are popular throughout the year. You must book accommodation 60 days in advance. Sir Harroon Hossenally, c/o Diane Liong Phew, Royal Road, Pointe aux Sables, Mauritius, tel. 234-4655.

If stuck for accommodation, ask for assistance at the police station. An officer can usually arrange something in a private house, or point you in the direction of a *pension*. These are not advertised and rely solely on word of mouth for custom.

Places to eat

Meals are available from the *Venus Hotel*, and the maids at *Hossenally's bungalows* will prepare meals, provided you buy the supplies. The best place for food is the *Tung Fong* restaurant on Royal Road. Serving enormous Chinese meals, it is a frequent lunch-time stop for tour buses. If you want to eat there at night, the management expects a reservation; about 24 hours' notice is sufficient, tel. 208-6279. Next to the Golden

Moon Nightclub is another small restaurant, but the food is of poor quality and the menu very limited.

MOKA

Regarded as one of the island's most beautiful settlements, Moka nestles below the 723 m Pic des Guibies about 10 km south-east of Port Louis. It is famous as the intellectual centre of Mauritius. Both the main campus of the university and the world-renowned Mahatma Gandhi Institute are located here. The setting of the town, among hills, forests and valleys, is in itself worth the visit. In the area travellers will find the Eureka Creole Museum, Domaine les Pailles nature park and Le Réduit, the governor's gracious mansion.

Getting there

Getting to Moka is no bother. Take any of the buses travelling from Port Louis to Quatre Bornes, Curepipe or Mahébourg, or a bus from any of those urban centres to Port Louis. Buses travel from most large towns from about 5h45-18h00. Moka is also one of the best places from which to hitchhike, especially to Port Louis, or east to Curepipe and Mahébourg.

Things to do

Travellers to the area should make every effort to visit Domaine les Pailles Nature Park. Just over 4 km north-west of Moka, Domaine les Pailles is one of the island's most famous nature reserves. Spreading across 1 250 ha of wilderness below the Moka mountain range, the park includes flora, fauna and historical exhibits. In addition, there are two fantastic restaurants, Le Clos St Louis and La Cannelle Rouge, and a small casino in the reserve.

Many tourists enjoy Domaine les Pailles in an ox- or horse-drawn cart, but it is far more interesting just to walk around the estate. You can also hire a horse from Les Ecuries du Domaine Centre Equestre stables. Even more costly than an ox cart, and a lot more exciting due to the terrain it covers, is a tour in a 4x4 Landrover. These vehicles take guests close to the summit of Pic des Guibies.

Drift down to the spice garden, or follow one of the forest paths that skirt clumps of ebony, mahogany, takamaka and palm trees. In the forest visitors are likely to encounter Java deer, samango monkeys and see such Mauritian rarities as pink pigeons and blonde bats. You may also visit a replica of the first sugar mill on the island, and try rum from its own distillery. For more details and restaurant reservations contact the park directly. Domaine les Pailles, c/o PO Pailles, Mauritius, tel. 212-6003, fax 212-4226.

The Mahatma Gandhi Institute, in Moka, will have a particular attraction for Hindus, or those with an interest in the Mauritian educational system. Set beneath hills and surrounded by forests, the institute is a place of silence and calmness.

Le Réduit is a beautiful 18th century mansion built by Frenchman Barthélémy David in 1778. Today it houses, not the governor, but the Mauritian army. Public visits are difficult to organise for one or two people. A group of you stand a better chance of being admitted, but only between 9h00-12h00, Monday to Friday. Tell the sentry that you would like to speak to the camp adjutant. This affable man usually agrees to your entry and provides written consent and a guide – who is, obviously, a soldier. You can find out more of the history of the building by speaking to the military historian at the museum in Port Louis.

There are several walks around the area that should be considered. There is an abundance of mountain streams, with waterfalls in the forests. Prepare a day-pack with some food and something to drink and set off north or north-west from Moka. Paths lead over mountains, across valleys and some go all the way down to Port Louis.

The Eureka Creole Museum, built in 1830, should be visited. Set in a rolling garden surrounded by mountains and steep valleys, the museum is a window on Mauritian history. An entrance fee is charged and a guide must be hired. The information offered by the guides is rather dull in itself, but the walk through the various rooms is fascinating. Different rooms have been assigned different displays, so that the French East India Room, for example, has collections of furniture and equipment used by the employees and directors of that company. The same is true of other rooms that have historical goods from China, India, Southeast Asia and Great Britain. Open daily from 9h00-18h00, the Eureka Creole Museum is highly recommended on any tour of Mauritius.

Curio shops have been set up in various parts of the museum and surrounds. Prices are high, but the quality of the pieces is equally high. You can eat light meals and snacks at the coffee shop on the wide veranda between 9h30 and 16h00.

Accommodation

There is no tourist accommodation in Moka and visitors will have to look for suitable lodgings in nearby Quatre Borne or along the south-west coast. There is, however, accommodation in **Belle Rose** at the *Riverside Hotel*, tel. 464-4957. **Rose Hill** has two places popular with islanders, *Villa Naheeb*, tel. 464-6495, and *Auberge de Rose Hill*, tel. 464-1793. To the south-west, at the settlement of **Beau Bassin**, spartan rooms are offered by the *Beau Bassin Vacances Hotel*, tel. 454-5249.

Places to eat

Finding snacks is no problem, as there are numerous street stalls around Moka. Meals are more difficult. Visitors should try the many restaurants in Quatre Borne or Rose Hill. **Rose Hill** has three restaurants worth trying for Chinese, Indian, Continental, Creole and seafood dishes. Reservations are recommended.

New Magic Lantern, Royal Road, specialises in Creole meals and seafood, tel. 464-2444

Blue Mauritius, Centre Commercial, for Continental, Creole, Chinese and Indian delicacies, tel. 464-4097

Le Pekinois, corner Royal Road and Ambrose Street, for Chinese specialities, tel. 454-7229

QUATRE BORNES

Mauritius's "Flower Town", Quatre Borne is a busy, vibrant town with a distinctive European atmosphere. Located about 16 km south-east of Port Louis, the town is passed by most visitors on their way to and from the airport in Mahébourg. Reaching Quatre Borne from Port Louis or other regions of Mauritius is relatively easy. There is a large bus depot opposite the market. Taxis may be hired from the taxi rank, near the bus depot.

Developing at a rapid rate in all directions, Quatre Borne is already almost linked to Vacoas, Phoenix and Curepipe. Although there is not a great deal to see in the town, it offers several good restaurants, low-medium tariff accommodation and is the frequent destination of foreign businessmen. Spend a few hours wandering through the tight jumble of stalls that comprise the market. Here you will find food, curios, clothing, fresh produce, traditional musical instruments and agricultural equipment.

There is a post office on the main road through town and several banks. The Hong Kong Bank and Bank of Baroda are near one another between the Gold Crest Hotel and St Jean Pharmacy. MCCB and Barclays Bank are situated in the vicinity of the modern Orchard shopping centre. The State Commercial Bank is near the Tropical pharmacy and King Dragon restaurant.

Basic medical assistance may be received from either the St Jean pharmacy or Tropical pharmacy. If you want natural medical treatment, then you cannot do better than visit the Himalaya Ayuvedic Medicine clinic near Pension Casablanca.

The Indira Gandhi Centre for Indian Culture puts on monthly Indian cultural events and has interesting displays of Indian history on Mauritius. Contact it for further information on its current shows and exhibitions: 85 St Jean Road, Newry Complex, Quatre Borne, tel. 464-3870.

Things to buy

Highland handicrafts are available from a wide selection at Spes Handicraft (take the lane opposite Total fuel station), and the Mauritius Alliance of Women Tourist Boutik, next to the police station.

Accommodation

There are several types of accommodation for tourists. It is not necessary to reserve rooms at any of the places. Top of the range is the *Gold Crest Hotel* (medium tariff), opposite the municipal building and near the centre of the CBD. The hotel is rather oddly arranged. There are rooms only on the third floor, with the restaurant, bar and reception all on the first floor. In between are administrative offices and private business firms. In the courtyard, the Gold Crest cafeteria offers breakfast and snacks. The main restaurant has a menu that includes Continental, Chinese and Indian cuisine. Gold Crest Hotel, St Jean Road, Quatre Bornes, Mauritius, tel. 454-5945, fax 454-9599.

In the low-medium price range is the *Pension de Famille,* on Trianon Avenue. Its rooms are clean, comfortable and inclusive of breakfast. Meals are provided, and vegetarians can ask the manager to arrange for special dishes. Pension de Famille, 43 Trianon Avenue, Quatre Bornes, Mauritius, tel. 424-2163.

Other hotels and guest lodges worth trying are:

Garden House (low-medium tariff). This small lodge, on the outskirts of the town, has four quaint rooms, tel. 424-1214

El Monaco Hotel (medium-high tariff). With 94 rooms, this is the largest hotel in Quatre Bornes. However, it is far from ideal, with rude staff and unkempt rooms. A swimming pool, restaurant and boutique complete the facilities, tel. 425-2631

White House (medium-high tariff). There are nine attractive rooms here. Situated close to both cultural and business facilities, this lodge is a favourite with businessmen, tel. 464-5835

Mountain View (low-medium tariff). Offering guests the best views in Quatre Borne, the Mountain View specialises in Creole food. Many of the guests are locals, always a sure indication of the character of the place. If you plan to stay here, it is recommended that you book about two days before arriving, tel. 426-3041

Auberge de Quatre Borne (low-medium tariff). Recently renovated and now with five rooms, the auberge caters for budget travellers and honeymoon couples. The staff are attentive and hospitable, tel. 424-2163

Places to eat

There are numerous restaurants and eating establishments around Quatre Borne. *Le Bon Choix* restaurant on St Jean Road has tasty Creole and European dishes, plus a daily special, all at very competitive rates. At the *King Dragon* restaurant, near the State Commercial Bank, diners may select from an exhaustive Chinese menu. Its seafood meals are particularly good. If you are planning to self-cater, then visit the market opposite the bus depot, or the Orchard Spar Supermarket, close to the Photo-Plus shop.

For snacks, *Café Singapore* on St Jean Road does a range of spicy traditional pastries from Creole and Chinese recipes. You can also find a good selection of light meals at *Café Dragon Vert*.

Visitors wanting to eat Chinese dishes must go to *Chopsticks* or *Happy Valley* on St Jean Road. There are at least three restaurants worth trying for authentic Creole food: *Rolly's Steak and Seafood House*, *Piment Rouge* and *Le Gavnor*, all on St Jean Road. At *L'Alibi*, there is a piano-bar and restaurant. It concentrates on Continental and Chinese foods.

At night, the places to go are the Palladium, or the Club Malibu. These nightclubs get very full on weekend nights. Both places offer loud music, drinks, flashing lights and are patronised by hundreds of joyous Creoles.

Between the large urban centres of Quatre Borne and Curepipe is the village of **Phoenix**. Curio hunters will find Le Front de Mer Ship Models here. If you speak directly to the manager of Lords and Cashmere Textiles, you will be taken on a tour of the factory and offered purchases from a variety of knits and cotton clothing.

CUREPIPE

The island's main urban centre, way up in the central highlands, Curepipe is a cool, bustling town of numerous shops, government offices, public transport depots and tea gardens. Many people who live in and around Curepipe make the daily trip to Port Louis to work. The climate is invigorating and healthy. It is frequently wet and a pleasant break from the heat and humidity of the coastal regions. Renowned for being the centre of the Mauritian tea industry, it also has a proliferation of model ship workshops.

Getting there

Buses travel to the town from south, east, central and western Mauritius. The bus station – which looks like a giant orange squeezer – is on the east side of the CBD, just off Sugar Road. Travellers will find signboards indicating the destination of each bus. Staff members at the transport office are helpful in finding you the correct bus.

Forest-Side post office is on the corner of Royal Road and D'Epinay Street, to the west of the main town. A larger post office, which keeps poste restante mail, is located at the entrance to the shopping mall, near the bus depot. Several banks have counters in Curepipe. Delphis Bank is near the Castel vegetable centre. The State Commercial Bank is situated near the Hannafee mosque in town. Mauritius Commercial Bank has its offices on the corner of Mahébourg and Chateauneuf Roads. Barclays Bank is on the opposite corner. BNP has facilities on Mahébourg Road.

Things to do

Most tourists come to Curepipe to see Trou aux Cerfs crater and the tea estates. To reach the crater, take Sir John Pope Hennessy Street south-west from the CBD. At Edgard Hugues Street turn right and follow the road for about 300 m. To the left is a road that goes through the trees to the rim of the water-filled crater. The caldera is an estimated

87 m deep and over 200 m wide. There are incredible panoramas from the rim. On cloudless days you can quite easily see most of Mauritius from up here, and far to the south-west, it is sometimes possible to see the north-eastern mountains of Réunion.

The tea gardens grow all around Curepipe. Many of the smaller plantations grow to the very edge of the suburbs to the north and west of town. There are no fences and visitors are free to wander about. To get to see a tea factory it will be necessary to make prior arrangements through the Ministry of Agriculture, Fisheries and Natural Resources. Speak to the manager of its Tea Board. He is able to arrange guided visits to the Ministry's Tea Experiment Station, tel. manager 464-8809, experiment station 696-1445.

South of the congested shopping district, between Botanical Gardens and Robinson Streets, is a small but pleasantly tranquil botanical garden. Entrance is free, and at lunch time, many of the town's office workers converge on the site to bask in the sun and eat their sandwiches. Paths lead around the various flowerbeds, and those visitors who have been to the Royal Botanical Gardens at Pamplemousses should be able to identify the plant varieties cultivated here.

The Royal College on Mahébourg Road is a magnificent old edifice. Nearby is the municipal building built in 1902. Outside are commemorative statues to Paul et Virginie, the writer Paul Toulet and famed Mauritian astronomer Abbé la Caille.

The huge Hannafee mosque is open Monday to Wednesday for visitors. The Sweet Spot is not a sweet shop, but worth looking into. It specialises in "Quick Marriages".

Curepipe has no tourist nightlife, aside from the small casino near the lake on De La Teste De Buch Street.

Things to buy

Curepipe is the place to find the island's finest model ships. There is a busy workshop on Celicourt Antelme Street. Called *Voiliers de L'Ocean*, it is one of the largest model-making sites on Mauritius. Its selection exceeds 100 vessels. Prices vary according to the size of the vessel, and the amount of sail and rigging displayed. The ships are beautiful but incredibly fragile. Instead of lugging one around the island, you can have it posted home in a special model-box. The shop pays the postage, and will issue a receipt and a guarantee of delivery within 21 days. Further south, on Gustave Collin Street, is the even bigger factory of *La Marine en Bois*. The management will not let visitors watch the crafters at work and tend to be a little pushy when you browse through the displays. A much smaller shop, with much friendlier staff, is *Comajora Ship Models*. On the same street as La Marine, this place encourages visitors to look around and will even offer you tea and a samosa. There is no pressure to buy any of the works.

For handicrafts, visit the *City of Peking* shop in the Salaffa shopping centre. It has an impressive array of art, handicrafts and souvenirs. All major credit cards are accepted.

Accommodation

Most of the accommodation in and around Curepipe falls into the low-medium tariff category. Not many tourists stay in the town, preferring the luxury hotels and beaches of the coast. Suggested hotels are:

Continental Hotel (low-medium tariff). With 50 rooms, the Continental has excellent service and offers Indian meals in its dining room. 256 Royal Road, Curepipe, Mauritius, tel. 675-3434, fax 675-3437

Shanghai Hotel (low-medium tariff). There are 38 functionally furnished rooms at this hotel in downtown Curepipe. It specialises in Chinese meals and its menu has an extensive selection. Impasse St Joseph, Curepipe, Mauritius, tel. 676-1965, fax 676-1965

L'Auberge du Petit Cerf (low-medium tariff). Just seven rooms are available at this lodge in the suburbs of Curepipe. Its restaurant prepares Continental, Creole, Indian and Chinese food. 23 Anderson Street, Curepipe, Mauritius, tel. 676-2892

Places to eat

Curepipe has literally hundreds of places to eat, from five-star meals at *Au Gourmet* on Avenue Bernardin de St Pierre, and *La Nouvelle Potiniere* in the Hillcrest Building on Sir Winston Churchill Street, to seafood delights at the *Golden Lion* on the corner of Sir Winston Churchill and Impasse St Joseph Streets. The tastiest Chinese dishes are found at the *Tropicana* and the *Chinese Wok*, both on Royal Road. Authentic Creole food is cooked at the *Asterix* on Royal Road and *Pot de Terre* along Impasse Pot de Terre. Indian specialities are offered at *La Pomme d'Amour* on Royal Road and the *Maharajah* in the Casa Maria Building along College Lane.

East of Curepipe, en route to Mahébourg, visitors will see signs to Union Park and Le Val Nature Park. In the province of Grand Port, Le Val Nature Park is worth a visit. Taking its name from the deep valley in which it lies, alongside the Rivière des Creoles, Le Val has a number of attractions. Its deer park offers close-up views of rare Java deer. Monkeys swing about in the tall trees, competing with the colourful local birds. In the natural pools, shellfish mix with carp and eels. The plant life includes scented frangipani and wild orchids. There are two greenhouses for the cultivation of anthuriums and andreanums.

MAHÉBOURG

Mauritius's main fishing port, Mahébourg – named after governor Mahé de Labourdonnais – lies on the east coast of the island near Plaisance international airport. Visitors seldom stop here, preferring to dash for the beach hotels. For those who take the time to explore the town, it will reveal many small attractions and rarely seen sites. Even the area surrounding Mahébourg is worth a few days' visit.

Getting to Mahébourg from the airport or Port Louis is facilitated by numerous taxis, and buses that arrive in the town every 30 minutes. One of the main stops is outside the Mahébourg RCA School on Rue des Creoles. The other is at the bus depot at the eastern end of Rue des Flamands. Hitchhiking from the airport is a pleasure, and you should not have to wait longer than 10 minutes for a lift. Car hire is available from several outlets in the airport terminal.

The post office is on the corner of Rue des Creoles and Rue Marianne. Barclays Bank is on the corner of Rue des Creoles and Rue des Cent Gaulettes. Mauritius Commercial Bank and State Commercial Bank are near one another on Rue des Creoles. The Hong Kong Bank is on the same street, next to the Total fuel station. There is also another office of the Mauritius Commercial Bank between the Shell fuel depot and the Tourist Rendezvous Hotel.

Emergency medical treatment is obtainable from the health centre near the police station.

Things to do

The Historical and Naval Museum is a must. It is one of the first houses you pass on entering the town along Mahébourg Road. It was to this colonial mansion, built in 1803, that the wounded British and French admirals were brought for treatment after a massive sea battle in 1810. The British and French navies engaged in what was to become one of the greatest victories in France's chequered history. It is the only naval battle inscribed on the Arc de Triomphe in Paris. Mementos of the event, from both sides, are kept in the museum. You can follow the course of the battle by a brilliant display that takes a visitor through each stage of the battle.

Other items of interest include some of the furniture of the most famous of all French Indian Ocean island governors, Mahé de Labourdonnais. The ship's bell from the wreck of the *St Géran* is also here, as are several etchings and lithographs depicting Paul et Virginie. Another exhibit has some of the items used by the survivors of the SS *Trevessa*, which sank south-east of Mauritius. A memorial to them stands on the beach in southern Mauritius (see chapter 9). Of particular interest are the maps used by Portuguese and Dutch navigators on their first visits to the island. Of course, there has to be a pirate story somewhere along the line. Here, it is the buccaneer Robert Surcouf who is honoured. His portrait hangs beside his weapons and a few he commandeered from luckless ships of the British East India Company. The museum is closed on Tuesday, Friday, Sunday and public holidays. It is open from 9h00 and closes at around 16h30 on Monday, Wednesday and Thursday; Saturday 8h30-12h00.

West of the museum is the Sri Sathya Centre. It has a large library of philosophical books and the pundits speak fluent English. Another Hindu site that warrants a visit is the Andrha Saba Mandir-Shivalay.

There is no suitable swimming beach directly off Mahébourg. From Pointe Jerome, south to La Cambuse, there are stretches of long white beach and safe, reef-fringed lagoons. Most of the tourist hotels are off Beau Vallon. Just walk across their grounds to reach the beach.

Accommodation

Accommodation in Mahébourg is low priced, clean and managed by attentive staff. On the south coast are the usual beach resorts, water sport facilities, restaurants and cafés. One of the cheapest places to stay in Mahébourg is the *Tourist Rendezvous Hotel*, near the police station. You do not need a reservation to stay here, but try to arrive before 12h00 during the Mauritian summer season.

On the seafront are numerous unadvertised *pensions* and guest lodges. Take a walk one block east of Rue Hollandais. If you are unsuccessful there, then try further into Mahébourg. There are also guesthouses along Rue du Bambou and Rue du Souffleur, cheaper but also less clean than those on the seafront.

Out at Pointe Jerome is *La Croix du Sud*. Graded as medium-high tariff, this hotel of 70 rooms has thatched accommodation and a long stretch of tropical beach. La Croix du Sud, Pointe Jerome, Mahébourg, Mauritius, tel. 631-9501, fax 631-9603. Self-catering accommodation is offered at *Villas Le Guerlande*, medium-high tariff. It has a restaurant and bar. Villas Le Guerlande, Route Royal, Pointe D'Esny, Mahébourg, Mauritius, tel. 631-9882, fax 631-9225. On the south-east coast lies *Le Blue Lagoon*, medium-high tariff. On one side is a reefed lagoon with safe swimming. On the other, windsurfers and sailors can pit their skills against the long rollers of the open sea. Le Blue Lagoon, Blue Bay, Mahébourg, Mauritius, tel. 631-9105, fax 631-9045.

Places to eat

Mahébourg has lots of restaurants and snack bars. At the hotel restaurants there is always a variety of dishes from which to choose, but do not let this stop you from venturing out to discover the diners of Mahébourg. The best-known restaurant is *Chez Joe*, on the seafront. Another spot worth considering is *Chez Jacqueline*, south-east of Rue de la Plaine. Most of the *pensions* provide breakfast and dinner as part of their rate.

Before reaching Vieux Grand Port, travellers will pass the tiny settlement of **Ferney**. It is here that one of the oldest sugar plantations on the island is found. If you ask at the estate's reception office, to the side of the village, you will be given a guided tour of the plantation. Relics from the early days lie amid wild flowers, sugar cane and trees.

Seven km north of Mahébourg is **Vieux Grand Port**. It was off this point, in 1810, that the British and French fleets met. There is nothing really to see to evoke images of the fateful battle. The area itself is a mass of eroded rocks, strips of white beach and surging waves.

The protected bay at Vieux Grand Port was once called Fort Frederick. The first Dutch arrivals set up their naval base here in September 1598. You can view a monument to them on the banks of the Rivière Champagne, not far from Pont Molino.

Near the viewpoint at Vieux Grand Port is a small memorial to the Dutchmen who brought the first sugar cane ratoons (shoots) to the island.

Behind Vieux Grand Port is Pic Lyon. Supposedly resembling a crouched lion, the summit offers impressive views of the surrounding area. Start a walk to the summit from the police station in Vieux Grand Port. The path is easy to follow but has some rather treacherous sections. Expect to take between one and two hours to reach the top.

North of Ferney is Le Domaine du Chasseur (sometimes known as Domaine des Grand Bois). Spread across 834 ha, this nature reserve and hunting area is situated deep in indigenous forest. There is high tariff accommodation in the thatched bungalows at the reserve. The reserve is between 200-500 m in altitude and cool breezes blow in from the sea in the morning and early evening. In the woods, patient watchers will spot deer, monkeys and occasionally tusked, wild pigs. The prolific plant life includes such beauties as ebony, colourful orchids, the Malagasy traveller's tree and several species of palm. A restaurant has a good menu that includes wild boar, venison and wild herbs. Reservations for accommodation are necessary. Le Domaine du Chasseur, Anse Jonchee, Vieux Grand Port, Mauritius, tel. 631-9259, fax 208-0076.

11 OUTER ISLANDS

The government of Mauritius also administers other islands in her territorial waters. Of these, Rodrigues is the best known, but other islands belonging to Mauritius are also worth visiting, despite the difficulties of getting to them.

Agalega and the St Brandon islands are remote, sparsely populated but suitable destinations for scuba divers and adventure travellers. There are, as yet, no viable tourist facilities on Agalega and the St Brandon isles. Most of the 600 inhabitants on Agalega island – which lies over 1 000 km north of Mauritius – are involved in the depressed copra industry, their future uncertain and the fate of their island dependent on the world's diminishing copra demand. The St Brandon islands (in Creole Cargados Carajos), 22 atolls nearly 372 km north-east of Mauritius, are used only by passing deep-water fishermen and yachtsmen en route to the Maldives or the Pacific. Rodrigues, on the other hand, has a rapidly expanding tourism industry. Just making contact with Agalega and St Brandon is a long complicated procedure. There are no telephone exchanges on these islands, which means that use must be made of the "Advance Notice" telephone system. Call 10092 in Port Louis for information about the current availability and operating times of Mauritius Telecom to the islands. Rodrigues does have a telephone exchange, and can be contacted directly by telephone or fax.

For information about ships to these islands, or possible short camping visits, contact the Outer Islands Development Corporation, 4th Floor, Jade House, Jummah Mosque Street, Port Louis, Mauritius, tel. 240-4061.

RODRIGUES

Lying about 560 km north-east of Mauritius, Rodrigues island is 18 km long by 8 km wide. Air Mauritius has a regular schedule of flights to Rodrigues. At the moment there are six flights from Monday to Saturday. Departure time from Plaisance is 9h30, with the return flight leaving Pointe L'Herbe, Rodrigues at 13h15. Once on the island, visitors make use of the local bus service to travel from the airport, at Pointe

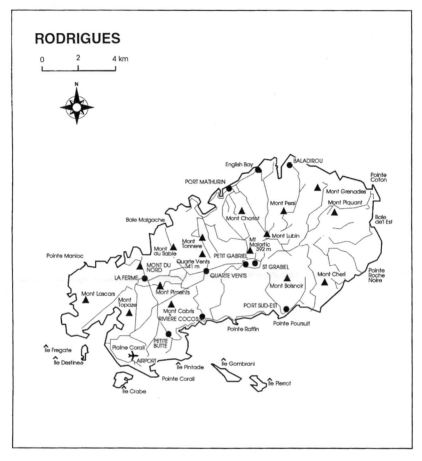

L'Herbe on Plaine Corail in the south, to the island's capital at **Port Mathurin,** on the north coast.

Detailed tourist information on Rodrigues may be obtained from the Ministry of Rodrigues on Jenner Street, in Port Mathurin, tel. 831-1504, fax 831-1815, or from its other office in Ricard Street, tel. 831-1695. On Mauritius, these details are available from the Ministry for Rodrigues, 5th Floor, Fon Sing Building, Edith Cavell Street, Port Louis, tel. 208-8472, fax 212-6329.

Port Mathurin has a post office along Mann Street. International and Mauritius telephone calls can be booked at Mauritius Telecom on Morrison Street. Barclays Bank has an office at Mount Lubin. The Development Bank of Mauritius is also represented in Port Mathurin. The Indian Ocean International Bank and Mauritius Commercial Bank are both located in Duncan Street, with the State Commercial Bank in Jenner Street.

Flights from Rodrigues may be confirmed through Air Mauritius offices at Plain Corail airport or on Ricard Street in Port Mathurin.

Medical assistance is available at the Queen Elizabeth hospital, Creve Coeur, tel. 831-1628.

Things to do

The three biggest attractions of Rodrigues for travellers are birdwatching, scuba diving and the long, empty, white beaches. Birdwatchers are in for a feast of rare bird species. Colonies of sooty, noddy and fairy terns return each year to nest on the island. A unique species is the endangered Rodrigues fody, found nowhere else in the world.

Scuba divers visiting the waters off the island are catered for by the island's only diving facility, La Licome Diving Centre. Under professional guidance, divers can explore the 20 marked dives in the surrounding ocean. Each dive is tailored to individual needs and prices are reasonable when compared to similar facilities on other Indian Ocean islands. It is suggested that you contact the dive centre prior to arrival. The manager will meet you at the airport, arrange accommodation and provide transport. La Licome Diving Centre, c/o PO English Bay, Rodrigues Island, Mauritius.

While many of the most beautiful beaches on Mauritius have been monopolised by beach resorts, those on Rodrigues are still untouched. To reach the really secluded stretches of beach such as Pointe Palmiste and St François involves considerable walking. Those not keen on lengthy excursions through dense bush can visit the easily accessible beach off Pointe Coton.

Hiking and trails through the lush vegetation of this still unspoilt island have yet to be developed by the tourist authority. You can spend hours walking along forest paths looking for wild orchids, the strange bottle palm or blonde bats. From the summit of Mt Malartic you look down on the entire island.

Things to buy

Visitors don't go to Rodrigues to shop. However, if you are interested in curios, then a trip down to Craft Aid on Victoria Street is worth the outing. It has a selection of handmade items specifically from Rodrigues. As it appears to work in cycles of crafts, call and find out what is presently being made, tel. 831-1766.

Accommodation

There is limited accommodation on the island. You do not have to worry about finding lodgings if the hotels are full. If you ask around the stores for assistance, within minutes a room will be organised with a local family. When staying with the islanders, it is considered good manners to supply some of the ingredients for a meal. Dehydrated food seems to be readily accepted.

Tourist accommodation on Rodrigues is found at the *Coton Bay Hotel*. With 40 standard rooms, six de luxe rooms and two suites, the Coton Bay Hotel also provides delicious meals from a menu that has a wide offering of fresh seafood. Reservations must be made. Coton Bay Hotel, c/o PO Pointe Coton, Rodrigues, Mauritius, tel. 831-3000, fax 831-3003.

Other possibilities include:

Hotel Relais (medium tariff). Overlooking the sea near English Bay, this lodge is built in the style of a Creole mansion, and includes breakfast and dinner in the tariff. Pointe Venus, Mont Venus, Rodrigues, Mauritius, tel. 831-1577.

Auberge Beau Soleil (low tariff). In the heart of Port Mathurin, on Victoria Street, tel. 831-1916.

Another place worth trying is the *Mauritius Telecom guesthouse* at Mont Venus. If there is no one there, the caretaker usually lets people sleep over for one or two nights. Details can be obtained from the residence, tel. 831-1531. The *Youth Centre*, at La Ferme, is able to assist travellers in search of cheap accommodation. Speak to the seniors at the club, tel. 831-1201. The police department in Port Mathurin will make every effort to locate suitable accommodation for you. Call at the office, or phone for information, tel. 831-1536.

Meals may be eaten at any of the hotels, but non-residents will have to pay an extra fee. Hardly anyone eats lunch, preferring to buy snacks at roadside stalls. These snacks have a distinctly African blandness to them, especially after one has eaten spicy Indian-influenced Mauritian cooking. Travellers who are camping or living with islanders can do their shopping at the Port Mathurin market.

Part 2

RÉUNION

12 INTRODUCTION

Imagine a lush, mountainous island, topped by a smouldering volcano, frequently cloaked in mist and hidden in the immensity of the south-western Indian Ocean – that is Réunion. Réunion is not a typical island in the sun. It is a place of mystery, where verdant green land, deep azure sea and pale blue sky merge in a festival of nature. From the bustle of sugar cane fields, busy highways and empty volcanic beaches, to modern towns, the silence of forests and echos of canyons, Réunion unites into one continuous celebration of life.

Réunion is the most expensive and European of the Indian Ocean islands. Visitors will find the capital, St-Denis, as enthralling as Paris, as captivating as Marseilles. The mixed cultural marriages have created one of the most hospitable nations on the planet. The human and natural splendour of the island serves to inspire and humble everyone who travels there. Nothing can ever prepare a visitor for the astonishing beauty of Réunion. For travellers in search of adventure, nature and a glimpse of heaven, Réunion is the place to go.

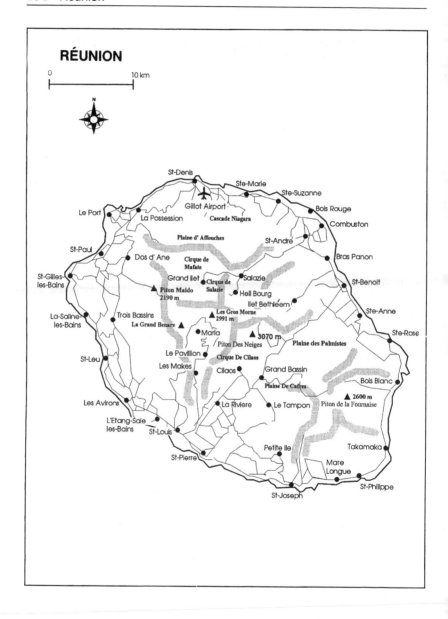

13 FACTS ABOUT THE COUNTRY

HISTORY

Known to Arab and Malay sea traders from about the 10th century, Réunion was never as attractive to them as the warm and protected lagoons of nearby Mauritius. Arab sailors occasionally landed, more out of curiosity than any desire to settle or find water and food. Alone and volcanically active, the island lay forgotten in the south-western Indian Ocean for another five centuries. In 1507, the Portuguese navigator and explorer Tristan Da Cunha, blown off course by a violent storm on a homeward journey from the Malabar coast, sighted the mountains of what he named Santa Appolonia island. Five years later, in 1512, Pedro de Mascarenhas, another Portuguese, rechristened the island Mascareigne. The Portuguese had no intention of settling. They were far more interested in developing and colonising their lucrative discoveries in India and Southeast Asia. Mascareigne Island languished without habitation until 1642. In that year a French East Indiaman landed at what is now known as La Possession, planted the French flag and annexed the island for France. Having planted the flag, the ship sailed off, leaving the island uninhabited once again.

In the meantime the French had claimed and settled the large island of Madagascar, north-west of Mascareigne. Jacques Seur Pronis, the governor, was having trouble with a dozen or so Frenchmen who refused to accept his laws and statutes, and were on the brink of instigating a colonial mutiny. Desperate to get rid of these troublemakers, he decided to exile them, but to where? 800 km east lay the remote island of Mascareigne, the perfect penal colony. So, in 1646 the first settlers arrived. Unceremoniously dumped on the beach near present day St-Paul, they were left without food, water, shelter or weapons.

For the next three years the men lived in cliff-side caves (which can be seen east of St-Paul, Grotte des Premiers), fished, hunted and explored what can only be described as one of the most beautiful places on earth. In December 1649 the exiles were surprised to see a fleet of five French ships drop anchor offshore. The French had finally come to settle. Commanding the vessels was Captain Lebourg, who had strict instructions from the king to start colonising the island. Administration was handed over to the French East India Company with one proviso;

that the name be changed to Île Bourbon, after Colbert Bourbon, foun-
der of the French East India Company. Under the leadership of Etienne
Regnault, the 20 volunteers and 42 Malagasy slaves set to work building
a permanent settlement on Île Bourbon.

Things seemed to stagnate after the initial rush for colonisation had
subsided. Pirates and corsairs saw Île Bourbon as the ideal replenishment stop, far from the French navy and troops. Returning from forays
in the Indian Ocean, they began using the island as their base. By 1685
the only port on the island was full of pirate ships weighed down with
bounty, stolen as much from French vessels as Portuguese, Dutch and
English. Swashbuckling legends like La Buse, Captain Kid and Diego
Vigo were regularly seen walking the muddy streets of St-Paul. The
settlers, glad of the boom, worked hard at supplying the buccaneers
with food, water, accommodation and information. It was a place of
safety, where the pirate captains had laid down a collective law; no
weapons ashore, no burying treasure on the island. Violence was treated
with savage cruelty and Île Bourbon became the equivalent of a pirates'
holiday resort.

The French East India Company had to regain control. Arriving with
a virtual armada in 1713, soldiers landed and men-of-war ships caught
and sank many pirate vessels. The French East India Company built a
garrison on the island and decided to improve conditions and make
the island profitable. Despite a clause in its own company constitution
forbidding it, the French East India Company transported hundreds of
slaves from Africa between 1715 and 1730 to work the coffee, spice
and cotton plantations. In 1735 the island's most famous governor,
Mahé de Labourdonnais, arrived. Administering both Bourbon and
Mauritius, he built schools, hospitals, roads and a successful export
infrastructure. Then, in 1746, Mahé de Labourdonnais resigned his post
and went off to fight the British in India. He was never to return to
the islands on which he had such a major influence.

During the first quarter of 1764, the failed business ventures of the
French East India Company reduced it to bankruptcy and by June of
that year, it had collapsed completely. The French Crown was forced
to take control. But trouble was brewing back in France. Île Bourbon
was forgotten as France was catapulted into the infamous French Revolution. With the king gone and an assembly formed, the island fell
under the jurisdiction of the Colonial Assembly and was renamed Réunion in 1794. The slavers however, who had not been ousted from
their feudal landlord positions, refused to call the island Réunion, pre-

ferring instead to give it the name Île Bonaparte in honour of Napoleon Bonaparte.

The situation in both France and her colonies got steadily worse. On Réunion, the catastrophic cyclone of 1806 destroyed the island's agriculture. Réunion was reduced to total dependence on France. Conditions in France were little better. After a series of empire-building wars and expeditions by Napoleon, France's resources were already stretched. By 1810 Napoleon Bonaparte had lost and surrendered to the British forces and German mercenaries. As part of the spoils of war Britain received Réunion as well. Arriving triumphantly on 9 July 1810, the British navy established a Royal Marine garrison but did not assign any governor to the island.

Britain never really showed any great interest in Réunion. Réunion had no proper port or harbour, and so Britain developed its colonies on the more protected islands of Mauritius and the Seychelles. In 1815 the British and French signed the Treaty of Paris, which included the return of what was officially called Île Bonaparte. France decided to pour funds into the development of the island. Sugar took over as the main agricultural crop, towns were built and immigration actively encouraged. Once again there was to be a name change. The Second French Republic was established in 1848 and one of the first commands given was that Île Bonaparte be known as Réunion. In the same year the atrocious slave trade was abolished on 20 December, liberating over 63 000 slaves.

By then a number of slaves had fled their masters. Living in the thick forests and maze of mountains that still cover Réunion, they waged a war of attrition against the French plantation owners. The Debassyns in particular had a reputation of cruelty to their slaves. The family mansion, church and terraced gardens can still be seen in the hills above Boucan Canot, near St-Gilles-les-Bains. With the freeing of the slaves, there was a sudden loss of labour for agriculture. To remedy the problem the Colonial Assembly indentured Indians, Arabs and Chinese, from 1848 to 1855, to work the fields and assist with trade.

From about 1850 to 1870 Réunion saw a surge of growth and development. Money poured in and the island administration extended the port facilities at the settlement of Le Port. Ships using the routes around Africa made Réunion a stop on their journey. Business flourished, sugar exports filled the coffers, France was happy and the future looked bright. Then, disaster. The Suez Canal was opened, shortening the time taken for ships to travel between Europe and the East. Sugar beet was being harvested in Europe, reducing the need for expensive imports. Réunion reeled under the multiple attack. Plantations were sold, sugar was left to seed and trade ground to a virtual halt. A mass exodus took place to France and the dream was turning into a nightmare.

To worsen the drain on the island, when World War I broke out, nearly 15 000 Réunionnais left for the trenches of Europe. Staggering to recover after the economic collapse and war, Réunion was once more crippled, this time by another world war. Crushing France was not enough for Nazi Germany. It also decided to blockade the French island colonies. For two years nothing left or arrived on Réunion. U-boats and battleships patrolled the offshore waters, throwing up a lethal curtain that few were prepared to cross. By the time the blockade was broken in the last months of 1942, Réunion was in the grip of a famine. Little could be done however. France was still occupied and most of the world was locked in mortal combat.

By 1945 the war in Europe was over. France stood up, shook itself and looked around at the devastation. Finally, in March the following year it got around to looking at Réunion. Shocked at what it saw and what had been reported, the French government officially made the island a Département Français d'Outre Mer on 19 March 1946.

Today Réunion is one of France's last colonies. Although there have been a few rumblings about independence from secretive factions such as the Comité d'Action Démocratique et Social, most Réunionnais are content for their island to stay part of France.

GOVERNMENT

Réunion is administered by a Prefect delegated by the French cabinet. A cabinet, secretary general and regional councils make up the island's political councils. Representing Réunion in the French National Assembly are five deputies, three senators and a proconsul for economics.

GEOGRAPHY

Réunion's geological beauty will quite literally take your breath away. It is a mountainous, volcanic island whose birth started an estimated 2,5 million years ago. Commencing with a fissure in the ocean floor crust, molten lava spewed out, building up successive layers. Réunion's oldest peak, Piton des Neiges (Snow Peak), was the first to rise the almost 4 000 m from the ocean bed. Four volcanic eruptions later, Piton des Neiges reached its present height of 3 069 m. A youth in geological time, this volcano became extinct 500 000 years ago. But the volcanic growth did not stop. Piton de la Fournaise (Furnace Peak), on the east coast of the island, rose more recently and continues to be active – its last eruption occurred in 1986. Balanced precariously on a stalk of solidified lava, Réunion has developed a unique and beautiful landscape. It lies in the path of moist weather pattern circulations and water plays a major part in the island's sculpture. Two mountain ranges give a rugged and wild appearance to the tiny island. A mere 2 512 km², Réunion's attraction is undoubtedly the interior. Cirques (natural bowls and amphitheatres) continue to erode, creating ever widening circular valleys and resulting in stunning scenery of waterfalls, rivers, cliffs and ravines.

Piton de la Fournaise can be climbed on the island's south-east side. It is onto the south-east coast that lava now spills whenever there is an eruption. Gushing from its misty heights, lava boils downhill to tumble into the ocean, where it remains glowing and steaming long after it has been submerged. This is the stuff of creation, the original matter of life itself. Two of the highest mountains in the Indian Ocean are to be found on Réunion, Piton des Neiges (3 069 m) and Gros Morne (2 992 m). Other smaller but no less impressive mountains can also be seen and climbed on Réunion. Many of these mountains are linked by a series of crests which, over consecutive eruptions, have left a way for the adventurous traveller to see most of Réunion's splendour.

Rivers and waterfalls are features of Réunion. Seeming to fall from the clouds, waterfalls can be seen virtually everywhere. Of particular beauty are those on the road to the cirque settlements of Cilaos and Salazie. Rivers on Réunion behave in a most peculiar way. Wide, empty, rock-strewn riverbeds belie the ferocity and suddenness of flash floods. A river that is raging today could quite easily be gone tomorrow. Hikers and campers need to be aware of this when sleeping out in wilderness areas overnight.

Réunion is very remote, almost 700 km from Madagascar to the west, 200 km south-west of Mauritius (her nearest neighbour) and over 13 000 km south-east from the seat of government, France.

CLIMATE

With cold, high mountain ranges, warm seas and in the path of southern weather circulations, Réunion suffers from climatic extremes. There are two distinct seasons inland, while the coastal regions – influenced by warm ocean currents – remain pleasant throughout the year. Réunion has its summer from about October to March. The weather is hot and humid and it's wet. Early April sees the start of the winter season which continues until about mid-September. Winters are cool and dry inland. Despite its small size, Réunion experiences a variety of weather conditions at different places at the same time. The east coast is generally damp and humid all year. During winter there is a noticeable drop in temperatures along the east coast (windward coast). Along the west coast (leeward coast), conditions are drier and warmer, making it more attractive to tourists. Winter temperatures along the west coast seldom drop below 22 °C, with the thermometer rising to a hot 31 °C during summer. Along the thickly forested east coast, visitors can expect winter temperatures hovering around the 19 °C mark, with summer frequently seeing readings of 28 °C.

Inland, visitors can expect low temperatures, even during mid-summer in the high areas around Piton des Neiges, Cilaos, Mafate and Hell-Bourg. Summer mornings in these regions have temperatures of about 15 °C, 25 °C at midday and evening temperatures as low as 12 °C. Winter brings frost, ice and wind to the mountains. On winter mornings, visitors will experience temperatures of 4 °C, with day-time highs of a little over 14 °C, dropping to as low as 0 °C at night. Sunny days on Réunion can be hit-and-miss affairs. While clear skies and bright sunshine could be found on the coast, mist, rain and storms might block any sight of the mountains and make hiking difficult. On the other hand, when it is pouring with rain on the coast, the mountains could be bathed in glorious sunshine.

There are an estimated 200 micro-climates on Réunion. This staggering amount of climatic diversification is both a boon and hindrance to travellers. The Réunion Tourist Authority advises visitors to see the island from May to October. Réunion is small, so visitors can choose their climatic preferences and be in a particular area within a few hours or, in some cases, even minutes. The one thing that could spoil a vacation on Réunion is a cyclone. Cyclones occur frequently from early November to the end of March. They will limit what you will be able to see and do. The islanders, however, are quite used to them and continue their daily routines undeterred while the cyclone rages around them. You should consider a visit any time from the beginning of April to the end of October. Unless, of course, you would really like to experience living through a cyclone. I did, and was able to see Mother Nature's awesome power and savage beauty unleashed.

POPULATION

With a population between 650 000 and 710 000, visitors may be surprised to notice that almost half Réunion's inhabitants are under the age of 20. This has resulted from France's policy of subsidising families. Some years ago, the government noticed that the country's birthrate was dropping dangerously. To encourage growth, numerous incentives, including reduced taxation, support for children and social services, were implemented. This policy, which was initially only intended for the French mainland, also found its way to French colonies throughout the world.

Réunion is a colourful melting pot of cultures. While the Indo-Réunionnais (known as Malabars) make up a large percentage of the population, the influences of Chinese, Arabs (Arabes), Africans and French (Oreilles – ears, or the eavesdroppers) have contributed to a harmonious intermingling of races. From this has come the common language and culture of Creole. Not really an ethnic group, the Creoles are a happy mix of mainly Franco-Africans. Creole is spoken all across Réunion and, for that matter, many of the other Indian Ocean islands. The language is an odd mixture of French and original ethnic tongues.

The most obvious differences are found between urban and rural, and coastal and mountain people. Thoroughly French, city folk are hip, market-orientated and generally affluent. In contrast, rural dwellers are traditional, poor, relaxed and polite. Coastal Réunionnais tend to be well educated, friendlier and more helpful to tourists. In the remote mountain areas visitors will encounter real "hillbillies". Quiet, suspicious and agricultural, these villagers make the best trail guides on the island.

After the Creoles, the pure-blooded French make up the largest group. Involved mainly in large business corporations and colonial administration, they are Réunion's elite. Descendants of the noble sugar baron families can still be found sipping rum at top-class hotels in St-Denis and St-Gilles-les-Bains. As on Mauritius, the Franco-islanders are a tight clique.

CULTURE

The culture too, is a creation of French, Indian, Chinese, African, Arab and a little British influences. All early arrivals brought their own special ways and traditions which were adopted and assimilated. This continuous adding on makes for a wonderful, dynamic culture that is always growing.

Dancing, music, art and the theatre are encouraged. An annual programme is scheduled for the arts. This listing, and a monthly entertainment pamphlet (RUN), are available from:

Institut de Formation aux Metiers Culturels (IFMC), 94 Avenue Leconte-
Delisle, Apt F, 97490 Ste-Clotilde, tel. 29.96.34, fax 29.31.03

Fonds Regional d'Art Contemporain (FRAC), Immeuble Camelias, Boulevard Doret, 97400 St-Denis, tel. 30.17.43

Centre Réunionnais d'Action Culturelle, Natural Museum, Jardin de
l'État (State Garden), Rue Poivre, 97400 St-Denis, tel. 21.69.75

Dancing

Traditional island dancing is called sega. But it is not identical to the
sega dance seen on other Indian Ocean islands. The original dance of
the slaves on Réunion became infused with European and Oriental
nuances as they assimilated different cultures. To the Creoles it is known
as the maloya. It is graceful and seductive, often accompanied by the
melancholy songs of a balladeer. Although modern musical instruments
are used today, two of the original instruments are still retained for the
unique Réunion Creole sound; the houler (hand-held drum) and caiamb
(maracas filled with rice). Most of the larger tourist hotels have at least
one maloya or sega show per week.

Music

Relatively few traditional music exponents appear live in Réunion. The
production of music cassettes seems a far better proposition to them.
However, a particularly good solo singer can be heard in the dining
room of the Sterne Complex hotel at St-Pierre. On certain evenings he
can be listened to around the swimming pool bar on the hotel's top
floor.

Art

Despite the vibrant culture, art is not a major form of expression for
the islanders. Good galleries are limited, and of those accessible to the
public, only one has anything of real artistic interest. The Leon Dierx
Museum, on Rue de Paris, St-Denis, is a must for the visitor who enjoys
the works of past masters. Centrepiece of the display is works by Paul
Gauguin (1848-1903). Other works of note are by Picasso, Rouault and
Le Gac. On the Rue La Bourdonnais is Galerie Montparnasse. In St-

Pierre, a dealer and artist sells and exhibits a small selection at 32 Chemin Archambaud, Ligne des 400. Along the west coast, at Trois Bassins, there is an eccentric character certainly worth visiting at Raymond Fontaine Gallery, 10 Allée de la Source. A permanent exhibition is on display at the East Coast Tourist Office on Rue Centre Commercial in St-André.

Theatre

Réunionnais love the theatre. Visitors will find both professional and amateur troupes giving shows at at least two popular venues. For a truly spectacular evening, see a show or concert at the open-air theatre in the hills above St-Gilles-les-Bains (Théâtre de Plein Air). The Théâtre de Champ Fleuri in Ste Clotilde regularly hosts groups from abroad. A small but intimate theatre hosts visiting groups to Le Tampon, at Théâtre Luc Donnat.

In the mountain villages especially, you will be able to attend local shows put on by schools and church groups. Local productions are usually held only in summer. The church group of Cilaos is famous for the quality and setting of its annual play.

ECONOMY

Very little is manufactured on Réunion. Most goods are imported from France at great cost, despite the fact that similar, and often better, goods are available much closer from Australia or South Africa. There is an odd symbiosis however. As much as Réunion imports from France, France in turn imports the same quantity of goods from Réunion, e.g. 5 000 kg of beans imported from France, 5 000 kg of sugar exported from Réunion to France.

Sugar, vanilla, geranium and vetiver oils are the island's main earners of foreign currency. The economy is in a bad state and rapidly getting worse. Depending more and more on the social structures in France, the Réunionnais see no need to work when they can be supported by unemployment benefits. Agriculture – mainly sugar – was once the backbone of the country's export strength. The sugar cane plantations cover most of the island's arable coastal land. Once a major supplier of high-grade sugar to Europe, the farms have seen a steady drop in demand from abroad. High transport costs, taxes and levies have contributed to placing the Réunion sugar industry in jeopardy. Production costs have soared without a rise in market prices. Many sugar estates are now understaffed, the owners seriously considering stopping production altogether. Although there are six sugar mills across the island, visitors may discover that several of them have virtually shut down. While Australia and South Africa continue to supply the world with large quantities of fairly low-grade sugar, Réunion struggles to produce enough for the large rum consignments that are ordered from France. As the sugar plantations are sold off for housing and plots, the old families search for new ways to earn an income. A few have turned to geranium and vetiver oil production.

The island is the largest supplier of geranium oil in the world. Used primarily by the perfume industry in Europe and America, the oil is used as the base for perfumes – the longer lasting its base, and therefore scent, the better the quality of the perfume. Flower oils are not exclusively produced by the nobility. In many hill villages, particularly on the mist-shrouded slopes between l'Etang and St-Gilles-les-Hauts, tenants plant flowers and distil the oils from moonshine-type copper stills. A few, very few, people still draw oil from Réunion's most beautiful scented flower, ylang-ylang. On warm nights, the darkness is filled with the heady scent of these yellow flowers.

Smaller quantities of other agricultural items are grown. Maize, beans, garlic and potatoes are grown on a small scale, as is tropical and subtropical fruit. Vanilla was a large revenue earner until the market became threatened by artificial vanillin. By cutting back on production, Réunion now lies well down the list of vanilla-producing countries – the main suppliers being Madagascar and Comoros. A magnificent museum of the vanilla industry can be seen in and around the old plantation mansion at St-André on the east coast.

Tea was once a lucrative enterprise, as were coffee and tobacco. These too have now disappeared from Réunion. Many of the planters have moved to Mauritius where dedicated and hard-working staff are easy to find. In the mountain areas, dairy and beef cattle are herded for both milk products and meat. Visitors who have been to the mountains of France, Italy and Switzerland will find an amazing similarity in livestock-farming methods. Animals wear bells around their necks, most milking is done by hand in wooden barns and lush meadows provide nutritious feed. Réunion's yoghurt is considered to be the best in the Indian Ocean islands.

Inflation is well into double figures, far outrunning that of France. Standards of living have correspondingly dropped and a sad sort of apathy seems to have infected the youth. Many of them flee to France, seeking a better life and higher wages, but, according to the Affaires Economiques, over 96% of those who leave return within nine months.

Looking for other ways of bringing in foreign money, the Réunion Tourist Board, together with the French Tourist Board, has poured a great deal of effort into selling Réunion to tourists. In France, special package deals and flights are available during school holidays. Yet, tourism figures remain below those of neighbouring islands, especially Seychelles and Mauritius. Another deterrent to tourists is the high cost of actually holidaying on Réunion. As the world economic recession continues to affect people, paying prices about 30% higher than those found in Europe is ridiculous.

A trickle of immigrants has recently been making their way to Réunion. The Département Français d'Outre Mer has encouraged the arrival of these foreigners, mostly businessmen. Subsidies, low taxation and extended loans have made the prospect particularly attractive to South Africans fleeing the intractable problems of that country. These new immigrants have brought a rush of enthusiasm to the Prefecture, which hopes that soon, Réunion will be able to compete favourably in world markets.

RELIGION, HOLIDAYS AND FESTIVALS

Réunion has a large number of festivals, public holidays and celebrations, with numerous rituals by Christians, Hindus and African faiths. Buddhists and Muslims too, have an annual programme of ceremonies. Along the east coast, where the European influence is less obvious, you will discover the practices of ancient Africa. Those living in the shadow of the volcano – notably in the forests between Ste-Rose and St-Philippe – are devotees of tribal lore. Spring and autumn see these remote settlements donning bright colours and holding animist rituals. They are not usually open to foreigners.

Christianity is the largest religion on Réunion. Over 96% of Christians are Roman Catholic. Churches and temples are open to all who visit. A large Hindu Ashrama in St-Louis welcomes visitors, and will even offer a bed and meal for the night. Leave a suitable donation when leaving. Islam is more restrictive towards non-believers. At the impressive mosques in St-Denis and St-Pierre it is extremely difficult gaining entrance.

Buddhism came to Réunion with the Chinese and Asians, as did Taoism. These religions have adherents on the island, and there are a few pagodas.

Réunion has 12 public holidays. While government facilities will all be closed, visitors can expect to find cafés and small supermarkets open from about 8h30 to 12h00.

1 January – New Year's Day
12 April – Easter Monday
1 May – Labour Day
8 May – 1945 Victory
20 May – Ascension Day
31 May – Pentecost
14 July – National Day
15 August – Assumption Day
1 November – All Saints Day
11 November – Armistice 1918
20 December – Abolition of slavery
25 December – Christmas Day

There are numerous town and city fairs held at different times of the year. These usually take place over weekends, but in some places, such as St-Paul, the fair in July lasts for two weeks. During the fruit season (December to February) the following fairs are held:

- Foire de St-Pierre, St-Pierre, early December, 10 days

- Fête des Letchis, St-Denis, mid-December, seven days

- Fête de l'Ail, Petite Île, mid-December, two days

- Street concerts on 20th December, to mark the abolition of slavery, fill the rural towns and villages in a festive and happy celebration

- Fête du Miel, Le Tampon, mid-January, seven days

- Pagodas are bedecked with flowers and red paper for the Chinese New Year in mid-January

- Hindus perform the famed fire-walking ceremony at temples in late January. The temple in St-Pierre, near the bus depot, has a lively and intriguing demonstration of devotees' faith

Starting in early March, events continue through until the changing of seasons at the end of May:

- Fête du Vacoa, St-Benoit, early April, seven days

- Ascension Mass, Piton des Neiges, mid-May, one day

- Fête du Chou, Hell-Bourg, early May, two days
- Fête de la Vanille, Bras Panon, mid-May, 10 days

June to August is winter on Réunion, when goyaviers, vanilla and sugar are harvested. Around the coast, conditions are pleasant and suitable for several fetes and fairs:

- Fête des Goyaviers, Plaine des Palmistes, mid-June, two days
- Street singers and bands entertain spectators in all large cities on the island on 21 June, Réunion's day of music
- Fête de la Canne, Ste-Rose, late July, two days
- Fête de St-Paul, St-Paul, mid-July, two weeks
- Foire du Bois, Rivière St-Louis, early August, 10 days
- Fête du Safran, St-Joseph, mid-August, 10 days

Known as the season of the Flowers' Dance, September to November see the return of the sun and the bursting forth of life:

- Flower show, Le Tampon, late September, seven days
- Fête de la Rose, St-Benoit, early November, five days
- Fête des Lentilles, Cilaos, mid-November, two days
- Fête des Mangoustans, St-Benoit, mid-November, two days
- Diwali, the Festival of Light. On an auspicious day in November, Hindus undertake "puja" in a celebration of purification and worship

WILDLIFE

Visitors to Réunion will immediately be struck by the wild appearance of the island. Plants, birds and animals will lure you into believing that you have stumbled through the gateway to the Garden of Eden. Réunion offers naturalists the opportunity for discovering coastal and alpine splendour and everything in between. Rainforests at Bélouve teem with birdlife. In the thickets of Salazie, hares and deer melt away at the approach of humans.

Nature conservation on Réunion is of major importance to both the administration and Réunionnais. A strongly supported forestry department involves itself in the protection and propagation of many rare plant and bird species. Nature trails, demonstrations, guides and advertising all assist in maintaining this tiny enclave of paradise in the Indian Ocean.

Flora

A botanist's dream, Réunion offers visitors a diversity of plant life that is astounding. Where agriculture has not intruded, the progression of natural plant life continues. Even on the edges of the most recent volcanic eruption, moss and fungi have taken hold. With frequent rains washing most of the island, tropical vegetation has flourished.

There are, however, striking contrasts. Carpeting the Plaine des Palmistes, cycads, tree ferns and dense vegetation thin out on the slopes of Piton de la Fournaise. Around the crater, in a dry, dusty, barren lunar landscape, nothing yet grows.

Although trees seem to be the predominant vegetation on Réunion, a little exploring will lead you into a fairyland of flowers. From the late 18th century, a host of botanists and environmentalists have cultivated as many tropical plant species as possible. Réunion is a scented garden of flowers and plants, from the explosion of colour of the Tahitian bougainvillaea to the alluring shapes and spots of wild orchids. The reds, pinks and whites of hibiscus bushes brighten many drab roadways. Purple jacaranda and red flamboyants brighten many otherwise dull neighbourhoods.

Fauna

As though to compensate for the lack of wild animals, birdlife is prolific. That is not to say that everything has always been that way. As on Mauritius, the dodo was hunted to extinction. So too was the mystical crested bourbon bird. Even today, certain species, like the crow – considered a pest – are in danger. The national bird of Réunion, the long tail-plumed paille-en-queue (white-tailed tropicbird), is threatened. This bird's habitat, the vertical coastal cliffs, is endangered. As many of the national roads edge these cliffs, engineers regularly blast the cliffs with dynamite, to prevent rockfalls onto the busy road, thereby also destroying the paille-en-queue's nests and often, fledglings too.

Undoubtedly the prettiest bird is the small, red-tailed virgin bird (Mascarene paradise flycatcher). Shy and alluring, it can be found in the thick forests of the eastern plains. Exotic species are also well represented by clutches of moorhens, quails and flocks of migrating swallows. On the coast, colourful puffins build untidy nests. Out over the ocean, petrels, seagulls and occasionally albatrosses can be seen gliding above the deep swells. Inland, falcons and papangue (Réunion harrier) soar on mountain thermals in search of prey. Partridges and francolins can be spotted scuttling for cover in hedges.

No dangerous animals inhabit Réunion, but then, neither do many animals at all. Rare for forested tropical islands, the deer and hare found are exotics, as are the rats and wild cats. Mainly from Southeast Asia, they were brought by ship and have thrived in the warmth of the tropics. Interesting specimens of what were once on the island can be seen at the State Garden (Jardin de l'État), Natural History Museum, Rue Poivre, St-Denis.

Marine life

Ignored for many years by scuba divers, Réunion's submarine wildlife flourished and diversified. Within the reefs along the west coast, snorkellers are in for a wonderful time. Fish are inquisitive and the plant life is colourful. Wear sandals or sneakers though – urchins and the odd stonefish can inflict severe and sometimes fatal wounds. There is no need for scuba gear when diving off Réunion. A face mask and snorkel are quite sufficient. Parrotfish, needlefish, clownfish and angelfish inhabit the shallow, plankton-filled waters around the island. Offshore lurk the rulers of these waters, marlin, sailfish and great white sharks. Protected from predatory attacks, inshore fish are surprisingly tame. They may nibble on a hairy leg or suck a finger, but no bites or stings threaten visitors. Snorkelling around the reef off St-Gilles-les-Bains is highly recommended. The water is warm and startlingly clear. Basic gear can be hired from the Hotel Coralia or VVF.

Trout are to be found in the mountain rivers, or so suggest a few guide books, but the villagers around Cilaos, Hell-Bourg and Mafate disagree. "Freshwater fish disappeared many years ago," says Claude Giraudeaux from Îlet a Cordes, near Cilaos. Conifer forests are said to be to blame, as well as intensive agriculture. Whatever the cause, it will no doubt soon be corrected by the capable and dedicated team of conservationists who are determined to make Réunion an ecological success.

Places that will be of special interest to nature lovers include:
- Natural History Museum, 1 Rue Poivre, St-Denis, tel. 20.02.19
- Eden Garden, Route Nationale 1, L'Hermitage-les-Bains, St-Gilles-les-Bains, tel. 24.49.16
- Botanical Garden of Mascarin, Domaine des Colimacons, St-Leu, tel. 24.92.27

- Spices and Perfume Garden. Contact the tourist office at 69 Rue Leconte de Lisle, St-Philippe, tel. 37.10.43
- The Home of Vanilla, 466 Rue de la Gare, St-André, tel. 46.00.14

Details of conservation programmes, parks, gardens, forests and reserves can be obtained directly from:

Comité de l'Environnement, 60 Rue Victor Mac Auliffe, 97400 St-Denis, tel. 41.44.12, fax 21.78.73

Service de la Protection des Vegetaux, Parc de la Providence, Boulevard de la Providence, 97400 St-Denis, tel. 48.61.00, fax 48.61.99

LANGUAGE

English-speaking visitors may find Réunion frustrating. The English cannot speak French and the French, in turn, refuse to speak or understand English. Getting by on English alone is only possible at the tourist-class hotels on the west coast, and one mountain hotel, Hotel Lallemand. Elsewhere, you have three ways to make yourself understood. Either speak French, Creole or use sign language. Creole is difficult without the correct accent and sign language is virtually impossible among this cosmopolitan conglomeration of cultures. (This excludes the required loud hand-clap when wanting a bus to stop.) This leaves French the only viable option. The Réunionnais are different to their mainland French cousins in one major regard. If you try to speak French and fail, they will make every attempt to converse in broken English. It is highly recommended that a smattering of French sentences be learned before arrival in Réunion.

Good morning	Bonjour
Good evening	Bonsoir
Do you speak English?	Parlez-vous Anglais?
Yes	Oui
No	Non
I don't understand	Je ne comprends pas
Goodbye	Au revoir
Where is the . . . Hotel?	Où est l'hôtel . . .?
Where is there a restaurant?	Où y a-t-il un restaurant?
Where is the taxi stand?	Où y a-t-il une station de taxis?
Where is the post office?	Où est le bureau de poste?
How much?	Combien?
What is your name?	Comment vous appelez-vous?
My name is . . .	Je m'appelle . . .

How far is . . .?	C'est a quelle . . .?
How long does it take?	Il faut combien de temps?
I should like to make a telephone call	J'aimerais telephoner
Can I change money?	Comment puis-je changer de l'argent?
Have you a room?	Avez-vous encore une chambre?
How do I send a telegram?	Comment dois-je faire pour telegraphier?

14 FACTS FOR THE VISITOR

VISAS

All arrivals need a valid passport. If you are a French or EU national, no visa is required. A return or onward travel ticket is needed and will be asked for upon disembarkation. French citizens can also get away with carrying just their national identity documents. Visitors from outside EU countries are required to have a visa. Visas are cheap and can be obtained at all French embassies. If there is no French consulate, you can usually find a representative at the British or Swiss embassy.

EU nationals may be asked to give exact reasons for their visit and their estimated date of departure. With high unemployment and vagrancy on Réunion, the authorities are trying desperately to keep the influx of possible immigrants under control. Extensions for visa holders can be a problem in view of the above. You will need a very good reason for wanting a visa extension if not from EU countries. Visa extension applications can be made to the Centre Regional de Documentation et de Controle, 9 Avenue de la Victoire, 97488 St-Denis Cedex, tel. 21.04.06, fax 41.09.81.

Current international certificates of vaccination are required by all visitors arriving from countries where yellow fever and cholera are endemic. This includes all African and Asian arrivals. You may not be expected to show this card, but if asked for and yours is not available or valid, you will either be refused entry or immediately taken to a government doctor for the "shots". Contact your nearest local government health department for these vaccinations at least 42 days before departure.

FOREIGN EMBASSIES AND CONSULATES

Honorary consul of Belgium
33 Rue Felix-Guyon, 97476 St-Denis Cedex, tel. 21.79.72, fax 41.40.93

Honorary consul of Germany
18 Rue Papangue, 97490 Ste-Clotilde, tel 28.04.00

Embassy of India
101 Rue Bois-de-Nefles, 97400 St-Denis, tel. 41.75.47, fax 21.01.70

Embassy of Italy
35 Chemin Commins, 97417 La Montagne, tel. 23.63.31

Embassy of Madagascar
77 Rue Juliette Dodu, 97400 St-Denis, tel. 21.66.00

Royal Norwegian Consulate
43 Rue de Verlaine, 97420 Le Port, tel. 43.30.48

Embassy of Switzerland
65 Rue Jules Auber, 97400 St-Denis, tel. 41.39.03, fax 41.63.50

Consulate of the United Kingdom (also representing South Africa)
Immeuble de la Compagnie des Indes, Rue de la Compagnie, 97463 St-Denis Cedex, tel. 21.06.19, fax 21.00.07

Visas for any of these countries can be obtained from the relevant consuls or embassies on Réunion. Applications must be accompanied by four passport-size photographs and the required fee, payable in French francs. Most embassies will take about two days to issue a visa, the exception being Madagascar, which can take anything up to seven days. If you are intending to visit countries for which a visa is required, it is far better to arrange the documents through a reliable visa service in your home country.

CUSTOMS

There are different customs and excise requirements depending on your point of embarkation. Visitors coming from EU countries are permitted to bring in 1,5 ℓ of liquor of more than 22% proof or 4 ℓ of under 22% proof. EU citizens can also bring in 5 ℓ of wine. Those from other countries are restricted to 1 ℓ of liquor of more than 22% proof, or 3 ℓ of under 22% proof and 2 ℓ of wine.

Perfume and cigarettes are allowed into the country in any quantity, provided they are either gifts or for personal use.

All animals require documentation. Only three animals per tourist is permissible. Several regulations apply to visitors who bring their pets along: the animal must be over four years old, a valid rabies vaccination certificate and a valid health clearance certificate, not older than five days, from a veterinary surgeon in the country of origin, must be submitted.

Any queries relating to the importation of foreign goods should be directed to Direction des Douanes, at least 90 days prior to departure. Direction des Douanes, 7 Avenue de la Victoire, 97488 St-Denis Cedex, tel. 21.04.06

Enquiries about animals or plants should be made at least 35 days before departure to: Direction de L'Agriculture et de la Forêt, Parc de la Providence, Boulevard de la Providence, 97400 St-Denis, tel. 48.61.00, fax 48.61.99

On leaving Réunion, visitors are only permitted to take out 1,5 ℓ of liquor over 22% proof, or 3 ℓ under 22% proof. It is expressly forbidden to remove any plant or animal from Réunion without written permission from the department of agriculture. Smuggling out cuttings or frozen semen is highly illegal and there are heavy penalties.

MONEY

Réunion is expensive, arguably the most expensive island in the western Indian Ocean. The unit of currency is the French franc. Prices are much higher than in France and visitors will find themselves spending money quickly. A franc is divided into 100 centimes. Notes are distributed in denominations of 500, 200, 100, 50 and 20 francs, coins in 10, 5 and 1 franc pieces. Centimes are issued in 50, 20, 10, 5 and 1 coins.

Make certain that you arrive with at least 200 francs in cash. This should cover the taxi fare from Gillot airport to St-Denis. Hard currency can be changed at hotels in St-Denis but handling charges are high and visitors should rather change at one of the numerous banks around the city. Banks and hotels will cash traveller's cheques, as will a few of the larger guesthouses. American Express is the most common traveller's cheque. There is a representative at Bourbon Voyages, 14 Rue Rontaunay, St-Denis, tel. 21.68.18. Personal cheques are useless on Réunion. Credit cards are accepted in even the smallest of places, and can also be used for drawing cash from automatic tellers and bank counters. Those readily accepted for payment and for drawing cash are Diners Club, Mastercard, Visa, American Express and Eurocard.

It is best to deal with banks in the larger urban centres. They are open Monday to Friday 8h00-16h00. Banks in St-Denis in particular are efficient and fast:

BNP (Banque Nationale de Paris), 67 Rue Juliette Dodu, St-Denis, tel. 40.30.30

Credit Agricole, 18 Rue Felix Guyon, St-Denis, tel. 40.80.00

Banque de la Réunion, 27 Rue Jean Chatel, St-Denis, tel. 40.01.23

There is a thriving black market in St-Denis and St-Pierre. Bear in mind that this is highly illegal.

COSTS

With so much being imported, import charges and local taxes raise prices way above normal market value. You will need lots of money, irrespective of whether you are backpacking or on an organised tour. Quality, however, is also very high, but service isn't. The high cost of living discourages budget travellers from visiting Réunion, which is a pity. To keep your expenses down it is advisable to keep away from the cities and tourist resorts. In the mountains and along the southern coast, guesthouses, local cafés and markets will provide for most travellers' needs relatively cheaply. Réunion is not for beach holidays. Trekking and adventure travel are the main attractions – their prices the main disappointment.

Adventurous travellers, willing to sleep in tents or with the locals, eat just fish and rice and travel by public transport, will be able to live the most cheaply on Réunion. But even for them, the price of holidays on the island will soon become prohibitive. The Réunion Tourist Board aims at people earning European salaries and used to paying high prices.

Budget carefully if you decide to visit Réunion. Many travellers opt for Mauritius – where things are at least 60-70% cheaper – and just take a two or three day trip to Réunion. For South African and Australasian visitors this is definitely a better choice.

TIPPING

As a thoroughly European country, tips are expected. In restaurants, 15% of the bill is customary. For bellboys, messengers and those delivering food, a few francs is enough. Up in the mountains, guides usually expect to be shown some sort of gratitude. The Creole guides are the easiest to please. Living in the cold of the cirques, for them jerseys are a favourite, as are woollen socks or thermal clothing.

TOURIST INFORMATION

Réunion has the most efficient and helpful tourist information service in the Indian Ocean. Customer-orientated staff go out of their way to assist those who visit. Airlines also provide prospective tourists with information. Air Austral has the largest selection of brochures and pamphlets, which it will mail to any destination. Its staff all have intimate knowledge of the island and can supply helpful itineraries. It can be contacted either in Réunion or South Africa:

Air Austral, Rue Nice, St-Denis, Réunion, tel. 20.20.20, fax 21.05.72

Air Austral, PO Box 41022, Craighall, 2024, South Africa, tel. (011) 880-9039, fax (011) 788-5440

Visitors will be sent an enormous supply of informative literature if they contact the Réunion Tourist Office direct:

Comité du Tourisme de la Réunion (CTR), BP 1119, 97482 St-Denis Cedex, Réunion, tel. 21.00.41, fax 20.25.93. Alternatively, go to its offices on arrival: CTR, 23 Rue Tourette, St-Denis

Each district also has a regional tourist office. These cover an area in detail and are certainly worth a visit upon arrival in the town. In St-Denis, go to the Tourist Office of St-Denis, 48 Rue Ste Marie (near the Musée Léon Dierx), tel. 41.83.00. For the southern parts of Réunion: Tourist Office of St-Pierre, 27 Rue Archambaud, tel. 25.02.36. Tourist Office of the West Coast, Galerieandine, St-Gilles-les-Bains, tel. 24.57.47. The north-east coast is under the control of the Tourist Office of St-André, 68 Centre Commercial, tel. 49.91.63. In the south-east and east, visit the Tourist Office of St-Philippe, 69 Rue Leconte de Lisle, tel. 37.10.43.

Inland, up around the cirques and mountains, maps, brochures, guide lists and pertinent information can be obtained at specific tourist offices.

Tourist Office of Cilaos, 2 Rue Mac Auliffe, tel. 39.62.99

Tourist Office of Salazie, Rue Georges Pompidou, tel. 47.50.14

Many of the hotels can be approached for tourist information, as can local police. The VVF in St-Leu has an amazing selection of pamphlets and information leaflets available. The village manager too, offers a wealth of hints and tips for making travel around Réunion easier.

Many of the travel agencies also provide visitors with valuable information. Top of the list for assisting prospective visitors is ERL Tours. Call on them or write for details about the region you are interested in:

ERL Location de Voitures, 24 Rue Leopold Rambaud, 97490 Ste-Clotilde, tel. 21.66.81, fax 24.06.02

In Third World countries, some information can usually be found at French embassies, consulates or representatives. Where Réunion is not represented, the local French Tourist Office will be of some assistance. Ask for a copy of the island's hotel guide and *Escapades* magazine, which is published biannually. In First World countries, Réunion has agents promoting the island. These agencies are known all over as Maison de la France.

Australia: BNP Building, 12 Castlereagh Street, Sydney NSW 2000, tel. 231-5244, fax 233-4576

Austria: Hilton Centre, corner Landstrasse and Haupstrasse 2A, 1033 Vienna, tel. 715-7062, fax 715-7061/10

Belgium: 21 Avenue de la Toison d'Or, 1060 Brussels, tel. 513-0762, fax 514-3375

Italy: Via Larga 7, 20122 Milan, tel. 583-16471, fax 583-16579

Spain: Gran Via 59, 28013 Madrid, tel. 541-8808, fax 541-2412

United Kingdom: 178 Piccadilly, London WIV OAL, tel. 491-7622, fax 493-6594

POST OFFICE

The main post office is at 60 Rue Maréchal Leclerc, tel. 21.12.12. As with most European post offices, the counters are well staffed and efficient. Postage is expensive. Parcels are usually sent by airmail, as surface mail can take up to three months to reach its destination.

All settlements have a post office which is open from 8h00-18h00 Monday to Friday, and on Saturday 8h00-12h00. Visitors can have their mail sent to poste restante at even the smallest of villages. Charges are levied against poste restante mail, so be prepared to pay. This mail is kept at the local post office for six months, then returned to the sender. Airmail is fast, with letters arriving in Europe within a few days of mailing. Most post offices have photostat machines which operate on franc coins.

TELEPHONE

The international dialling code for Réunion is 262, which is preceded by your own country's access code.

Réunion is linked via cable and satellite to the rest of the world. There is no need to pre-book long-distance calls. Even from public phones, visitors will be able to immediately link up with a subscriber. Telephone books covering the island can be found at all post offices and pay-phones. Phone-cards (Telecard) can be bought from several shops and the post office. They work out cheaper than paying for individual calls, provided you make full use of them. Forget about making long-distance calls, or any call for that matter, from a hotel or guesthouse. They all charge exorbitant fees.

Cellular phones are quickly becoming the rage. Visitors will find their meals, tours and sleep regularly disturbed by that annoying tinkling sound. If you take your own cellular phone along, remember that, because Réunion is so remote, charges are very high due to the many relays and link-ups.

TIME

Standard time is four hours ahead of Greenwich Mean Time. This alters during winter and summer. Réunion is three hours ahead of Paris during winter, and two hours ahead in summer. Réunion is two hours ahead of South African time and four hours ahead of the UK in winter, and three in summer.

ELECTRICITY

The voltage throughout the island is 220 volts. Large, tourist-class hotels have adaptors for three and two-pin plugs, plus square plugs. The St-Alexis Hotel at Boucan Canot has square-to-round adaptors and transformers for visitors with appliances from countries with different voltage requirements.

BUSINESS HOURS

Hours of business for government and administrative offices are Monday to Friday 8h00-12h00 and 14h00-18h00. These offices are closed on Saturday and Sunday. Commercial institutions' hours are Monday to Friday 8h30-12h00 and 14h30-18h00; Saturday 9h00-12h00. Closed on Sunday.

Banking houses, excluding the foreign exchange counter at Gillot airport, are open Monday to Friday 8h00-16h00. Some banks, such as Credit Agricole, are also open on Saturday morning from 8h30-11h00. At Gillot Airport, the banking counters are open Monday to Saturday 10h00-19h00 and Sunday 13h00-19h00.

Shops, excluding cafés and restaurants, are usually closed on both Sunday and Monday morning, but are open Monday 13h00-18h00; Tuesday to Saturday 8h30-12h00 and 14h30-18h00.

Markets are open each day, except Sunday, 6h00-15h00.

Cafés, bistros and restaurants are open daily 10h30-14h00 and 18h00-0h00. Coffee shops are open 7h00-16h00.

MEDIA

Everything is in French. Occasionally, in the larger bookshops of St-Denis, English-speaking visitors will find something to read. Four newspapers are printed daily. The most informative concerning local events is *Le Réunionnais*. Mainly reporting on Réunion current affairs, it also has a section on neighbouring Indian Ocean islands. Newspapers which cover world events are *Journal le Réunion, Le Quotidien de la Réunion* and *Témoignages*. They can all be found in St-Denis at Cazal, 42 Rue Alexis de Villeneuve. At other centres, you will find dailies at Librairie Papeterie Alizes, 58 Rue Marius et Ary Leblond, St-Pierre; Librairie de St- Philippe, 43 Route Nationale, 2 Basse Vallee, St-Philippe; Mangrolia, 118 Avenue le de France, St-André.

Each regional centre also puts out a weekly or fortnightly paper with news of local happenings. These can be obtained from hotels or the Hôtel de Ville enquiry counter.

International newspapers are delivered a week after publication. These include both English and French editions.

Local magazines are limited, and most readers buy the glossies arriving from Europe, America or South Africa. Periodicals published in Réunion are *Visu, L'Enjeu* and *Télé 7 Jours*. *Plein Sud* magazine is published bimonthly.

Television falls under the auspices of French Television, and has a good selection of movies, news, chat shows and sporting events. RFO, the local television station, has two channels. Movies in English are dubbed into French, while documentaries are usually screened with French subtitles. Recently, a number of tenders have been put forward for the opening of independent television stations, but the government is still negotiating this.

Radio programmes are popular on Réunion. Music is played loud and everywhere. Unlike television, pirate radio stations are common.

Broadcasting mainly music, they aim large amounts of advertising at their listeners. Government-controlled radio is more serious. It broadcasts regular news, light music, plays and talk shows.

ACCOMMODATION

Réunion offers visitors a bewildering selection of accommodation. From luxury-class hotels through mountain guesthouses to family homes and camping, there is something for every budget. There are definite high and low seasons and travellers should book well ahead if they plan to arrive during a peak period. Inland, in the cirques, you will find accommodation fairly simple to locate even without reservations. In the tourist areas of St-Gilles-les-Bains and St-Denis, the worst months for finding accommodation are July and August. Low season starts around February and runs through to March. Réunion's busiest time is during the European school holidays. The Christian festive season is surprisingly quiet on the island. Irrespective of when you plan to visit, make reservations 60 days before arrival and confirm them by telegram 20 days before leaving.

There are an estimated 42 tourist-class hotels on Réunion, and new establishments are springing up virtually monthly. When requesting information on Réunion, ask for a copy of the latest listing of classified hotels.

High tariff

At the top end of the market are two hotels. The most luxurious is undoubtedly the newly built Le St Alexis on Plage de Boucan Canot. Undeniably the most expensive tourist accommodation on Réunion, it is European luxury at its best. It is followed by the Coralia at St-Gilles-les-Bains.

Medium tariff

For the average tourist, there is little sense in spending hundreds of francs on a room. If looking for a medium-priced room, there is nothing to beat one of the chalets of Villages Vacances Familles (VVF). These establishments offer clean accommodation, with meals, at reasonable rates, in pristine areas. VVF's reputation is so good that during the annual international surfing competition that takes places at St-Leu each year, all the contestants and their supporters refuse to use any other accommodation but VVF. It has chalets at St-Gilles, St-Leu and deep in the mountains at Cilaos.

There are several mountain huts or "gîtes" as they are called in French. If you are planning on hiking, write to Relais Départemental des Gîtes de France, 18 Rue Ste-Anne, 97400 St-Denis, Réunion, tel. 21.83.36, fax 21.84.47, and ask for a copy of its latest gîte edition. This agency will also arrange accommodation in local family homes. Reservations for the mountain gîtes must be made at least 90 days prior to arrival. These isolated cottages are a favourite among walkers and trekkers.

Next in price is a room with a family which is not registered. Known as chambres d'hôte, they introduce visitors to the life styles of the islanders. Ask at any rural café or store and you will be directed to the nearest place. Not as numerous on the coast, in the mountains and highlands they occur every few hundred metres. These rooms are advertised by small, unobtrusive signs hanging from the gate. There is seldom any need to book ahead. Breakfast is always included, and lunch and dinner will be provided at an additional charge. This is one of the joys of Réunion, for you will find that the islanders are not French at all, but a nation on their own, with their own unique behaviour and traditions.

Hiring an apartment or room on a long-term basis will be out of reach of most tourists. Rents are astronomical on an island that has limited residential land.

Low tariff

There is really only one way of staying cheaply in Réunion. Camp with your own tent. Around the larger urban centres it is inadvisable to camp, but away from the coastline, campers will find a multitude of suitable sites. In the forests you will only have birds and wildlife for company. On the cirques and mountains, only silence. Along the flatter agricultural estates, planters will gladly allow camping near their homes – and may even invite you in for dinner and breakfast.

A few campsites have been developed by regional councils, but they are in unsuitable locations and very exposed. Should you use these sites, especially along the west coast, at St-Gilles-les-Bains or St-Leu, be careful about your gear. Up at Cilaos and Bois Court there are specific tourist campsites. Also council built, they cater well for the camper.

Washing facilities and protected sites are provided, and hot food is available nearby.

Do not worry unduly about accommodation on Réunion. It is highly unlikely that a tourist will ever have to sleep outdoors. If desperate, go to the local police who will arrange a room at a chambre d'hôte that you were unaware of.

FOOD

Cuisine at hotels and restaurants is mostly French. Specialist restaurants are however a feature of the larger centres. In St-Denis, diners can choose from Chinese, Indian and Italian meals. You will be given a restaurant guide at the airport tourist information centre on arrival.

Away from these haunts, Creole cooking is the norm. Rice and spicy chicken stew make delicious food in the cold highland areas. Chicken is the staple meat. Beef is expensive and pork not common. Rice accompanies all Creole meals, with noodles and chips (*frites*). Fresh produce is available in abundance. Although much of the fruit is exported to France, you will find enough subtropical varieties on sale at local markets. Vegetarians are well catered for, and cooking will be done for them at all tourist accommodation – just let your host know on arrival. Chilies and spices are an integral part of vegetable dishes on Réunion. Legumes and beans are popular with midland families, and you should not miss the opportunity of trying a bowl of steaming haricots mixed with grilled chicken at the cafés in La Plain des Cafres.

Seafood is available along the coast from a wide selection of Indian Ocean specialities. Marlin is served in hotel restaurants, while tangy fish stew is sold at takeaway shops. Excellent calamari is offered in punnets from any number of roadside vendors along the swimming beaches.

Tourists can eat in private homes as well as restaurants. Many hang a table d'hôte sign outside. Although there are registered tables d'hôte on Réunion, you will find literally hundreds more across the island. They serve full Creole meals and sometimes have a wine cellar as well. Most of these places make their own cold meats, which, when accompanied by a glass of wine, make ideal snacks on the road.

Street vendors ply their trade along the island's beach areas. Set up in vans, they make enormous sandwiches and long rolls, with a variety of fillings. Visitors can also buy beer and cold drinks at these stalls.

Supermarkets are located in most towns and have well-stocked shelves. Bread is usually baked daily, as are cakes and buns. The Score supermarkets are recommended. In rural areas, travellers will be able to buy food from cafés and occasionally farms. Visitors will not go hungry on Réunion, except if caught in St-Denis on a Monday, when most restaurants and cafés are closed.

DRINK

The islanders have two passions when it comes to drink: rum and beer. Cheap and tasty beer is made by Biere Brassee a la Réunion in St-Denis. Rural cafés brew their own rum. Locals usually make their rum with the addition of some fruit. At the remote mountain bistros visitors will be offered a dash of rum with their coffee as well.

Pure rum is also available, but from commercial distilleries. The best white rum, Rhum Blanc de Plantation, is made by Charles Isautier. A good dark rum, Rhum Langevin, is made by Distillerie J Chatel.

Imported alcohol is available in all hotels, restaurants and large stores. Liqueurs as well as rum have fruit added. The most famous of the Réunion liqueurs is Paul et Virginie, with a variety of fruit flavours. Visitors are welcome to visit Distillerie de Vue Belle, where it is made.

Beer is light and tasty, with a distinct European flavour. Lunch times see the promenades and cafés filled with people sipping the local beer. It is known as "dudu", after the extinct bird on the label.

Wine is offered with all meals, and can be selected from comprehensive wine lists that include the best of French, Italian and South African wines, plus a few bottles produced on the island at Cilaos. Island wines are very sweet.

Both tea and coffee were once grown on Réunion, but the planters have long since gone to Mauritius or Africa. Most of the tea and coffee is imported now. On week-day mornings visitors will see cafés and bistros spilling over with office workers sipping cafe au lait. Tea is far less popular. You can buy a cup after a Chinese meal, but that is about it.

BOOKS

As is to be expected, most books are in French. English editions are limited to those required at schools and universities. Many tourists arrive without a guide book and rely totally on the informative brochures handed out by the tourist office. If you are only visiting Réunion and if you have sufficient funds to follow the suggestions, these are adequate.

Glossy picture books are popular with visitors. Highly recommended is *La Réunion, Île de Ocean Indien*, by G Coulon, Editions Pacifique.

Good bookshops are:

Librairie Autrement, 14 Rue Edmond Rostand, Champ Fleuri, Ste-Clotilde, tel. 41.51.57

Librairie de la Réunion, 29 Avenue de la Victoire, St-Denis, tel. 21.07.58

Librairie des Îsles, Rue Cayenne, St-Pierre, tel. 35.33.39

Visitors can get numerous free booklets directly from the tourist offices in St-Denis. See if you can obtain a copy of the latest issue of *Destination Réunion*. It has everything to help a prospective tourist's planning. The *RUN le Guide* booklet has long lists of accommodation, sites, restaurants and activities. RUN is a cultural journal available free to tourists. English copies of *Destination Réunion – Intense Island* can also be obtained at tourist offices. The annual edition of *La Réunion Annuaire International Prive* can be useful if you are interested in more than just tourism. For this you must visit the Delegation Ocean Indien, at 150 Rue de General de Gaulle, 97400 St-Denis, tel. 21.67.19, fax 21.84.75. The Réunion Tourist Board's monthly newsletter provides changes or updates to existing tourist brochures. Contact them at BP 1119, 97482 St-Denis Cedex, tel. 21.00.41, fax 20.25.93.

MAPS

These are freely available from the tourist offices at the airport or in St-Denis. They will issue you with a general map with a scale of 1:160 000. It includes main roads, points of interest, hotels and larger settlements. A table of distances is included.

Travellers planning to hike in Réunion should get hold of the Hiking Map which details routes, mountain huts and gradients. At the same time ask for a copy of the *Hiking in Réunion* booklet. The closest you are going to get to obtaining a topographical map is by asking for photocopies of the relevant area from the military. The adjutant of the paratrooper barracks north of St-Pierre is very helpful in this regard. Alternatively, contact hiking guide Yves Vignerte at 1 Ruelle des Lianes, 97413 Cilaos, tel. 31.72.57, fax 31.78.18.

THINGS TO BUY

Handicrafts on Réunion have a distinct African and Creole influence. Until recently, Creole families made their own handicrafts, which were not for sale but rather for everyday use by the people. Selling Réunion as a tourist destination has persuaded the local tourist committees to exploit their unique crafts. In the main cities you will find most items have been mass produced at some sweatshop and are expensive. Instead, go to the isolated villages and settlements along the east coast or in the hidden valleys around the cirques.

One item often on display is turtle shell. Some turtle species are endangered. There is a turtle farm outside St-Leu, but it is unlikely that everything on sale is from there, indicating that turtles in the wild are still being slaughtered. Please don't assist in the extinction of these animals by supporting such sales.

Each region has its own brand of handicraft. The most famous of these is the fine embroidery done at Cilaos. Started in the early 1900s by Roman Catholic nuns, this work is now done by several local women. A school of embroidery has been established in Cilaos. No visit to the town is complete without a trip to Maison de la Broderie, 4 Rue des Ecoles, 97413 Cilaos, tel. 31.77.48. The museum-cum-workshop and sales office is open Monday to Saturday 9h00-12h00 and 14h00-17h00; Sunday 9h00-12h00.

Tourists intent on shopping in St-Denis have a good selection of places to choose from. You must not miss the Grand Marche on 2 Rue Maréchal Leclerc, open Monday to Saturday 6h00-19h00.

At Galerie Artisanale in Ste-Clotilde visitors can choose from the full range of Réunionnaise craft. This handicraft centre is located at 75 Route du Karting, 97490 Ste-Clotilde, tel. 29.56.66.

At St-Joseph visitors will find the best handicraft selection on Réunion. In the Cramar Centre d'Exposition de Langevin, on Route Nationale, Langevin, 97480 St-Joseph, tel. 56.22.31, there is an amazing display of items for sale. The centre is open Monday to Friday 10h00-12h00 and 14h00-16h30; Saturday 9h00-12h00. Perfumes are also sold here. One can select from distilled scents made from local flowers and plants. Geranium is a favoured ingredient, while ylang-ylang blossoms impart a unique and lasting fragrance. All the prices are negotiable and the perfumes much cheaper than the same items in overpriced duty-free shops.

For those who enjoy the smell of vanilla and would like to buy some for flavouring, or worked into a figurine, the place to visit is Parfums Vanille, 21 Route Nationale, 97412 Bras Panon, tel. 51.50.62. It sells pure vanilla essence, flavoured rum, vanilla figures, sweets and literature. Open Monday to Friday, 8h00-12h00 and 13h45-17h15.

In the mountain villages around Hell-Bourg, the people make quilts, statues and preserves. These are all available at Cazanou, Rue Charles de Gaulle, Hell-Bourg, tel. 47.88.23.

The duty-free shop in Gillot Airport has most typically Réunionnais products on offer, but the prices are incredibly high. If at the last minute you do need a gift, rather visit any of the regional tourist offices. They all stock curios from their areas. The large Réunion Tourist Office in St-Denis has a particularly extensive selection of quality products.

THINGS TO DO

Réunion is a mecca for the adventure sport enthusiast. Tourists who are not partial to jumping off cliffs or scuba diving can go walking and sailing. Still too demanding? Then try scenic drives, viewing volcanoes or suntanning.

The tourism councils have made a great effort to supply visitors with a holiday that will never be forgotten. The Réunion Tourist Board has divided activities for tourists into three categories:

- On the ground – trekking, mountaineering, horse trails, cycling and golf.
- In the air – hang-gliding, microlighting and paragliding.
- On the water – scuba diving, windsurfing, game fishing and waterskiing.

Trekking

For many people, trekking is the reason for visiting Réunion. Each year hundreds of walkers and hikers arrive to explore the island's majestic wilderness areas. Prospective hikers should contact the Maison de la Montagne, 10 Place Sarda Garriga, 97400 St-Denis, tel. 21.75.84, fax 41.84.41. Here you will be able to get suggested routes, maps, advice on clothing, equipment and food, plus – should you require one – an experienced guide for the region you plan to walk. Guides from official organisations are costly, so, if travelling on a budget, contact Yves Vignerte for assistance. He is the most experienced hiking and mountain biking guide on Réunion and usually freelances. Reserve his services at least 60 days prior to arrival. 1 Ruelle des Lianes, 97413 Cilaos, tel. 31.72.57, fax 31.78.18.

Eco-tours are becoming the rage on Réunion. For the most informative trip, whether a hike or short walk, contact Ecologie Réunion, 1 Lotissement Payet Gillot, 97438 Ste-Marie, tel. 53.51.83, fax 28.09.53.

Cilaos, Salazie and the volcano are the most popular areas for hiking. If you prefer the untrodden trails, head into the forests between Plaine des Cafres and Plaine des Palmistes. This is virgin wilderness. Few trails cross the forest, but by linking up with those marked on the hiking map, trekkers will find their way. The most challenging and rewarding hikes are around Cilaos. A well marked trail circles the Cirque de Cilaos. Starting at Palmiste Rouge, take the path to the right that climbs through forests to Bras Sec. From Bras Sec swing left, pass above Cilaos and loop south along the crater rim to Illet a Cordes.

It is also possible to make the arduous trek from Cilaos to Hell-Bourg. This hike is only recommended for experienced hikers. From Cilaos follow the road for Illet a Cordes. About 3 km west of town there is a split in the road, one road going on to Illet a Cordes, the other turning north and becoming a track. Turn along this track going north. Once down the Col du Taïbit, the path leads to a mountain hut at Marla. From here there are excellent views of the highest mountain on Réunion, Piton des Neiges (3 070 m). Leaving the hut, hug the base of Le Gros Morne (2 991 m) onto the Plaine des Tamarins. A good path now edges along the Crete des Calumets into the Cirque de Salazie. At the tarred road turn right (south-east) and take the footpath to Hell-Bourg and on to Salazie.

To reach the volcano, start from Plaine des Cafres. Take the tarred road to Vingt Septieme Bourg-Murat. Turn east at the settlement and go up to the mountain summit at 2 138 m. This good road traverses a huge gash in the landscape to the viewpoint above Plaine des Sables. This is the end of the line for most vehicles. If you have hired a 4x4, then cross the lunar-like Plaine des Sables to the lookout point at Pas de Bellecombe (2 309 m). Leaving the viewpoint, walk down onto the arid surface of the volcano. A mountain hut (self-catering) has been built here – book well in advance if you plan to sleep over. Visitors can walk all the way to the crater of Piton de la Fournaise at 2 631 m.

These are just a few of the numerous hikes, walks and rambles that visitors can take on Réunion. Local hotels are a good source of mountain trail and route information. Hotel des Thermes in Cilaos will go out of its way to arrange every assistance for a trekker.

Mountaineering

Mountaineering, being the highly specialised activity it is, inevitably requires the services of a guide. Contact Compagnie des Guides de la Réunion, Maison de la Montagne, 10 Place Sarda Garriga, 97400 St-Denis, tel. 21.75.84, fax 41.84.29. Abseiling is also gaining in popularity, called canyoning by the Réunionnais. No specialist knowledge is needed for this exciting and adrenalin-filled pursuit. Speak to Aventure Ocean Indien, Souris Blanche, 97434 La-Saline-les-Bains, tel. 24.13.42. Rock climbing needs technical skill and the equipment associated with cliffs. Route guides can be obtained from the Maison de la Montagne. There are several graded climbs around Le Belier, Grand Bassin and Illet a Cordes.

Horse trails

These are becoming a regular activity for tour groups. Exploring Réunion on horseback is an enjoyable and relaxing way of doing things. No previous riding experience is necessary. For rides along the coast, visit the large Centre Equestre De L'Hermitage, ZAC de L'Hermitage, 97434 St-Gilles-les-Bains, tel. 24.47.73. If you want to ride into the mountains and around the volcano make reservations 30 days ahead at La Diligence, 28e km Bourg-Murat, 97418 Plaine des Cafres, tel. 59.10.10. Be prepared for a sore bottom if you ride the volcano route. It takes all day, and while often uncomfortable, is the easiest and most pleasant way of reaching the volcano.

Cycling

Cycling is popular in Europe and in the mountains of Réunion. Europeans love to hire cycles and tackle the routes. You can hire bicycles for day outings from any number of local shops. If you are planning to try a mountain route over a few days, you should hire both a guide and a reliable mountain bike. Try one of the following organisations for assistance:

Cilao-Fun, Place de L'Eglise, 97413 Cilaos, tel. 31.70.02

VTT Evasion, 113 Chemin de Ceinture, 97442 St-Philippe, tel. 37.06.72

Golf

Very few visitors go to Réunion for the sole purpose of playing golf, but as all golfing addicts know, the temptation is always there. To cater for these people, a full 18-hole course has been constructed at Étang-Sales-les-Hautes. Bookings should be made at least 48 hours before arrival. Call the club manager at Golf Club de Bourbon, Route Nationale 1 Les Sables, tel. 26.33.39. You will be charged green fees – which are raised over weekends. Hiring golf equipment is a problem. The manager at the club is sometimes able to arrange basic equipment.

Aerial activities

Hang-gliding and paragliding are usually administered and provided by the same organisation. Full training courses, plus free introductory flights, are available. The most experienced company is Parapente Réunion, 2 Rue Alexandre Begue, 97416 La Chaloupe, St-Leu, tel. 44.33.25. It has its own training slopes and offers visitors equipment hire and detailed information on where to find the best sites.

Microlighting is gaining members almost daily, and Réunion is no exception. Although training is offered, few visitors ever bother, and instead take a two-seater tour with a pilot. Sunrise and sunset are surely the best times for taking a microlight trip. With the wind in your face and a feeling of unimagined freedom, this is one activity that even shoestring travellers should make an effort to try. Book your flight about three days in advance with Club des Pulms de Sud, BP 182, Aerodrome de Pierrefonds, 97456 St-Pierre Cedex, tel. 39.56.29, fax 25.54.71.

Water sports

Tourists expect water sports and the tourist councils have made several activities available.

Scuba diving, although not as good as off the Seychelles, is offered. It makes little sense to go out scuba diving when simple snorkelling is so good. Off the beach at the Coralia Hotel, visitors snorkelling will see more marine life than in the open sea. A face mask, snorkel and a pair of shoes are all you need to explore the shallow, life-filled reefs of western Réunion. Those determined to venture out to deep water should count on it being an expensive desire. Both day and night dives can be arranged through Centre International de Plongée Sous-Marine, BP 466, 97400 St-Denis, tel. 24.34.11.

Windsurfing is offered by most beachfront hotels, but do not expect instructors. Wear shoes when windsurfing, as sea urchins and other ocean nasties could inflict a serious wound should you fall off. If not at an hotel that offers windsurfing, contact the local VVF or chat to the fishermen who are always on the beach early mornings.

As on other Indian Ocean islands, game fishing is promoted. There are none of the environmental controls found in the Seychelles or Mauritius, and fishermen are welcome to cart their prizes back home. According to the Réunion Fishing Club, the best time for game fishing is between October and May. Charter boats charge astronomical hire fees and additional fees for landing a catch. Hotels can arrange fishing trips through their contacts, but this will cost at least 40% more than doing it directly yourself. For details contact the Réunion Fishing Club, 60 Chemin des Sables, 97434 St-Gilles-les-Bains, tel. 24.36.10, fax 24.39.46.

Waterskiing has never reached the popularity it has on Mauritius. West coast hotels usually offer it for a fee. Boats specifically for waterskiing can be hired from Ski Club de St-Paul, 1 Rue Croix de L'Etang, 97460 St-Paul, tel. 45.42.87. It will also arrange for instruction. You must hire the boat for a minimum of 60 minutes. In other locations ask the fishermen to find a local who has a boat with skiing attachments.

15 GETTING THERE

AIR

International flights connect Réunion with Antananarivo, Johannesburg, Mauritius and Paris.

The airlines servicing these routes are listed below, with their addresses and telephone numbers in St-Denis on Réunion. For their latest flight schedules and fares, contact a travel agent or these airlines' representative in your own country.

Air Austral, 4 Rue de Nice, tel. 20.20.20
Air France, 7 Avenue de la Victoire, tel. 40.38.40
Air Liberté
Air Madagascar, 2 Rue Victor Mac Auliffe, tel. 21.05.21
Air Mauritius, corner Rue Alexis de Villeneuve and Charles Gounod, tel. 20.25.00
AOM, 77 Rue Roland Garros, tel. 21.53.00

Passenger flights are expensive, and budget travellers should consider asking the air cargo companies for a flight. The regulations concerning passengers change frequently, and you will need to contact the airline at least 30 days ahead of intended departure. Two air cargo companies offer possibilities for independent travellers. You will need to make an application to the operations manager.

Corsair Cargo, 87 Boulevard de Grenelle, 75738 Paris Cedex 15, France, tel. (1) 42.73.10.64

Air Cargo Réunion, 152 Rue du General de Gaulle, St-Denis, Réunion, tel. 41.70.70

The offices of Air Austral keep loads of useful information on Réunion for visitors. The staff are all experienced in planning and organising suitable journeys to and around the island. Solo travellers should set up an appointment to meet the manager. Once you have decided what you want to do on Réunion, the manager will gladly assist you in putting together a route, plus provide details on sites, transport and accommodation.

There is no airport tax on Réunion. The international airport, Gillot, is about 11 km from the capital, St-Denis.

SEA

Getting to Réunion by sea is almost impossible. Unless they find a yacht or charter a vessel it is unlikely that visitors will arrive this way. Cargo vessels do sail between France and Réunion, but with the new legislation regarding passengers on French cargo ships, you need to be employed by the ship's company to make the passage. Yachts seldom cruise to Réunion – it's right in the path of cyclones and storms. You may be fortunate enough to sail on a yacht to Mauritius though. From there it is a short hop to Réunion on one of the regular Air Mauritius flights. Note: You will need to have purchased this air ticket outside Mauritius, and produced it when arriving in that country.

16 GETTING AROUND

Getting around Réunion is simple. Visitors can experience the whole gamut of transport while visiting the island, from hiring a car, catching the bus or flipping about in helicopters.

AIR

The international airport is Gillot, a few kilometres east of St-Denis. Visitors should contact the aero club at Gillot for information on fixed wing flights from there or out of towns further south. Aero-Club Roland Garros, tel. 28.40.03. You can expect to pay heavily to hire a private plane.

Although few people travel between towns by air, most tourists try at least one tour in a helicopter. Helicopters have become all the rage on Réunion. Several companies offer flights that take in the volcano, cirques and rugged coastline. Helilagon have the most comprehensive itinerary. Its tours include flights over the cirque de Mafate, cirque de Salazie, Réunion's highest peak, Piton des Neiges, Piton de la Fournaise (volcanic crater) and Plaine des Palmistes. Specialist trips are made during the holiday season over Plaine des Cafres, Le Dimitile, cirque de Cilaos and St-Gilles-les-Bains. To reach the company's heliport, l'Eperon, you travel to Boucan Canot on the west coast and turn inland, following the signs for St-Gilles-les-Hauts. The heliport is along a diabolical gravel road, just above La Ravine St-Gilles. Visitors should arrive on Réunion with a pre-booked helicopter ride, as attempting to get aboard during the vacation season is virtually impossible. Ask about the special fares on group bookings and reservations made for the low season. Contact the company about 60 days before leaving home. Included in the charge is transport to and from your hotel. Helilagon, Altiport de l'Eperon, 97460 St-Paul, Réunion, tel. 55.55.55, fax 22.86.78.

BUS

Using luxury coaches that speed along at well over 120 km/h, travellers will find it a pleasure getting around Réunion. Passengers are not permitted to carry their heavy luggage aboard. It will be stored in cavernous compartments in the lower section. These coaches run from about 6h30 through to 21h30 along national roads and 6h00-18h00 in the rural districts. There is, however, one major quirk that all foreigners travelling by bus need to know about. There are no bells for signalling when you want to get off. You must clap your hands together once or twice, as loud as possible, to make yourself heard above the din of French music. If this does not work immediately, whistle and clap to attract the driver's attention.

Most long-distance buses fall under the jurisdiction of Reseau Départemental Alizes, the buses being known as Alizes. There are principal routes and secondary routes, each identified by a coloured stripe. Principal routes are: blue – St-Denis to St-Benoit; yellow – St-Benoit to St-Pierre via St-Philippe; green – St-Denis to St-Pierre; purple – St-Benoit to St-Pierre via Le Tampon. Secondary routes are usually served by smaller buses. Red and green – St-Pierre area and around St-Louis; orange – St-Pierre to Cilaos, run by private contractors belonging to Transporteurs Interurbains du Département; red – St-Pierre to Cilaos. Visitors can collect timetables, which are strictly adhered to, from any of the bus depots, known as gares routières. St-Denis, tel. 41.51.10; St-Paul, tel. 22.54.38, St-Pierre, tel. 35.40.91.

The Réunionnais bus service is regular, cheap and highly recommended. Along the coastal routes to and from the capital of St-Denis, you will find at least eight buses per day travelling the main highways. Off the national roads, frequent small buses service the areas in the mountains and along the remote south and east coasts. Major bus depots are located at St-Denis, Le Port, St-Paul, St-Louis, St-Pierre, near Raphael Babet, St-Benoit and St-André. To reach the isolated villages in the mountains, visitors may need to first take a bus to the nearest large town. From there change onto the secondary route to your destination. Bus rides worth taking, even if just for the trip, are St-Louis to Cilaos; St-André to Salazie and St-Pierre to Grande Ferme.

In tourist resorts such as St-Gilles-les-Bains and Boucan Canot, the hoteliers have joined together and formed their own small transport company that whisks tourists around the coastal areas in a minibus. You can catch one by waiting at any official bus stop in these two villages. They do not travel further than the city limits but are wonderful when you want to go from the hotels of St-Gilles to the only good beaches on Réunion at Boucan Canot. If you are not a hotel guest, you are required to pay a small fee, which is the same irrespective of the distance covered.

TAXI

Taxis are the most expensive way of getting around Réunion. They are as much as 120% more expensive than a bus covering the same distance in the same time, and in the same degree of comfort. They have fare meters and a charge of around Ff12 when the journey starts. Over weekends and public holidays a surcharge is added to the starting fee.

Lines of taxis wait outside Gillot airport. In towns they can usually be located around the bus depot. Taximen are a vociferous lot. They bully, plead, cajole and beg prospective passengers. They are harmless though, and a smile, firm shake of the head and a few words of choice French end their tirade in roars of laughter. Budget travellers will find anything longer than a ride from the airport to St-Denis a real financial burden. The main attraction is that taxis are available 24 hours a day. All hotel reception desks have at least two local taxis on their phone list.

Off the main roads and highways, older model cars make up the taxi industry. These taxis are also expensive, but the drivers have an intimate knowledge of local accommodation, sights and places to eat. In a place like Bois Court or Le Pavillion, they can be helpful if you are looking for lodging in the area, as there are no guesthouses, hotels or restaurants advertised.

BOAT

Not many visitors try offshore sailing. As a result, you will be hard-pressed to find a yacht or charter vessel just for cruising. The best bet is to try and contact one of the game fishing or scuba diving charter companies (see Things to Do in chapter 14). Another alternative is to ask one of the local fishermen if you can hire him and his boat for a day's sightseeing around the coast. Excursions can be had by speaking to the fishermen in the small villages along the south-eastern coast. Good places to try are near Bois Blanc and south at Mare Longue. At Mare Longue, a meal and a bottle of Cilaos wine at lunch time will be included in the charter of the little fishing boat.

CAR RENTAL

This is the most popular way for visitors to get around Réunion. Car hire companies have proliferated in recent years and the competition has resulted in reasonable prices and attractive packages being offered.

You will need an international driving permit or a French driver's licence. Location de Voitures signifies a car hire firm. There are the usual international car rental agencies at Gillot Airport, with their respective representatives also at top-class hotels in St-Denis and St-Gilles-les-Bains. You may arrange to have a vehicle waiting for you on arrival. To do this contact the nearest branch of Europcar or Hertz. On Réunion they can be contacted at: Europcar, 1 Rue Doret, 97400 St-Denis, tel. 21.81.01; Hertz, 82 Rue Republique, 97400 St-Denis, tel. 21.22.52.

Of the local firms, AGR offer the most reasonable packages, with incentive discounts the longer you keep the car. Although it is based in St-Pierre, 17 Rue François Isautier (opposite the bus depot) tel. 25.48.48, fax 35.02.33, it will gladly deliver the vehicle anywhere on the island. Other firms worth trying are:

Location St-Gilles, 216 Rue General de Gaulle, St-Gilles-les-Bains, tel. 24.08.18, fax 24.05.63

Citer, Gillot Airport, and 69 Boulevard du Chaudron, Ste-Clotilde, tel. 48.87.87, fax 48.87.99

Au Bas Prix (the name alone makes it an attractive possibility), 35 Rue Suffren, St-Paul, tel. 45.43.36, fax 22.54.27

Credit cards are the preferred method of payment, which must be made when you collect the car. Check the company's insurance details before zooming off. Sometimes a slightly higher rate, that will cover any damage you incur, is offered – otherwise the hirer carries the cost. Ask them to also give you a map of Réunion and the necessary proof of ownership papers. As in continental Europe, drive on the right-hand side of the road. Fuel is supplied in Super and Premium grades. Drivers are usually given the car with a full tank of petrol, and are expected to return it full as well. Make a physical inspection of the vehicle, with the agent, and write down any faults or damage already on the car prior to departure.

BICYCLE

You will either love or hate cycling in Réunion. Mountain biking is popular around the cirques, but you will need experience if hoping to go off-road. Along the coast, cycling is dangerous and not advised. The roads are busy, drivers speed and the whole experience can be traumatic. Cycling is enjoyable in the rural areas. The scent of farms, flowers and forests wafts around you as you explore the backroads. In Cilaos, speak to the owner of Hotel des Thermes about hiring a bicycle. Hotel des Thermes, Rue des Sources, Cilaos, tel. 31.70.01. You can also try Cilaos-Fun, Place d'Eglise, Cilaos, tel. 31.70.02. At Plaine-des-Cafres, the Lallemand Hotel is able to provide guests with cycles. Visitors wanting to cycle in Salazie must travel further up to Hell-Bourg, and there ask at the Auberge de la Jeunesse d'Hell-Bourg, Rue Cayenne, tel. 47.82.65.

MOTORCYCLE

Instead of a bicycle, consider hiring a small motorbike. The hire charges are on the same basis as car hire; the longer you have the bike, the cheaper it is. Agents seldom ask for a rider's licence, but take it along anyway. Visitors can cover most parts of Réunion within two or three days by motorcycle. The bikes are light on fuel and offer a wonderfully free feeling to adventure travellers. Call L'Île en Moto, 216 Rue General de Gaulle, 97434 St-Gilles-les-Bains, tel. 24.05.63, or Nickel Moto, 17 Rue Bonier, 97400 St-Denis, tel. 20.15.25.

HITCHHIKING

Hitchhiking around Réunion is difficult. It is also illegal on national roads. In the mountains, lifts are slightly more frequent, but they seldom go very far and you are likely to end up catching a bus in the end.

Getting out of St-Denis is a nightmare. Rather take a bus to St-Paul and try from there. Both St-Leu and St-Paul offer good possibilities over the weekend, but are useless during the week. The easiest coastline to hitchhike is the east. From St-Philippe to St-Benoit, heavy vehicles will occasionally stop. Hitching to Cilaos or Salazie is virtually impossible, unless you manage to get a through ride from St-Louis or St-André.

To reach the really remote destinations, visitors should ask around the markets in St-Pierre and St-Benoit. Farmers regularly drop off produce with the vendors, and are delighted to have some company on the journey home.

TOURS

Most visitors come with a group on a tour package but surprisingly few of these tours include sightseeing, and it has been left to the ingenuity of the locals to organise tours. There are about 12 registered tour operators, plus numerous private operators. ERL offers the widest selection of island tours, plus deals on 4x4 vehicle hire. Its most popular tour is the fly-'n-drive trip which includes helicopter flights, off-road exploration and coastal sightseeing. It specialises in tailor-made tours, aimed at the adventure visitor, that include hiking, windsurfing and paragliding. Contact it a minimum of 30 days ahead. ERL, 24 Rue Leopold Rambaud, 97490 Ste-Clotilde, Réunion, tel. 21.66.81, fax 24.06.02.

Another tour operator worth considering is Bourbon Voyages. It can handle all incoming tourists' planning, from booking hotels through to personalised excursions and helicopter flights. Bourbon Voyages, 14 Rue Rontaunay, 97400 St-Denis, tel. 21.68.18, fax 41.03.09. Visitors under 25 can have their tours planned and arranged by VVF Tourism, BP 20, 97434 St-Gilles-les-Bains, tel. 24.39.78, fax 24.05.77. It is experienced at organising cheap youth accommodation and exciting island tours. For a detailed list of all tour operators in Réunion, call at the Tourist Office, 23 Rue Tourette, St-Denis.

Overseas agencies also plan and lead excursion trips to Réunion. Many of these agencies are able to offer tourists excellent packages at prices way below what an independent traveller would have to pay. If you book through one of them, request that sightseeing and touring be included. Contact a reputable travel agent in your own country.

17 ST-DENIS

The Paris of the Indian Ocean, St-Denis, named after a French naval vessel, has blossomed from a village to the most vibrant and colourful town on Réunion. It took over from St-Paul as the capital in 1738, and today St-Denis still reflects an era of grace and gentility that has all but disappeared elsewhere. As immigration to Réunion from France increased, numerous members of the French nobility settled in St-Denis. Walking along Rue de Paris, visitors will still see their beautiful mansions and manicured gardens. The age of French colonialism has never left St-Denis. Today, centre of the seat of governorship, St-Denis pulses with a European vitality found nowhere else in the Indian Ocean. Here you will find the latest fashions from Paris and Milan, café society, motorbikes and techno-funk discos. Few tourists feel indifferent about the Réunionnais capital. Most travellers enjoy exploring the old cobbled alleys that once saw ox carts and carriages trundling along them. There are statues, museums, government buildings and boutiques which offer visitors the opportunity to do shopping, sightseeing and business transactions. In the evening, elderly couples walk their poodles along the promenade, and lovers sit kissing in the flower-filled parks.

GETTING THERE

Most visitors arrive on Réunion by air, flying in from Africa, Europe or neighbouring islands. Occasionally, a cruise liner will make the trip from Africa – usually as part of a voyage to Mauritius. If coming by ship, visitors will disembark at Le Port, about 25 km south-west of St-Denis. Tourists arriving by air land at Gillot International Airport, about 11 km from the city.

To reach St-Denis from the airport will involve the use of a taxi, bus or shuttle service. Taxis line up outside the main doors of the arrivals terminal. Each taxi has a fare meter, so there is little chance of negotiating a lower price. A cheaper option would be by bus. Walk out of the airport terminal and go south along the road that exits the airport. Just before the bridge is the bus stop for Alizes buses going into St-Denis (the St-Benoit to St-Denis blue route). Get the driver to drop you at the main long-distance bus depot on Joffre Boulevard. A shuttle bus

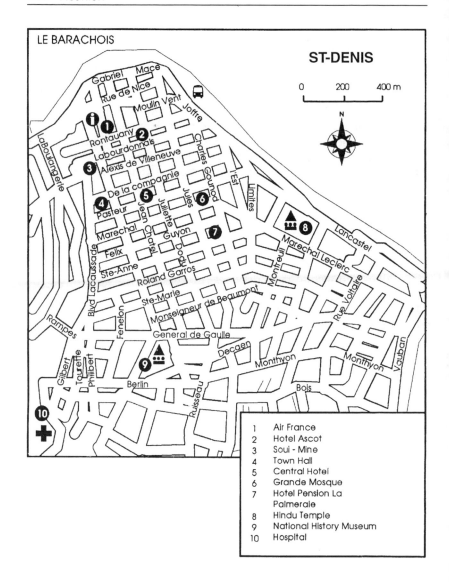

LE BARACHOIS

ST-DENIS

0   200   400 m

1	Air France
2	Hotel Ascot
3	Soui - Mine
4	Town Hall
5	Central Hotel
6	Grande Mosque
7	Hotel Pension La Palmerale
8	Hindu Temple
9	National History Museum
10	Hospital

service is available whenever large international flights arrive. There is usually a mad rush to get on, and unless you find a seat you may be left behind – no standing passengers are allowed. This blue shuttle bus drops tourists off either at the St-Denis bus station or outside the Meridien Hotel. Two hours before the departure of international flights, the same shuttle leaves from the Meridien Hotel for Gillot. Most hotels in St-Denis provide their guests with airport transport anyway.

From Le Port, walk into Le Possession and wait at the gare routière in town. The green route Alizes bus, from St-Pierre to St-Denis, stops here. Alternatively, approach one of the taxis that wait outside the Caltex garage, near the mosque.

GETTING AROUND

Getting around St-Denis is best done by walking. Even if you stay at hotels that are out of the city, the walk into the CBD is enjoyable and easy. A local city bus service (Transports Dionysiens) does travel the routes from the city centre out to the suburbs. Like the Metro in Paris, the routes of buses are graphically shown inside each bus and at each large bus stop. For rides to and from the CBD to the southern suburbs, wait along Rue de la Victoire. If wanting to go east, wait on Rue Maréchal Leclerc. Buses on Rue du Pont go west. Alternatively, wait at the gare routière Urbaine bus depot, on Boulevard Joffre. Should you use the bus, make certain to keep the ticket you purchase on the first ride. The same ticket can be used anywhere on that route for the next hour, either into or out of town.

Taxis dash about the city at high speed, but tend to miss out on the smaller, interesting alleys and lanes that make up the heart of St-Denis. Tourists can also hire a taxi for the day, specifically for a sightseeing tour of the city. Contact Paille-en-Queue Taxis, tel. 29.20.29. Hiring a bicycle or motorcycle can be fun, provided you travel around the city on Sunday or in the evenings. The weekdays and Saturday see traffic jams and neurotic drivers. Max Moto, 11 Onyx Bellepierre, tel. 21.15.25, hires out motorcycles and can arrange bicycles as well.

Getting yourself orientated in St-Denis is pretty much a matter of trial and error. A good idea is to choose two long streets which cross at some point in the centre of town. Travellers who have spent any length of time in St-Denis unanimously agree that Rue Maréchal Leclerc (from west to east), and Rue de Paris (north to south) are the best streets to use as reference points. Boulevard Gabriel Mace, which becomes

Boulevard Joffre further east, is the main road that edges the sea, immediately north of the city. At the southern end of the CBD, Rue du General de Gaulle cuts from east to west. Using the St-Denis river in the west, Butor ravine to the east, the sea in the north and Ravine des Noirs in the south as boundaries, visitors can comfortably walk St-Denis and its environs within a few hours. A simple grid pattern has been used in the planning of the capital, which makes things a lot easier for walkers and tourists. There is a large graphic city map on display along Rue des Moulins.

TOURIST INFORMATION

You can obtain detailed tourist information at the regional tourist office. Tourist Office of St-Denis, 48 Rue Ste-Marie, tel. 41.83.00. To find this small but informative tourist office, go south along Rue de Paris. Just past the Musee Léon Dierx, turn right into Rue Ste-Marie. The office is on the left, about 50 m from the corner, and is open Monday to Friday 8h00-12h00 and 14h00-18h00. It has a good selection of pamphlets, brochures and excellent service-orientated staff. Ask for the free map, *Plan de la Ville* of St-Denis. The map is useful and simple to use. It has a scale of 1:11 000, and tourist attractions are clearly marked. If you plan to use local buses, also ask for a *Plan Schematique du Reseau de Transports Dionysiens*, which indicates in different colours the routes that city buses take. Information on other parts of Réunion can also be found at this office. For specific details of activities on Réunion, visit the headquarters of Réunion tourism at 23 Rue Tourette, St-Denis Cedex, tel. 21.00.41. Walk south on Rue de Paris to the circle on Place de Metz. Turn right (west) along Rue General de Gaulle. The third road you cross is Rue Tourette.

Tourist information is also available at Gillot airport. The staff tend to be rude to travellers arriving with backpacks and travelling independently, so rather visit the more helpful tourist offices in St-Denis. Another place to get tourist information is at Tropica Pro-Photo, near the Air Mauritius offices on Rue Charles Gounod. The manager has a delightful manner and years of experience in travel around this island he obviously loves. Adventure and budget travellers will find his help and information particularly useful.

Hikers and mountain climbers can get pertinent information and assistance from Maison de la Montagne on Place Sarda Garriga, tel. 21.75.84, near the Radio and Television Française (RFO) building on

Rue Jean Chatel. Its information and orientation centre is well-staffed and helpful. It is open Monday to Friday 8h00-12h00 and 13h00-15h00.

Banks are a feature of St-Denis. Several mainly French banking institutions have set up branches in the city. You can cash traveller's cheques and change hard currency at virtually all these banks. You may have to ask around the banks if you want to use your credit card to draw money. Not all banks accept all cards. For example, Banque Nationale de Paris Intercontinental will not handle Mastercard, but Credit Agricole is quite happy to do so. Credit Agricole also has the most efficient and helpful foreign exchange counters. Its staff are always a delight to do business with. Its exchange counter at Gillot is highly recommended, both for arrivals and when changing francs back into the original currency on departure.

The banks are:

Banque Française Commerciale, 58 Rue Alexis de Villeneuve, tel. 40.55.55

Banque Nationale de Paris Intercontinental, 67 Rue Juliette Dodu, tel. 40.30.30

Banque de la Réunion, 27 Rue Jean Chatel, tel. 40.01.23

Credit Agricole, 14 Rue Felix Guyon, tel. 40.84.00

Visitors using American Express traveller's cheques or cards will find the American Express office on Rue Rontaunay.

Numerous international tour operators and local travel agents have offices in St-Denis. It is prudent to make all your tour reservations prior to leaving the capital. Outside of St-Denis and St-Gilles-les-Bains it is almost impossible to arrange tours. Independent visitors intending to go up into the mountains should make their bookings at least five days ahead, and three days in advance for tours of the coastal areas, including reservations for helicopter flights and car hire. ERL, although based in St-Gilles-les-Bains, has an office in the Ste-Clotilde suburb of St-Denis. Adventure travellers should contact them for tour guidance and planning assistance.

ERL, 24 Rue Leopold Rambaud, Ste-Clotilde, tel. 21.66.81.

Air Vacances Réunion, 22 Rue Felix Guyon, tel. 41.81.41

Bourbon Voyages, 14 Rue Rontaunay, tel. 21.68.18

Reucir Voyages, 74 Rue Juliette Dodu, tel. 41.55.66

Tropic Voyages, 15 Avenue de la Victoire, tel. 21.03.54

Several post offices are scattered about the suburbs of St-Denis, but the best one at which to do any mailing or postal business is in the centre of town on Rue Maréchal Leclerc, tel. 21.12.12. Open Monday to Friday 7h30-18h00; Saturday 8h00-12h00. To find poste restante mail, visitors must enter through the Boites des Commerce door around the corner on Rue Juliette Dodu. You will be charged for the poste restante service.

St-Denis offers the best selection of bookshops and newsagents in the country. Prices are high for non-French books, and the choice of English literature is limited to text books and large format books.

Librairie Cazal, 42 Rue Alexis de Villeneuve, tel. 21.32.64
Librairie L'Entrepot, 82 Rue Juliette Dodu, tel. 21.90.99
Librairie Papeterie Gerard, 5 Rue de la Compagnie, tel. 21.34.51
Librairie de la Réunion, 29 Avenue de la Victoire, tel. 21.07.58

Photographic equipment and repairs are available from several shops. Tourists can buy both print and slide film, batteries, have repairs carried out, and have their photos developed at one-hour facilities.

Photo 2 000, 6 Rue Alexis de Villeneuve, tel. 21.10.83
Photo Express, 90 Rue Juliette Dodu, tel. 20.01.65
Photo Shop, 83 Avenue De Lattre de Tassigny, tel. 29.67.88
Photo Varietes, 12 Rue de la Compagnie, tel. 21.06.82

St-Denis has an abundance of medical practitioners, from GPs to specialist surgeons. The ambulance service can be summoned throughout 24-hours, tel. 43.43.43. Medical service is costly and hikers especially should consider taking out a travel-health insurance policy before leaving home. Foreigners cannot simply turn up at a hospital or clinic and expect treatment. You will have to be referred by a doctor, unless involved in a life and death situation. The same applies to visiting a specialist; a letter of introduction from a GP is necessary.

The main hospital serving St-Denis is on Route de Bellepierre, tel. 21.24.90. A day hospital is located down Rue Labourdonnais; Centre Hospitalier Specialise de St-Paul, tel. 21.34.59. Many private doctors have formed partnerships that run clinics. These are expensive, but the service is excellent. Visitors will find a comprehensive list of doctors and clinics in the yellow pages of the telephone book. Look under Medecins Generalistes – St-Denis section.

Pharmacists can provide for minor problems such as influenza, diarrhoea, sore muscles and headaches. Pharmacie Moderne on Rue Maréchal Leclerc has a good reputation. The nearby dentist, Dr Pascal Cadet, tel. 20.02.24, is recommended.

St-Denis has five libraries worth visiting. You must however be able to read French to reap the full benefit of the library services. Municipal and educational libraries, known as bibliothéques, are open to the public:

Bibliothéque Départemental, 52 Rue Roland Garros, tel. 21.13.96

Bibliothéque Municipale de St-Bernard, 146 Chem Père Raimbault, tel. 23.61.30

Bibliothéque Municipale, Chaudron, 2 Rue Jean Bertho, Ste-Clotilde, tel. 29.94.30; La Motagne, 32 Route Palmiers, La Motagne, tel. 23.71.23

Université de la Réunion, 24 Avenue de la Victoire, tel. 20.20.07

Confirmation of flights is essential well in advance of departure. This can be done by phone through a travel agent or directly with the respective airline representative on Réunion:

Air Austral, 4 Rue de Nice, tel. 20.20.20

Air France, 7 Avenue de la Victoire, tel. 40.38.40

Air Madagascar, 2 Rue Victor Mac Auliffe, tel. 21.05.21

Air Mauritius, corner Rue Alexis de Villeneuve and Charles Gounod, tel. 20.25.00

AOM, 77 Rue Roland Garros, tel. 21.53.00

THINGS TO DO

Any walking tour of St-Denis should start on Boulevard Gabriel Mace, along the seafront. Over weekends this area is full of families relaxing. On Sunday afternoons the road along Place du 20 Decembre 1848 is closed to traffic and only strollers are allowed. Men play boccie (bowls) in the park on Boulevard Gabriel Mace. Snack vans sell hotdogs, beer and takeaways. Buskers wander about singing their ballads and the island's elite spill out onto the pavements from the cafés and bistros. It is vibrant, busy and joyfully European.

French cannons point north-west over the sea at Le Barachois, opposite Place Sarda Garriga, where the statue of Réunion's most famous son is located. The daring aviator Roland Garros was born in St-Denis, 6 October 1888. He was awarded France's highest military accolade, the Croix de Guerre. This area is tranquil parkland, with palms, lawns, flowers and gentle ocean breezes.

Turning west, follow the boulevard to Hôtel de la Préfecture. This is not an hotel in the English sense. It is actually the Prefects' administration offices for Réunion. To the east, Place du Gouvernement is marked by an enormous French flag, armed soldiers and security fences. There is a small park alongside the impressive edifice. Cannons, chains and flowers create an ironic setting. A statue in honour of the island's greatest governor, Mahé de Labourdonnais, is located in the park. Air France is across the road on Rue de la Victoire.

Further along, another monument has been erected to Réunion's most famous poet and writer, Leconte de Lisle. From the park, go east along Rue du Mat to Place Charles de Gaulle, honouring the French leader. Turn right into Rue de la Victoire and continue south, through Place Leconte de Lisle and up to the cathedral, opposite Place Jean Paul II. A beautifully sculpted fountain pours a shower of water into a pond. The atmosphere is peaceful, and students from the nearby university often lie under the trees studying. To the south stands a monument dedicated to islanders who have suffered racism and abuse.

Continuing up Rue de la Victoire, visitors will pass the old stone building of the Secretariat General, on the right. At the southern end of Rue de la Victoire is the Monument aux Morts, a memorial to Réunionnais soldiers who died in both world wars.

Go around the circle and continue along the same road, which becomes Rue de Paris. This is where the wealthy suburbs of St-Denis start. The abandoned and ruined Hôtel de Ville is located on the west side of the road. On the corner of Rue Maréchal Leclerc and Rue de Paris is the mansion in which the writer, artist and poet Léon Dierx was born on 31 March 1838.

Turn right (west) along Rue Maréchal Leclerc to the market (Grand Marche), opposite the police station. This is a good place to look for authentic island curios, and to stock up on fresh produce if you are going hiking in the mountains. Swing south into Rue Lucien Gasparin and then first left, down Rue Felix Guyon. On the corner of Rue Felix Guyon and Rue de Paris, visitors will see the magnificent Creole mansion of the Secretariat General. Walk along Rue de Paris again. Splendid colonial houses line either side of the street, hidden behind weatherworn shutters and filigreed balconies lined with flower boxes. Across Rue Ste-Anne, the College de L'Immaculée Conception stands in a park-like setting of trees, hedges and blossoms.

Further south, past the Villa Mancini, is the art museum, Musee Léon Dierx. Founded in 1911 by Marius and Ary Leblond, this gallery is not only the first, but also the most renowned, art museum in the Indian Ocean region. Original works by Gauguin, Picasso and local artist Vollard are on display. Housed in an old episcopal mansion, the museum is open from Tuesday to Sunday 10h00-12h00 and 13h00-18h00.

Entrance is free. Weekend group bookings can be made, tel. 20.24.82, fax 21.82.87.

Leave the museum by the Rue Ste-Marie exit. Directly across the road is the regional tourist office of St-Denis. Rue de Paris ends at a circle, in whose centre is a statue of Conte FG Bally of Monthion. Stretching away to the right and left is Rue General de Gaulle. On the far side (southern side) of the circle is the entrance to the botanical gardens of Jardin de L'Etat (State Gardens) and the natural history museum. Open daily 6h00-19h00, the park is worth visiting. Started by botanists Joseph Huber, Nicolas Breon and Jean Claude Richard, there are over 2 000 botanical species and 7 000 plants growing in the garden. There are long fish ponds, fragrant flowers, orchids and a host of strange-looking palm trees from all over the tropics. If you are looking for a place to restore your sanity after the congestion of the central city, head for the Jardin de L'Etat. The natural history museum, open from Tuesday to Friday 10h00-16h00, weekends 10h00-17h00, is a disappointment. Displays are decaying, dust coats everything and the staff are far from helpful. An entrance fee is charged, but it hardly seems worth the expense.

This route covers most of the sights that will interest visitors to St-Denis. For a bit more sightseeing, return down Rue de Paris to Rue Ste-Anne. Turn right into Ste-Anne and walk east to the corner of Rue Chinois, where you can find serenity in the Buddhist pagoda. Continue walking east on Rue Ste-Anne until it meets Rue Maréchal Leclerc. Turn right and less than 150 m on the left is the colourful Tamil temple. Heading north-west, back towards town, follow Rue Maréchal Leclerc. The road turns left (west) and crosses Rue Charles Gounod. On the second block on the right is the Grand Mosque, Noor-E-Islam. Suitably dressed visitors are welcome every day except Friday, when the Muslims have weekly worship.

Continue west on Rue Maréchal Leclerc until reaching Rue de Paris. By turning right you will return to where you started the tour. Expect to take about three to four hours to cover the route thoroughly and see this wonderful city.

Arranging a sea cruise around Réunion is difficult. In St-Denis, visitors should speak to travel agencies about an island cruise:

Bourbon Voyages, 14 Rue Rontaunay, tel. 21.68.16, fax 41.03.09

Comète Voyages Réunion, corner Rues Jules Aubert and Moulin a Vent, tel. 21.31.00, fax 41.37.71

Euro Voyages, 20 Rue de L'Est, tel. 21.89.00, fax 41.30.00

Along the coast, at St-Gilles-les-Bains, St-Leu and St-Pierre, yacht owners are usually willing to provide a cruise for the right price.

THINGS TO BUY

Traditional handicrafts are limited to the tourist office on Rue Ste-Marie, the market and two specialist shops in the capital. The largest selection of typical Réunion craft work can be found at Galerie Artisanale, Centre Commercial Continent, 75 Route du Karting, in the eastern suburb of Ste-Clotilde. This delightful shop is open Monday, Wednesday, Thursday and Saturday 9h30-20h00; Tuesday 9h30-20h30 and Friday 9h30-21h00.

Extremely expensive, but worth a visit, even if just to get an idea of what is available, is the tourist shop known as Galerie Lacaze at 10 Place Sarda Garriga. It has an extensive range of handiwork, but the prices are absolutely ridiculous, especially if you have seen and priced similar work in the mountain villages.

The Grande Marche – market – on Rue Maréchal Leclerc, is also a good place to search for local curios. Many of the items are mass produced and not worth the prices asked. Just keep looking and bargaining.

Exquisitely crafted model ships can be purchased from Galerie des Mascareignes on Rue Maréchal Leclerc.

If you have only just arrived in St-Denis and are still planning to tour Réunion, try and find curios in the rural areas. They are not only cheaper, but made with an attention to detail and workmanship that is lacking in city-made craft.

ACCOMMODATION

Accommodation in St-Denis is expensive. The less time you remain in the capital, the better it will be for your pocket.

Le Meridien Hotel (high tariff)

Tourists who are not concerned about hotel rates should try this four-star hotel. This is where the wealthier package-tour visitors stay. Prices are prohibitive for annual vacationers, but group bookings make it more reasonable. There are 122 bedrooms; singles, doubles and suites. Each room has air-conditioning, telephone, television and mini-bar. Bars, discos, an airport bus service and traditional dances are among the facilities offered. The Mascarin restaurant is open during the week, but closed on Saturday and Sunday afternoon. Make your hotel reservation a minimum of 60 days before arrival. Le Meridien, 2 Rue Doret, 97462 St-Denis Cedex, tel. 21.80.20, fax 21.97.41.

While several tourist-class hotels serve St-Denis, only two are really worth consideration by the medium-budget traveller.

Ascotel (medium tariff)

In the very heart of St-Denis, this three-star hotel has 52 air-conditioned rooms with telephone, mini-bar, television and en suite bathroom. Breakfast is included in the rate. This is arguably the best value for money hotel in the city. Staff are cordial and helpful, going out of their way to speak English if a guest requires it. There is security, covered parking and two restaurants. French food is available in the quaint Le Verger restaurant, and excellent Chinese meals can be eaten in the highly acclaimed Le Pont du Ciel restaurant. Vegetarians should inform the restaurant of their preference on booking, and a delightful vegetarian platter will be cooked for you. Within a few minutes' stroll of the most important tourist areas, the Ascotel is the ideal hotel at which to spend your first or last night on Réunion. Book well ahead. Returning guests often reserve a room six months in advance. Ascotel, 20 Rue Charles Gounod, 97400 St-Denis, tel. 41.82.82, fax 41.71.41.

Hotel Bourbon (medium tariff)

Owned by the wealthy Apavou family, the Hotel Bourbon caters mainly for business people. As a result, the service tends to be a little poor. Woe betide anyone who arrives and cannot speak French. Be patient and the receptionists will, after a while, try and help you. Despite the service, the Hotel Bourbon provides a wonderful break from the noisy confusion of town. Up in the hills to the south of the city, along Rampes de St François, the hotel commands incredible vistas of St-Denis. There are 197 rooms, all with small bathrooms, telephone and television. Breakfast is not included in the rate. A restaurant provides French and some Creole dishes from an à la carte menu. Perhaps the hotel's two biggest attractions for tourists are the free shuttle service between airport and hotel, and the magnificent swimming pools. Tennis courts, billiards room and a cavernous conference room complete the facilities. To reach the city by bus, you must walk north-east along Rue du Verger to Rue des Camelias. There is a bus stop on the hill alongside the shabby housing estates. Take the Camelias bus which travels through town to the gare routière on Joffre Boulevard. Hotel Bourbon, Rampes de St François, 97400 St-Denis, tel. 40.72.40, fax 30.32.28.

Low tariff

There is none of the low-tariff accommodation which travellers are used to. The closest you will come to this in the capital is one of the *pensions de famille*. *Pension Touristique les Bougainvilles*, out near the airport in Ste-Clotilde, has rooms for the more affluent backpacker. Call it from the airport. Occasionally it provides transport if there are more than two of you, tel. 29.12.96. *Pension du Centre*, at 272 Rue Maréchal Leclerc, tel. 41.73.02, is possibly the best bet for low cost accommodation. It is, however, very popular with French students, and a room should be booked about 60 days ahead. Another place for budget travellers is *Balnaik*, with cosy rooms at 30 Rue General de Gaulle, tel. 20.29.11. The manager goes to great efforts to please guests and has an amazing knowledge of local folklore, history and places of interest.

PLACES TO EAT

There is no danger of going hungry in St-Denis. From street vendors and snack bars, to bistros and restaurants, there is food to satisfy everyone. Chinese, Italian, Indian, and of course, French cuisine, is offered from sidewalk cafés, vans and the smartest of dining rooms. On virtually every city block visitors will find some or other eating establishment. By far the best way of finding a place to eat is to just wander about, stopping to read the menus and prices which each restaurant is required to display outside. A few are listed below.

Low prices

Le Palmier Pizzeria: low prices and a good selection of toppings, plus Creole food; 54 Rue Victor Mac Auliffe.

Mac Burger: burgers at reasonable prices. A fairly good American-style menu of fast foods; 63 Rue Maréchal Leclerc.

Medium prices

Le Pekinois: a comprehensive menu that leans heavily towards Oriental dishes and spices. This restaurant has a relaxed ambience and top-rate service. Prices may be considered high by African and Australian guests, but the meals are lavish and delicious; 78 Rue Alexis de Villeneuve.

Restaurant Aziz: specialises in Mauritian dishes, which are a lot closer to authentic Creole cooking than you can get anywhere else on Réunion. Popular and nearly always full at lunch time and for dinner. Patrons are advised to reserve a table for evening sittings; 122 Rue Monthyon, tel. 21.53.20.

High prices

The higher the price for a sit-down meal, the less likely you are to get traditional island cooking. The highest graded restaurants all concentrate on Continental dishes and shun local fare. After several weeks on Réunion, you may find yourself longing for something other than rice, chicken and fish. Haul out your credit card and splash out on an expensive dinner.

Bambara: dine and dance in this retreat-from-reality restaurant. It concentrates on meat dishes, especially thick beef steaks. There is no need to make a reservation, the dining room is seldom full; 160 Rue Monthyon.

Le Gratin: with numerous house-specials, an internationally acclaimed chef and enormous servings, this restaurant is certainly value for the prices charged. The service is attentive and prompt. Call well ahead for a reservation; 59 Rue Monthyon, tel. 21.30.60.

Brasseries and cafés form an integral part of St-Denis café society. Over weekends the beachfront along Boulevard Gabriel Mace is filled with Réunion's "beautiful people". No-one who visits the capital should miss out on lounging about for a few hours over an aromatic cup of café au lait or espresso. Street vendors sell hot snacks, drinks and light meals from any number of vans that park around Pointe des Jardins. Make sure you taste the delicious ice-creams made in St-Denis. Liberty Ice-creams has the biggest selection; 149 Rue Maréchal Leclerc. Another recommended place is the Café de Paris Glacier; Avenue de la Victoire.

18 WEST RÉUNION

This stretch of coast is in the lee of the high mountains that make up the highlands of Réunion. It is also where the best swimming beaches are found. There is about 27 km of beach along the west coast. At the settlements of St-Paul, St-Gilles-les-Bains, St-Leu and St-Pierre, visitors will find beaches of sparkling white sand alternating with black volcanic sands common to young volcanic islands. The biggest attraction of the west coast is its tourism infrastructure. While the east coast is sparsely populated, mostly forest wilderness and in the path of lava flows, the west coast has hotels, beach resorts, areas of historical and natural interest, and offers an abundance of restaurants, banks and curio shops. The largest, most developed urban centres are also located on the west coast.

LA POSSESSION

A tour of the west coast starts at the town of La Possession. It was here, in 1642, that a ship of the French East India Company raised the flag to claim Réunion for the French crown. Not many visitors stay here, preferring to see it on a day trip of the north-west region. Two restaurants worth considering for lunch or dinner are: Hai Phong, 32 Rue Raymond Mondon, tel. 22.39.80; Restaurant Le Boucane, 1 Rue Lacaussade, tel. 22.20.05.

A striking feature of the area between St-Denis and La Possession is the tall volcanic cliffs topped with lush vegetation. The dual carriageway from St-Denis offers quick travel between the two towns. To reach La Possession from the capital, take the green-line Alizes bus going to St-Pierre. Buses run frequently throughout the day in either direction.

LE PORT

This is another town that few tourists visit. Réunion's main harbour, it has little to interest general visitors. It is an industrial town, full of pollution, trucks, ships and dock-workers. Just before reaching Le Port, visitors will pass Nelson Mandela stadium, where international sporting events are hosted. At the entrance to Le Port is an exhibition of local sculpture. The most startling thing that many visitors will notice is the extremes between elite and working class. While the working class struggles in shanty settlements and depressing housing estates, the rich live in cool splendour on the hillsides above town.

Le Port and La Possession are reached in the same way. The main bus depot in Le Port is in the CBD. Look for the Banque Française Commercial Indien Ocean; the bus stop is directly behind it.

The post office is on Rue Glaciere. There is a branch of the BFC (Banque Française Commerciale), at 1 Avenue 14 Juillet 1789. The BNP (Banque Nationale de Paris) is on Avenue Commune de Paris, with Banque de la Réunion along Rue Evariste Parny. Credit Agricole is at 16 Avenue Commune de Paris. Travellers wanting sea transport from Réunion to other Indian Ocean islands should visit Compagnie Generale Maritime, at 2 Rue Est. The travel agent to contact for tours of the port and mountains to the east is Havas Voyages, 22 Avenue Commune de Paris, tel. 42.22.42, fax 43.29.96.

Worth a visit are the sugar terminal warehouses near the port and the small mosque near the colourful fresh-flower market. Out along the N1 motorway, there is an enormous nursery at Hyper Jardin. Flowers and plant species from all over the Indian Ocean are cultivated here. Only here will tourists who want to take plant material home get clearance and a certificate indicating their purchases are disease free. Two of the top restaurants in the country are located at Le Port. The one specialises in fresh seafood, while the other is rated the best Chinese restaurant on Réunion. For delicious shellfish and line fish, try *Ecume des Mers,* 13 Rue Evariste Parny, tel. 42.18.55. The unique taste of Sino-Creole cooking can be experienced at *Le Jade Restaurant,* 41 Rue Evariste Parny, tel. 42.17.28.

Snacks and takeaways are available from *Le Bouef Pizzeria and Grill,* on the edge of town near the palm and bamboo groves. Another place that has a good range of European fastfoods is *Le Korail Snack Bar,* near the mosque and flower market. *Les Jardin des Îles* restaurant, close to the Shell fuel station, has a good menu, but is rather costly and the staff really rude. Its seafood dishes are popular with tour groups, but you will have to endure the poor service before tasting the delicious food.

ST-PAUL

St-Paul is a favourite weekend destination of city dwellers, having the closest beach to St-Denis. Almost 3 km of volcanic beach line the sea off St-Paul. It is also home to the Réunion yachting fraternity and regularly hosts international yacht racing events.

Once the capital of Réunion, St-Paul saw the arrival of the first French settlers – albeit they were not there voluntarily – and execution of the last Indian Ocean pirate, Olivier le Vasseur. It is a picturesque town, nestled between mountains and the sea. St-Paul is a place of tranquillity, where tourism's hectic influence has not yet reached. St-Paul is the flower town of Réunion. Not only is there a bewildering variety of cut flowers for sale, but the residents spend a great deal of time working in their beautiful gardens.

You will find the post office on Rue Rhin et Danube. Credit Agricole bank is along Chausse Royal, with Banque Française Commercial Ocean Indien on Rue Rhin et Danube. Banque de la Réunion is on Rue Evariste de Parny. The BNP is down Rue Marius et Ary Leblond. Tourist information pertaining to the St-Paul area may be obtained at the information centre on the corner of Rue de la Baie and Rue Surcouf. Treatment for minor ailments is available from the chemist at Pharmacie Dupuis on Rue du Commerce.

Getting there

Reaching St-Paul from south or north is relatively simple. It is one of the few places in Réunion where hitchhiking is easy. Simply stand near one of the bus stops on the N1 motorway on-ramp and stick out your thumb. Buses travelling between St-Denis and St-Pierre all stop in St-Paul. The bus depot (gare routière) is on the eastern side of the CBD. Another company also operates buses south from St-Paul to the many hill villages of Trois Bassins and down to Piton Mairie. They leave from the same place. There is an information kiosk at the bus depot.

Things to do

The main places of interest in and around St-Paul are the old Creole buildings along the seafront, the sugar mill at Savannah, Cimetière Marin, the weekly street market, caves where the first French lived, blowholes along the volcanic coastal cliffs, the short walk around Trou des Roches and perfumed plant nurseries.

Along the coast road, Quai Gilbert, are numerous gracious old Creole mansions, many of which have now been converted into government administrative offices. Opposite Maison de Justice is a small palm and *filaos* tree park that has several old French cannons pointing out to sea. These cannons were to protect the original settlement on Réunion, but were never used.

Out in the sugar cane fields of Savannah, tourists can take an informative guided tour of the sugar mill. The tours are run Monday-Friday, beginning at about 9h30. The mill does not provide individual tours and there must be at least two of you. On Rue de la Caverne is a war memorial to the brave soldiers from St-Paul who died in the Great War.

The Cimetière Marin is the town's main tourist attraction. Visitors should spend a while walking around the signposted tombstones of some of the island's most famous and notorious characters. Turn at Rue de la Baie and go south on Rue des Filaos. The volcanic-rock-walled cemetery is where the road nears the black sand beach. The local fishermen land their daily catches here and at the bottom of Rue Surcouf at about 7h00 – another thing to see if you are in the area. The first grave you will see on entering the cemetery is that of the most notorious of all Indian Ocean pirates, Olivier le Vasseur (La Buse). He was executed in July 1730 and his tombstone has a skull and crossbones etched into it. His vessel, *La Victorieux*, was scuttled off the west coast of Madagascar, but the cannon, Le Batailleur, was kept and now sits alongside its owner's grave. Mysterious visitors still leave bottles of rum and encoded messages on the tombstone. The famous Réunionnais poet, LeConte de Lisle, was also buried here in 1894. His grave is marked by a small bust and several lines from his poems. Perhaps the most bizarre grave in the cemetery is that of Captaine Au Long, who "Died of his own generosity". Born in St-Malo in 1801, the sea captain arrived in St-Paul on 17 February 1830. In that same year he died, defending the honour of a woman. This in itself is not surprising, but what is, is the manner of his death. In a duel, his opponent's weapon misfired, so, in the manner of cavaliers, Au Long lent him another handgun. It was a bullet from this gun that killed the 29 year old Capitaine Au Long.

On the very edge of town, travelling south, across the national road from the Cimetière Marin, is the Grotte des Premiers Français (Caves of the first French). Visitors with their own transport should park their vehicle either at the Elf fuel station or outside the Cimetière Marin and walk to the site.

The first French settlers of Réunion were not here by choice. Accused of mutiny, they were exiled to Réunion from Madagascar. For over three years they lived in the large caves in the cliffside opposite the beach. Damp, windy and relatively exposed, it must have been miserable living there. The cascades that spill over the cliffs swell in summer rains, often flooding the shallow caves of the abandoned exiles.

Walk along the beach, either south or north of St-Paul, and you will discover blowholes in the porous lava rock that hangs out over the ocean. Take care, the rock is brittle, lined with fissures and severely eroded. The blowholes in the cliffs to the south are particularly impressive. Try and get to see them at high spring tide, when the higher tide levels and big waves force tall columns of spray through the blowholes.

Those who do not mind walking can take a short hike along the Tour des Roches. There are direction signs along the walk, which starts just east of the N1 motorway. Along the walk, which should take about two hours, visitors can inspect the ruins of a French water mill, and spend time drifting through the cool palm and wild banana plantations. At the highest point on the path, there are magnificent views of St-Paul, its volcanic beaches and surrounding lush vegetation.

One of the highlights of a visit is a walk through the perfumed plant nurseries of Réunion. Around the hills of Le Bois-de-Nefles to the east, Bellemène and Le Guillaume to the south-east, and along the road to Piton Maido, notably Petite France, there are several flower farms that distil their own essence. These farms concentrate on the production of geraniums and their oil for the world's perfume industry. Prior appointments are not necessary. Just ask the owner or manager for permission to walk through.

Things to buy

On Friday afternoon and all day Saturday, the streets of St-Paul come to life with a large street market. Saturday is the busiest day. In the main road, and the sidestreets, visitors will find colourful stalls selling items ranging from fresh produce to clothing and curios. All prices are negotiable and the quality of goods impressively high. Self-catering travellers would do well to stock up on food at the market. Traditional

Creole snacks are sold from small stalls that line Quai Gilbert and stand among the trees in the park.

Once shoppers have exhausted all the possibilities at the street-market, they should visit the pottery workshop on Rue Hubert D'Isle. Ingar Cassim Réunion Souvenirs, down Rue Suffren, is worth a look for local crafts and curios. Prices at both these places are much lower than in St-Denis or St-Gilles-les-Bains.

Accommodation

St-Paul does not yet have tourist accommodation, and finding any accommodation is difficult. If you find yourself stuck here, the police, on Quai Gilbert, will let you sleep in an empty cell, and even provide you with washing facilities and something to eat. Some travellers have reported finding accommodation by speaking to the snack van vendors along the beachfront. You could also try the Auberge de Jeunesse du Bernica on Rue Fatima Bernica, tel. 24.64.32.

Places to eat

St-Paul has a few good restaurants, apart from the several street vendors that offer hot and cold snacks in the CBD. The *Auberge Restaurant*, tel. 22.66.05, on Rue de la Caverne has a Continental menu at fair prices. At 26 Rue du Commerce, diners will find *Le St-Paul Restaurant*, tel. 45.62.06, which has a *plat du jour* and a good selection of fresh seafood. *Au Tamarin*, 93 Rue Marius et Ary Leblond, tel. 22.65.73, has set menus and à la carte from a predominantly Creole and French selection. Specialising in vegetarian dishes is *L'Oasis*, tel. 22.58.98, along Route Mafate. Pizzas and fast foods can be ordered from *Savane Pizzeria*, tel. 55.65.69, in les Arcades Plateau Caillou. Along the Tour des Roches route, walkers will see several houses advertising table d'hôte. These family-run eateries usually have traditional food at low prices, and provide a wonderful opportunity for meeting the rural people of north-western Réunion. There are well-stocked grocery shelves at *Discash Supermarket* on Rue du Commerce.

ST-GILLES-LES-BAINS (referred to as St-Gilles)

The holiday capital of Réunion, St-Gilles has everything to attract the visitor in search of sea, sports, top-class accommodation, restaurants, adventure tours and nightlife. With the sea temperature ranging between 22 °C and 28 °C, the long swimming beaches of St-Gilles are popular with tourist and islander alike. Covered with large-grained white sand, the area around the 15 km lagoon south of town is a hive of tourist kiosks and hotels.

Car hire is available from: SGM Car Rental, tel. 24.03.48, opposite Le Recif Bar and Restaurant in **L'Hermitage-les-Bains**; Hertz Car Rental, tel. 24.08.18, near Le Borsalino Restaurant in L'Hermitage-les-Bains; Budget Rent a Car, near Prisunic supermarket in town. Motorcycles may be rented from L'Île en Moto, at 216 Rue General de Gaulle, tel. 24.05.63. Bicycles are available from VTT Location on Place Paul Julius Benard.

The post office (La Poste) is near the Roches Noires public beach opposite Chris Beach Shop. There is a Tourisme Réunion office between the riding club and Alamanda Hotel in L'Hermitage-les-Bains. It has a good selection of pamphlets, maps and suggested tours of the area. If staying at a private home or camping, this is the place to come and arrange your helicopter flight of the island. The office is open Monday-Friday 9h00-18h00 and Saturday 9h00-12h00. The reception desk of the VVF, at the southern end of Avenue de Bourbon, is even better than the tourist office. It is much more helpful, has many more tours on offer and will also assist you in finding suitable accommodation. There is a tourist office on Place Paul Julius Benard in the CBD. It has a number of local handicrafts for sale, but the prices are exorbitant and the range limited. On Roche Noires beach promenade, near La Poste, there is a large map of St-Gilles-les-Bains, which indicates restaurants, snack bars, shops and points of interest in and around town.

Foreign currency and traveller's cheques may be cashed at the tourist-class hotels in L'Hermitage-les-Bains and Boucan Canot, or for a lower commission at one of several banks in town. Credit Agricole is at 48 Rue General de Gaulle opposite Naf Naf Clothing. Also on Rue General de Gaulle is the BNP, near Riz Supermarket. Banque de la Réunion is on N1 La-Saline-les-Bains, L'Hermitage-les-Bains. Drug prescriptions may be filled at the small pharmacy near the BNP in town.

Getting there

There is lots of public transport serving St-Gilles. Buses from St-Pierre and St-Denis travel through St-Gilles from about 7h00-18h30. If you are visiting the area around Boucan Canot, north of St-Gilles, or the tourist facilities on Boulevard Leconte de Lisle, south of the CBD, you will have to get off the bus on the N1 highway and walk from there. There is an SGM minibus service that takes a circuitous route from the south of St-Gilles, through town and north to Boucan Canot. These vehicles start their journey near the Coralia Hotel, at L'Hermitage-les-Bains in the south, and leave every 40 minutes between 6h30-16h00. To reach the open-air theatre, Musée de Villère, the helicopter airport and the ravines, take the Reseau Pastel bus company's transport along ligne G, from St-Gilles bus depot.

Things to do

Besides lying on the beach all day, there is a multitude of activities and things to see for holiday-makers. A favourite among beach visitors is snorkelling in the reefed lagoon, south of town. There is an amazing variety of sea life within 10 m of the surface. All you need is a face mask, snorkel and a pair of shoes. There is often a strong backwash where the sea meets the beach shelf. To avoid this, walk about 20 m out on the shallow sea bed, where there is less current and where most of the fish and aquatic plants are. Along these southern beaches, visitors will find pedalos, windsurfers, boogie-boards and canoes for hire from beach stalls. The beaches at **Boucan Canot**, to the north, are more suitable for surfers and tanning. There are buses from town to Boucan Canot, with a departure every 30 minutes, from outside Chez Seraphin Fresh Fruit on Rue General de Gaulle. You will be dropped off about 150 m south of the beach.

Tourists who want to try scuba diving in the sea off the reef should speak to the people who hang about at the Gloria Maris Scuba Club on Saturday and Sunday. The clubhouse is on the pier alongside the fishing harbour, south of Place Paul Julius Benard. It has all the equipment for hire at very reasonable rates and usually throws in the boat ride for free. For game fishing, contact the Réunion Fishing Club, 5 Rue Grand Large, tel. 24.34.74.

Near the Blue Beach Hotel in L'Hermitage-les-Bains tourists will find Le Tropiclub sports facility. You can take out temporary membership of this club and make use of the tennis courts and other amenities. Sain Gym (Adventures Indian Ocean), opposite St-Gilles-les-Bains Casino, is a sporting centre that includes such facilities as a climbing wall, tennis courts, Olympic swimming pool, gym, squash courts and clubhouse. Tourists are permitted to use the sports equipment and grounds from 10h00-14h30 Monday to Friday.

Horse riding has not quite caught on yet, but is a wonderful way of discovering the wilderness areas east of St-Gilles and the beach. Interested visitors, irrespective of experience, should contact the Centre Equestre et Pony Club de L'Hermitage, tel. 24.47.73. The entrance to the stables is near Score Supermarket and the Tourisme Réunion office.

The Marinarium, 167 Rue General de Gaulle, has an interesting collection of Indian Ocean seashells, a small marine aquarium and other items relating to the ocean off the west coast of Réunion. Open daily from 9h30-18h00, the Marinarium also offers guided tours of the displays on Tuesday and Thursday.

St-Gilles-les-Bains is also the closest centre to the heliport at L'Eperon. Along the same road you will find the entrance to the Ravines de St-Gilles, open-air theatre and Musée Villère. Take the road to Boucan Canot, go around the circle and proceed east up the hill, along Chemin des Cormorans, following the signs for Musée Villère. The open-air theatre is set atop a hill amid a jumble of volcanic boulders, palms and sugar cane. The stairs in the complex are made from a colourful mixture of coral and cement. Regular musical and theatrical events are staged here during summer. It has seating for 1 000 people. Phone the Office Départemental de la Culture for details of the current performances, tel. 24.42.01. There are impressive views out to sea and across the *filaos*-lined beaches of Boucan Canot.

East of the theatre, up a twisting road, is the entrance to La Ravines de St-Gilles. The site is not well signposted and visitors should rather look for L'Eperon Café, which is at the start of the path to the ravines. There are three waterfalls: Malheur, Aigrettes and Cormoran. The topmost waterfall is the only one accessible year-round. The other two can be reached during the dry season when it is possible to cross the rivers. Aigrettes is reached by scurrying along an irrigation canal that was dug by slaves, at great cost to life, several decades ago. The ravines get very crowded on the weekend, and it is advisable to rather visit the site during the week. Although it is not officially allowed, take a plunge into the deep pool at the bottom of Aigrettes. Avoid getting caught by the guards though, they throw an almighty tantrum in colourful French. The water is icy cold and the depth can make some people feel uncomfortable. Up the road from the ravines is a ruined sugar mill, which is now a base for local artists and craftsmen. You may watch them at work in the various rooms that have been converted into workshops. A small Hindu temple can be found higher up the hill, but it is often closed during the week. On Saturday and Sunday morning the doors are opened and casual visitors are allowed access to the quiet satsang hall.

The entrance to the Musée Villère is at the top of this road, where it crests the hill and starts south towards St-Gilles-les-Bains. There is a car park near the bus stop and ruined sugar mill, but the main entrance to the site is at the blue crucifixion statue, opposite Chapelle Pointue. In the car park there is a detailed map of the Musée Villère, showing the various buildings, houses and gardens.

Built in 1787, the plantation was to become home to one of the most mysterious and enigmatic colonial residents of Réunion, Mme Desbassyns. Legends abound about her cruelty to her slaves, while in other stories she is almost canonised for her gentle treatment of her large workforce. There are no records of her deeds, or misdeeds, only of her success as a sugar and coffee planter. Some stories are, however, noteworthy. One tells of her sending slaves to drag back ice blocks from the top of Réunion's highest mountain, Piton des Neiges. Over 300 slaves were involved in this task alone! Another tale is of her setting a man and his family free, simply because he brought her the reddest roses from her extensive gardens. The gardens are still lovingly tended by gardeners, some of whom claim to be direct descendants of the original slave gardeners. There are groves of bananas and pawpaws, fragrant flower gardens and trimmed hedges. Inside the house, the original furniture is on display. Also on show is a large clock, given to the family by the emperor Napoleon, and a hand-painted crockery set portraying the story of Paul et Virginie. Opposite the house are the outbuildings that include a large flagstone kitchen full of copper cauldrons and iron cooking utensils. The kitchen is not open to the general public, but the staff will let you in, and delight in telling stories about the history of the Desbassyns estate.

In the ruins of the sugar mill, visitors can see the original equipment (from Liverpool), blind corridors and, nearby, the crumbling slaves' quarters. Open daily from 9h00-18h00, except Tuesday.

Across the road is the Chapelle Pointue. Blue gum trees and flowers create a scented corridor to the chapel entrance. To the left of the entrance, visitors can view the grave of Mme Desbassyns.

Out on the N1 route nationale is Eden Garden. The garden has over 500 species on display. Among the plants, visitors may be able to identify medicinal plants used by traditional healers on Réunion. There is a tranquil Zen Garden to wander about in, ponds and even a Creole rice field. Open Tuesday-Saturday 9h30-12h30 and 14h30-18h00.

St-Gilles-les-Bains has numerous nightclubs, discos and casinos. The Elysée-Matignon Nightclub, in L'Hermitage, is open every evening, except Monday and Thursday. It only really gets going from about 23h00. Le Chat Noir Restaurant and Disco, opposite the Grand Écran cinema, offers delicious meals and dancing. Next door to Le Chat is Moulin du Tango nightclub. This caters for an older crowd. It opens at about 21h30 on Wednesday, Friday and Saturday, but closes early at 1h00. It has theme evenings on Wednesday and Saturday. At the Johnny Walker Opera Club, next to the Chinese restaurant in L'Hermitage, diners can relax and listen to sedate music and pieces from great operas. St-Gilles-les-Bains Casino, opposite the Sain Gym Club, has full gaming facilities and demands formal wear at night. The casino is open Monday-Thursday 17h00-2h00 and Friday-Sunday 17h00-3h00.

Things to buy

Curio shopping in St-Gilles is interesting and often bemusing. Near Score supermarket, visitors will find Art Cado Souvenirs. It has a wide range of Creole artworks on display and prices can be negotiated on the smaller items. On the way to Musée Villère, you will pass the old sugar mill occupied by Centre Artisanale de L'Eperon. Although the selection is not as wide here, the quality of work is high. The pottery and silk-screening must rate among the best in the Indian Ocean. Opposite Carterie du Lagon Post Cards is Menthe A L'Eau Art Gallery. Prices may be high, but the Gauguinesque art has a magical quality that will continue to enthral long after your return home.

La Tee-Shirterie in town has hundreds of silk-screened shirts, beach clothing, hats and a few local curios. Also in town is the Atelier Art Ecaille. Located on the second floor of the Forum de St-Gilles-les-Bains, it has displays of west coast crafts and jewellery. It seems to concentrate on works made from turtle shell. Turtles are endangered and trade in turtle products should not be encouraged. The tourist office, the Galerie Amandine, which is open from Tuesday-Saturday, offers locally made jams, dolls and island perfume. The prices are ridiculously high and budget travellers should rather wait until going further south or into the highlands and buying similar curios much cheaper there.

Accommodation

There is lots of accommodation in and around St-Gilles-les-Bains. All visitors will find suitable accommodation.

Le St Alexis (high tariff)

This is considered the top hotel on Réunion. Situated near the tourist beaches of Boucan Canot, Le St Alexis is the preferred hotel of affluent visitors. Still new, many of the final touches have still to be added, but even incomplete, the hotel offers luxury and superb service. Tour groups are not permitted at the hotel; only individual guests are catered for. All of the rooms have a jacuzzi, air-conditioning and television. A central swimming pool provides an alternative to the beach on which the hotel is situated. A sauna is on the top floor. Free airport transfers are provided in a shuttle bus, and guided excursions may be arranged at the reception desk.

The hotel has two restaurants, but meals are not included in the tariff. La Brigantine offers Creole and European dishes, while Le Grand-Hunier serves *nouvelle cuisine*. The staff at Le St Alexis is attentive and speaks several languages, including English, German, Italian and, of course, French. From Friday to Sunday it can be difficult finding a room, as the elite crowd from St-Denis escape the city for the peace and space that Le St Alexis provides. Make reservations a minimum of 30 days before arrival. Le St Alexis, 44 Route de Boucan Canot, 97434 St-Gilles-les-Bains, tel. 24.42.04, fax 24.00.13.

Hotel Coralia (high tariff)

This is one of the top hotels in St-Gilles, 40 km from St-Denis, and 50 km from Gillot airport. The Hotel Coralia offers exclusive accommodation in 115 air-conditioned rooms overlooking a magnificent 3 ha garden. The beach is just beyond the fence, and snorkelling gear is available from the hotel. All rooms have television and a safe. Included in the tariff is a huge English breakfast from a buffet that is open at 6h00. Lower tariffs are charged for groups and children under 16 who share with parents stay free, with 50% off all meals. Meals are taken in the restaurant named after that famous pirate, La Buse. Non-residents are occasionally allowed at the restaurant. Call to make a booking at least three days in advance. On Monday, dinner is a seafood buffet, and on Wednesday evening a Creole buffet is followed by traditional dancing.

In the reception area, guests will find travel agents, car rental firms and tour operators. A small shop offers a range of clothing, postcards, emergency needs, curios and the latest European magazines. Baby-sitting is offered on an hourly rate. There is a swimming pool in the grounds and water sport equipment can be hired from reception. On the beach, the hotel has set up the Case Coralia boathouse, where hotel residents are provided with free windsurfers, pedalos and kayaks.

There are three flood-lit tennis courts, which must be reserved at least 24 hours ahead. A tennis pro is on duty to help out. There is a bowling green with a tournament on Friday afternoon. Fishermen can hire light tackle from the boathouse. Game fishermen must book through the reception office or one of the travel agents. The hotel tour desk is able to arrange 4x4 tours of the mountains, blue-water sailing and helicopter flights. A favourite with package tours, the hotel is frequently booked out. Make your reservation at least three months ahead. Hotel Coralia, Les Filaos, 97434 St-Gilles-les-Bains, tel. 24.44.44, fax 24.01.67.

VVF (low-medium tariff)

On the edge of a lagoon, surrounded by casuarina trees, the VVF St-Gilles is situated on 4 ha of parkland at L'Hermitage. Flowers are a feature of the facility, with a profusion of cascading bougainvillaea, bright hibiscus, tall flamboyants and gracious palm trees. Accommodation is provided in 129 studios and 60 bungalows. Air-conditioning is available at certain times of the day. There are washing facilities in each room and self-catering equipment comprising stove, crockery, cutlery, pots, pans and a small fridge. A restaurant offers a tasty and cheap selection of Creole specialities. Breakfast is served in front of the swimming pool, where light lunches are also available from 12h30.

Traditional island dancing and locally produced plays are performed on selected weeknights, while those who prefer a quieter vacation may choose a book from the well-stocked library or watch a video in the television lounge. Full sporting facilities are available within a few hundred metres of the VVF, and it is able to arrange for guided island tours, scuba diving and fishing. The VVF is often full, and bookings are recommended at least 90 days prior to arrival. Villages Vacances Familles, BP 20, 97434 St-Gilles-les-Bains, tel. 24.29.39, fax 24.05.77.

Other accommodation worth considering in and around St-Gilles includes:

Blue Beach Hotel (high tariff)

34 rooms, restaurant offering Creole and French meals, swimming pool and expensive boutique. Avenue de la Mer, Les Filaos, 97434 St-Gilles-les-Bains, tel. 24.50.25, fax 24.36.22.

Cutty Sark Hotel (medium-high tariff)

This three-star hotel on Chemin Carosse has 14 rooms and six studios. Each room has a television, bathroom en suite, air-conditioning and sea views. Self-catering facilities are provided in each room, making the hotel popular with long-term guests. There is a minimum stay of two days, which can impose restrictions on travellers. Still, it does offer the opportunity of good accommodation and low cost self-catering near the beach resorts. Cutty Sark Hotel, Ilot Bleu, Chemin Carosse, 97434 St-Gilles-les-Bains, tel. 24.05.24, fax 24.34.32.

Alamanda Hotel (medium-high tariff)

You will find the two-star Alamanda Hotel between the Tourisme Réunion office and VVF in L'Hermitage. There are 58 rooms, all with air-conditioning, washing facilities and television. Numerous excursions are offered by the hotel, including scuba diving, hiking and glass-bottomed boat trips over the reefs. A restaurant serving Creole and French food is open daily. The rates are lower in June, July and September. Alamanda Hotel, Chemin Ceinture, L'Hermitage, 97434 St-Gilles-les-Bains, tel. 24.51.00, fax 24.02.42.

Commune de St-Paul campsite (low tariff)

There are full ablution facilities available at this beautiful campsite right on the edge of the beach. Surrounded by casuarina trees in a park-like setting, this is undoubtedly one of the best campsites on Réunion. It is situated on Chemin Ceinture. Reservations are not necessary, but give the staff a few hours' warning if possible, especially over the European holiday season. This can be done on arrival in St-Denis, tel. 24.42.35.

Places to eat

Equally prolific are the number of places to eat in St-Gilles. From snack bars to formal restaurants, there is something for every pocket and taste. Visitors who are self-catering will find well-stocked supermarkets, fresh produce stalls and bakeries available. To the south, in L'Hermitage, you will find *Score* supermarket, with its large selection of local and European foods for sale. *Riz* supermarket, in the CBD, has a good selection of groceries and bakes fresh bread daily. Almost directly across the road from Riz is *Chez Seraphin Fresh Fruit,* with its enormous tables of fresh produce. On Place Paul Julius Benard visitors may choose from the bewildering selection of produce available at the market stalls. East of Le St Alexis hotel in Boucan Canot, across the N1 motorway, is a small shopping centre with a large *Prisunic* supermarket. Prices are a little higher than in St-Gilles, but the selection of groceries is large and quality is high.

Snacks are sold throughout the day at *Le Club*, in L'Hermitage. *Le Pitalugue Snack Bar*, between the Sain Gym and casino, does a good range of fast foods, pizzas and ice-creams. In St-Gilles there are several snack bars and coffee shops where takeaways and light meals may be bought. *To Ten Snacks*, near the market on Place Paul Julius Benard offers cheap lunches and afternoon teas. Along the promenade of the beach at Roches Noires, carts and vans sell enormous sandwiches, ice-creams, cold drinks and beer. At *Plats a Emporter*, near the post office, visitors can select from a takeaway menu of light meals that includes fresh fish, hotdogs and shellfish stew. In the shopping centre at Boucan Canot the *Boulangerie Patisserie* makes fresh bread, pastries and cakes each morning. Along the beach of Boucan Canot is another army of pie carts and snack vans, offering sandwiches and drinks.

Le Chat Noir Restaurant and Disco, near Grand Écran cinema in L'Hermitage, has an expensive menu of European food. The main attraction, however, is not the rather tasteless meals, but the exciting disco that rages after dinner. *L'Auberge du Bonheur* is a Chinese restaurant between the opera club and campsite. Its dishes make for a pleasing change from French meals smothered in sauces. It has set menus and an à la carte selection, the prices are reasonable and the staff pleasant. *Le Borsalino Restaurant*, near the campsite at L'Hermitage, is set in a beautiful tropical garden. Tables are placed beneath flowering bushes and shady trees. At night, candles are spread about the garden.

At the *Fish Café Alpha*, on the edge of the harbour, diners can indulge in fresh seafood while being fanned by the ocean breeze. *La Bourdon Restaurant* in St-Gilles is also popular and offers seafood and meat dishes made with Creole recipes. Near the shopping complex east of Boucan Canot beach, *Le Delice Kreol Restaurant* has a good variety of expensive, but really tasty local dishes.

ST-LEU

This is Réunion's surf centre. Each year surfers from around the world gather for one of the competitions on the professional surf circuit. The town itself is quiet and laid back, with a local set of surfers frequenting the cafés and beaches. It is highly recommended to visitors in search of quiet and wilderness areas. The area around St-Leu is still very much devoted to fishing and farming.

To reach St-Leu take the St-Denis to St-Pierre bus from either of these towns. The main road runs through St-Leu and the drivers are usually willing to drop you off outside the campsite or VVF village. Hitchhiking to St-Leu is also easy, provided you do not try and hitch along the N1 during the morning or evening rush hour, from about 7h00-9h00 and 16h30-19h00. Tourists arriving in February and March should come prepared for lots of warm, wet weather.

The post office is opposite the port, near the small-craft harbour. Banque de la Réunion is at 52 Rue General Lambert, and Credit Agricole is up at Piton St-Leu. Wel'come Travel Agent is not far from the Hôtel de Ville (town hall) at 57 Rue General Lambert, tel. 34.74.66, and is able to confirm air tickets, arrange island tours, including helicopter flights, and make hotel reservations. Medical attention is available from the doctors who have their surgeries next to Pharmacie de la Salette, near the municipal buildings.

Things to do

Visitors can spend time wandering about the small forest before going to the flower-filled park. The gate to the park is often closed. Just hop over the low gate and walk among the palm and casuarina trees, exploring the garden with its flowers, shrubs and exotics. The main attraction in town is the cathedral of Notre Dame de la Salette. Built in 1760, this is one of the oldest and most sacred churches on the island. Turn east on Rue ND de la Salette and continue to the steps at the base of the cliff. Walking up the stairs, you pass through a small forest before arriving at a chapel. A waterfall trickles over rocks below the effigy to the left of the chapel. The water is said to be holy. Ice cold, it is wonderfully refreshing after the climb. The chapel is the site of an annual pilgrimage in September for Roman Catholics of St-Leu. They come to give thanks to God for sparing the inhabitants of the town during the catastrophic cholera epidemic of 1859. Taking the steps to the south, visitors will encounter several shrines to Christian martyrs and saints. Candles can be bought from the women at the bottom of the stairs, who also sell Christian mementos such as rosaries, pictures, icons and Bibles.

North of town is a turning east that leads to the disgusting city dump and La Roche Pate ravine. The area around and behind the dump is still indigenous forest, with trails leading up to the wooded summits. Take along a day-pack, some water and wet weather gear and set off for an hour or two of hiking. The view from the top of the hills extends out to sea and over St-Leu.

Caverne Thomas is a place of legend. Stories tell of pirates, curses, treasure and slaves being involved with the deep cavern. Visitors can try to decipher the writing and strange markings on the cavern walls. No definite conclusion has been reached by Réunionnais historians, and the cave remains shrouded in mystery.

Further north, about 2 km from the CBD, is the Coral Turtle Farm, alongside the national road. This depressing site is open daily 8h00-18h00, breeding marine turtles for the consumer market. There are a few curios that include seashells and, of course, turtle shell products.

South of St-Leu, along the coastal cliffs, you can see some of nature's works of art, Le Souffleur and Le Gouffre. Le Souffleur is about 5 km from town, above the sea, on the N1 national road. Through decades of erosion by the sea of the permeable volcanic rock, a giant blowhole has formed. The best time to see the impressive sight is on a night when the moon is full. There is a path that goes from the road to the very edge of the blowhole. It is an amazing feeling to stand looking over the hole as the spray explodes through. About 10 km further south is Le Gouffre. A canal has been sculpted by the sea through the soft rock. On either side are stretches of volcanic sand. Between the polluted town of St-Louis and St-Leu is a nature conservancy. The N1 is reduced to single-lane traffic and trees make a cool corridor of green. Although not open to the general public, you may visit the conservancy with one of the guided tours that leave from the top hotels in St-Gilles-les-Bains on Tuesday and Friday afternoons.

At Piton St-Leu, the Stella Matutina Agricultural and Industrial Museum is worth a visit. Go along Allée des Flamboyants to find the museum. There are displays showing the advances that Réunion's agricultural and industrial concerns have undergone since the 16th century. There is a permanent exhibition pertaining to the island's sugar production industry, several practical displays aimed at informing children about Réunion and a restaurant. The museum is open Tuesday-Sunday 10h00-18h00.

The Domaine des Colimacons has the famous Botanical Garden of Mascarin. Although visitors are encouraged to discover the gardens alone, guided tours in English, German and French are available on Tuesday, Wednesday and Thursday. It is more of a research centre than a public garden and you will be permitted to visit the laboratories and vast library. The garden is only open to the public on the first and third weekend of each month from 10h00-17h00. Entrance is free.

Accommodation

Accommodation in St-Leu is more geared for travellers than tourists. The best place to stay – whether self-catering or preferring served meals – is the VVF village, between the beach and main road. Campers are in for a treat. The campsite is virtually on the beach, with clean washing facilities and many snack vans.

Villages Vacances Famille (low-medium tariff)

The main entrance to the VVF is on Rue de la Lagon, near the beach. A membership card, valid for one year, is required from the central reservation office of VVF in St-Gilles-les-Bains. This is usually included when your confirmation notice is mailed to you prior to arrival. Accommodation is provided in 32 fully equipped self-catering bungalows, either side of a tree-lined avenue. Air-conditioning is provided, but runs only at certain times of the day. The village is not intended for holiday-makers who want to spend all day in their rooms. The management encourages visitors to try snorkelling, climbing, hiking, parascending, glass-bottomed boat trips and surfing. They are able to arrange guides, excursions and supply water sport equipment at nominal rates. Both scuba and game fishing can be organised at the VVF. Airport transfers are offered for a small fee. All meals may be taken in the dining room, and takeaways are available throughout the day.

The VVF in St-Leu plays a vital role in maintaining the unity and peace characteristic of Réunion by accommodating groups of underprivileged islanders. Each evening there is some form of entertainment presented by staff or a visiting troupe. Traveller's cheques and credit cards may be used for payment, but as yet, the facility does not accept foreign currency. The VVF is the ideal place to mix and make contact with Creoles from all over the island. Reservations are necessary, and the management recommends that these are made at least 60 days in advance. VVF St-Leu, 97436 St-Leu, tel. 34.81.43, or the central reservations office, fax 24.05.77.

Camping (low tariff)

Visitors with their own tents should make use of the excellent facilities available in St-Leu. The site is along the beachfront one block west of the CBD. A guard arrives each morning to charge for your pitch. No reservations are necessary.

Places to eat

Catering for the surf crowd and casual visitors, St-Leu offers numerous places to eat. On Rue General Lambert is the most popular snack bar in town, *Lee Ah Naye Snack Bar*. It sells fast foods and light lunches of fresh seafood and rice. Between the Elf fuel station and the park is *Le Palais d'Asie* Chinese restaurant. It concentrates on Chinese seafood dishes, and offers huge servings accompanied by noodles or rice at reasonable prices. Along the main road is *Au Ble Dore* bakery, near the church. Its daily-baked bread is delicious washed down with a litre of milk or "dodo" beer (pronounced dudu). The *Piment Bleau Restaurant and Snack Bar*, opposite the local surfing spot, is busy with surfers at breakfast and lunch time. This diner has a comprehensive seafood menu at low prices.

Along the beach are numerous snack vans. They sell sandwiches, drinks and spicy Creole snacks. Visitors who are self-catering should visit the *Geant 2 000* supermarket, near Club Korrigan (Scuba) and the fresh-produce market next to the Benedicta sign. *Restaurant Souffleur*, south on the N1, offers relatively tasteless meals from a rather expensive menu that leans heavily towards European cuisine.

ST-PIERRE

St-Pierre is a sprawling town of over 62 000 people on the south-west coast. A popular destination for Creole vacationers, St-Pierre has good accommodation, many restaurants and a strip of white beach. South of town are long beaches at Grand Anse and Manapany les Bains to St-Joseph. Separating the beaches are tumbling volcanic cliffs full of blowholes and canals.

The bus depot is on Rue François Isautier, behind the Hindu temple. The information office hands out free timetables to visitors.

La Poste (post office) has three branches. The main post office is on the corner of Rues Suffren and des Bons Enfants. Another office is located on Youri Gagarine, while the third is along Boulevard Hubert

Delisle. Banque Nationale de Paris is on Rue des Bons Enfants, near the mosque. Banque de la Réunion is at 18 Rue Bons Enfants and also on Rue Desire Barquiss. Credit Agricole has a branch on the corner of Rue Four a Chaux and Rue Victor le Vigoureux, while Banque Française Commerciale is at 4 Rue Augustin Archambaud. There is a small tourist office at 27 Rue Augustin Archambaud, but the staff are not very helpful. Of interest is its curios from southern Réunion.

Car hire is available from AGR Location, opposite the bus depot on Rue François Isautier. It has weekend and mid-week specials. ERL, on Rue August Babet, concentrate on the hire of 4x4s, but also arrange for guided adventure trips into the surrounding mountains and up to the volcano.

Things to do

Two of the main attractions in town are the mosque and the market. The mosque, on Rue François de Mahy, is closed on Thursday afternoon and all day Friday. Visitors are welcome on other days and will be conducted on an informative tour. St-Pierre's main market is on Rue Victor le Vigoureux. Another, much more informal market, takes place every Saturday along Boulevard Hubert Delisle and Rue du Boulevard, along the beachfront.

The small-craft port is always filled with local and international yachts. Each summer a regatta is held which draws competitors from Réunion, other Indian Ocean islands and from as far away as South Africa and France. The beach and lagoon off St-Pierre are safe for swimming. To reach the beaches at Grand Anse and Manapany les Bains, take the N1 motorway south, continue through the village of Grand Bois, and then turn right at the first tarred road to the right after the village.

St-Pierre's nightlife is busy and lively. Next to the Hotel Sterne, on Boulevard Hubert Delisle, is the Casino du Sud. This new casino is open daily from 21h00-3h00. Three nightclubs provide tourists and locals with a delightful way of spending an evening (or night and early morning!). Le Star Club on Rue du Presbytère is open from 21h30-sunrise Friday and Saturday. L'Acropole, at 36 Boulevard Hubert Delisle, opposite the small-craft harbour, follows the same schedule but seems to attract mostly teeny-boppers. Le Chapiteau, at Montvert les Bas, is only open on Saturday night, from 22h00-5h00. This disco fills up with Creole locals from about midnight, and is probably the most enjoyable nightspot outside of St-Denis.

Things to buy

Cramar Centre d'Exposition de Langevin, along Route Nationale, has a wide selection of local crafts for sale. Of particular interest are its perfumes and leather belts and handbags. The centre is open Monday-Friday 10h00-12h00 and 14h00-16h30; Saturday 9h30-12h00.

Curios from the area are also sold at the market in town, and at the sprawling Saturday market along the beachfront. Silk-screened T-shirts and cloth are sold from Muslim-owned fabric shops in the southern part of the CBD. Art works and fine jewellery are offered at Galerie Atelier Version Ecaille, 12 Rue Auguste Babet. This busy gallery and shop is open Monday-Friday 9h30-12h00 and 14h15 18h30.

Accommodation

Accommodation in and around St-Pierre ranges from three-star hotels, through self-catering cottages to *pensions*. The top hotel is Hotel Sterne, on Boulevard Hubert Delisle-Front de Mer. Self-catering travellers should consider the Demotel Residence Club, near the village of **Grand Bois**. The Tropic Hotel, along Rue Auguste Babet, is a favourite with budget travellers, but is due to raise its tariffs soon. There are cheap lodgings at the *pensions* on Rue Caumont and Four a Chaux.

Hotel Sterne (high tariff)

The Hotel Sterne is often host to tour groups, international sports teams and visiting dignitaries. It has 50 air-conditioned rooms, all with sea views. All the rooms have bathroom en suite, television and telephone. Car rental is available from the desk in the foyer, and excursions can be organised through the management. Its excursions include horse riding, visits to the high amphitheatres and volcano and helicopter flights over southern and central Réunion. A roof-top swimming pool, solarium and pool bar provide welcome havens from the bustling streets of St-Pierre. The Vanille et Lambrequin restaurant is well known, and top-class tour operators regularly take their clients to lunch or dinner here. The menu is extensive, with several Creole meals available. An expensive boutique and cavernous conference hall complete the facilities. Very much in demand throughout the year: it is advisable to book accommodation 60 days in advance. Hotel Sterne, Boulevard Hubert Delisle-Front de Mer, 97419 St-Pierre, tel. 25.70.00, fax 35.01.41.

Demotel Residence Club (medium-high tariff)

A fairly new concept to the area is the self-catering bungalows of Demotel. Located south of St-Pierre near the village of Grand Bois, Demotel is perched on the edge of a jumble of volcanic boulders overlooking the sea. Each of the 16 bungalows has an equipped kitchen, bathroom and television. Tours of the volcano, cirques of Mafate, Salazie and Cilaos and helicopter flights around the island, from the club's own helipad, can be arranged at reception. The club is also an agent for Eurocar rental. In the carefully landscaped tropical garden there is a swimming pool, jacuzzi and bar. Growing in popularity, especially with recession-hit French visitors. It is advisable to make reservations a minimum of 60 days ahead. Demotel Residence Club, 8 Allée des Lataniers, Grand Bois, 97410 St-Pierre, tel. 31.11.60, fax 31.17.51.

Budget travellers may find it difficult to locate anything cheaper than a *pension*. Inevitably owned and managed by a family, the local *pensions* are thoroughly enjoyable. You will get to meet the family and, occasionally, even be expected to fulfil some duties, like drying dishes or sweeping the house. The two recommended *pensions* are: Nativel, 13 Rue Caumont, tel. 25.07.19; Pension Touristique, 27 Rue Four a Chaux, tel. 25.64.87.

Other accommodation in St Pierre includes:

Les Hibiscus (medium-high tariff): 18 rooms with television and minibar. 56 Boulevard Hubert Delisle, 97410 St-Pierre, tel. 35.13.10, fax 25.81.95

Les Chrysalides (low-medium tariff): 16 rooms all with air-conditioning and en suite bathrooms. 6 Rue Caumont, 97410 St-Pierre, tel. 25.75.64, fax 25.22.19

Places to eat

The *Boulevard Pizzeria* is on the beachfront Boulevard Hubert Delisle. It has a wide selection of pizza toppings at very reasonable prices. Along Rue Auguste Babet is *Chez Jack* snack bar, where the lunch time menu includes, among other things, fresh shellfish and rice. *La Detente Bar*, next to the Hindu temple, does a wonderful range of Creole dishes and gives massive servings. The *China Express*, 69 Rue Marius et Ary Leblond, has a varied Chinese menu that includes cheap set menus and daily specials. Lavish Breton dinners and delicious lunches can be eaten at *Creperie St-Malo*, 1 Rue Port. *La Jonque* restaurant, 2 Rue François de

Mahy offers unusual Chinese fondues. *Restaurant da Baffi* specialises in Italian dishes that are filling and reasonably priced. You will find this homely trattoria at 8 Rue Auguste Babet.

Along the seafront there are always several snack vans selling the usual assortment of sandwiches and light lunches, plus cold beers and cold-drinks. There is hardly a street in the town that does not have at least two restaurants or snack bars.

If self-catering, visit *Tigre Supermarket* on Rue des Bons Enfants, the fresh-produce market along Rue Victor le Vigoureux or *Superco* super-market on Rue Auguste Babet. All have high quality goods and a large range of groceries.

ST-JOSEPH

St-Joseph sits on the southern promontory, near Pointe de St-Joseph and the mouth of the Rivière des Remparts. It is the ideal place from which to start a drive or hike up to the volcano viewpoint at Grand Galet on the Rivière Langevin. To the north, the majestic valley of the Rivière des Remparts offers scenic walks, forests, fields of sugar cane and flower nurseries. St-Joseph is one of the most important agricultural centres on the island, with quaint villages nestling in the folds of steep valleys. The few tourists who venture this far prefer to lie on the beautiful white beach at **Manapany les Bains**, or the black beach between **Langevin** and **Basse Vallee**. This area offers visitors the chance to escape the tourist resorts and over-utilised trails in exchange for indigenous forests and spectacular waterfalls. The least used route to the summit of Piton de la Fournaise volcano is here.

St-Joseph can be reached from either St-Pierre on the west coast or St-Benoit on the east coast. Yellow-line buses leave from St-Benoit every two hours between 7h30-15h00. The route follows the coast to St-Pierre. From St-Pierre, also on the yellow-line route, the Alizes buses travel along the southern coast to St-Benoit from 9h30-16h30. All the buses travelling this route stop for passengers in St-Joseph. Make certain that you catch the yellow-line route buses. Other buses on the route between St-Pierre and St-Benoit travel across the island, missing out the southern coast.

The post office is along Rue Raphael Babet, near Snack Bar des Remparts. Banque de la Réunion is at 78 Rue Raphael Babet, and Credit Agricole is at 5 Rue Maury. Bourbon Voyages travel agency has an office at 1 bis Rue Leconte de Lisle. Medical attention is available from

Cabinet Medical, 149 Rue Raphael Babet. Tourist information can be found at the Centre Locale d'Information et d'Orientation, 176 Rue Raphael Babet, tel. 56.54.16.

Tourists wanting to find crafts of the area will find a small collection of artifacts at the Centre Artisanal, along Route Nationale 2, De Jubilé, in the fishing village of Langevin, a few kilometres east of St-Joseph.

Things to do

To reach the Caverne des Hirondelles, turn towards the beach, at the church near the post office. The gravel road passes the soccer field and skirts the rubbish dump before stopping west of the cavern entrance. The cave is neglected and is now dirty and occupied by several tramps.

Visitors are welcome to visit the anthurium farms in the area of Langevin. It is advisable to phone before arriving though. The most progressive of these farms is Anthuriums Réunion Export, tel. 56.10.10.

There is a Scandinavian-style church, built of wood in 1875, that is worth seeing. It is across the bridge over the awesome Ravine Manapany. The area around St-Joseph is full of interesting routes for hikers to explore. For those in search of Réunion's vanishing wilderness, shoulder a pack, tent and food and follow the Rivière des Remparts north. A single track path follows the river through the deep forested valley all the way to the remote settlement of **Îlet de Roche Plate**. The hike should take about two days to reach the hamlet, with an overnight camp along the way. This is very much a solitary hike, and you are unlikely to encounter another person until near Îlet de Roche Plate. The walk winds through beautiful alpine scenery and passes several deep pools on the river, where one can swim. By taking the trail east of the settlement, fit hikers can continue up the col to Plaine des Sables and to the crater rim of Piton de la Fournaise.

Another region worth discovering is around the viewpoint at Grand Galet. You can catch the local bus up to **Grand Coude** and walk the few kilometres to the viewpoint above the dramatic Rivière Langevin valley. Following the ridge north-east, walkers arrive at the western edge of the rim of Piton de la Fournaise. Few people come this way and you will hike through remote, flower-filled meadows until reaching the barren slopes of the volcano. Skirt the caldera to the north-west until arriving at **Pas de Bellecombe**. From there it is a relatively easy walk up the volcano, or west down to Grand Ferme and the bus stop.

A far more strenuous but rewarding trek can be made from **Plaine des Gregues**. Take the local bus from St-Joseph through Les Lianes to the village of Plaine des Gregues. Walk east until reaching the steep edge of the Rivière des Remparts valley. There, turn north and continue along the ridge until meeting the tarred road above Plaine-des-Cafres. It is easy hitchhiking from here to Le Tampon and St-Pierre or east to St-Benoit. The hike from Plaine des Gregues to Plaine-des-Cafres takes about two days.

Accommodation

Accommodation is hard to find in and around St-Joseph. There are no tourist lodgings and the only rooms available are in pleasant, family *pensions*, more suited to travellers and those visitors on a low-medium budget:

Rose-May Gîte Rural, Chemin Piton Bel Air, tel. 37.56.89

Auberge de Langevin, 116 Chemin Passerelle, Langevin, tel. 56.60.23

Pension André-Benoit, Lianes, Bel Air, tel. 37.52.64

Le Dodo Restaurant, 57 Rue Raphael Babet, tel. 56.01.46, has eight comfortable rooms. Meals are included.

If stuck for accommodation, contact the assistant at Studio Pearl, 95 Rue Raphael Babet, tel. 56.58.80.

Clean camping facilities are available at Grand Anse Point, near the beach, for a small fee.

Places to eat

St-Joseph is famous for its restaurants. The *Coelacanth Restaurant*, northwest at **Grand Bois**, along Rue Regis Fontaine, offers a staggering diversity of seafood dishes at reasonable prices. *Le Manapany Restaurant*, on Boulevard Ocean, in Manapany les Bains, is one of the few four-star restaurants on the island. Its prices are quite high, but the quality of the food is equally high. Try the fresh line fish for a real treat. *Restaurant Le Dodo*, at 57 Rue Raphael Babet, is popular with locals and a good place to get a *plat du jour* at reasonable prices. *Restaurant L'Arcade*, 1 Rue Paul Demange, has a limited menu of American and European-style items. *Le Tropicana Restaurant*, 115 Rue Raphael Babet, is the favourite stop for tour groups. Prices are fair, the service excellent, and the selection of Creole and Continental dishes amazing. There is something for every taste here. Vegetarians are catered for with spicy meals cooked to Creole recipes.

Snacks, takeaways and light meals are offered by *Snack Bar des Remparts,* near the post office on Rue Raphael Babet.

Travellers who are camping along the coast or intending to hike up into the mountain valleys should do their shopping at one of the well-supplied supermarkets. *Champion* supermarket is opposite the dairy as you enter town from the west. *Score* supermarket is near the Esso fuel station, and has the biggest choice of groceries in St-Joseph. *Tigre* supermarket is along Rue General Lambert, and has a similar range of supplies to Score but at slightly higher prices.

19 EAST RÉUNION

Réunion's east coast is a sparsely populated, sea-lashed and lava-swept region of stark beauty and lush vegetation. It is also the stretch along which visitors have the best chance of meeting the villagers who still fish and farm in the traditional manner. The east coast has been the victim of numerous cyclones, tidal waves and volcanic eruptions in its turbulent history. Along this coast many slaves and Indian migrants found safety from the cruelty and oppressiveness of plantation owners. The area is steeped in history and offers travellers several interesting sights. Alizes buses travel the route throughout the day, and this is one of the easiest districts to hitchhike.

From St-Denis take the national road to **Ste-Marie**. Take the blue-line bus to St-Benoit from the main bus depot along the seafront. Hitch-hikers are advised to first take the local bus to Duparc. Note that the local St-Denis bus service also operates all the way to Ste-Marie.

En route to Ste-Marie is the settlement of **Rivière des Pluis**. To the south, as you cross the bridge, is the wide riverbed, the scene of raging waters and destruction during the cyclone season. At the settlement named after the river is La Vierge Noire (The Black Virgin). No-one seems to know by whom or why this unusual shrine was erected. Neither the museum curator in St-Denis, nor the Vatican's chief historian, who visited in 1992, has been able to unravel the Creole myths that surround the origins and power of La Vierge Noire. The villagers say that on full-moon nights you can hear the beat of slave drums, and see strange shadows that appear to be kneeling and bowing before the shrine.

There is not much to see in Ste-Marie and most travellers continue straight through and into the sugar cane fields before reaching Ste-Suzanne.

STE-SUZANNE

Once the centre for the northern sugar industry, Ste-Suzanne has a few sites worth visiting. The ruined sugar mill and rum distillery, on Rue de Cambuston, may be explored for free. Crumbling and forgotten, this historic site recalls some of the earliest refining techniques used on Réunion.

The post office is on Rue Desprez. Just past the Esso fuel station is a greyhound race track. Events are run on Wednesday evening and Saturday afternoon. It seems as though most of Ste-Suzanne's inhabitants attend the Saturday races, turning the event into a colourful family outing.

There are several exquisite colonial mansions around the town, and it makes for an interesting walk to simply drift about the streets.

At the church of Père Laval, take the path that hugs the Rivière Ste-Suzanne. If you follow this path through a small forest, and continue for another 2 km, you will come upon the Cascade Niagara. Tour operators do not seem to have discovered this little gem yet. You are unlikely to be disturbed should you swim in the shallow pool below the falls.

Visitors are allowed to visit the splendid mansion of Grand Hazier, but only if they make a booking at least seven days in advance, tel. 52.32.81. Constructed in the 1800s, this house still has some of the original furniture on display, and much of the cooking equipment now hangs from the walls and ceiling in a permanent exhibition. The flower gardens and fruit orchards are still cultivated and offer cool shade for the cocktails that the staff offer after the tour.

ST-ANDRÉ

Two things to see are La Maison de la Vanille, and the remains of the church, destroyed by the tsunami of 1962, on the coast at **Champ Borne**.

Travellers may take the bus between St-Denis and St-Benoit from either town, and jump off at the bus depot, near the church, in the CBD. There are five buses per day in each direction.

The post office is at 108 Rue Gare. Credit Agricole has a branch at 183 Rue Bourbon and the Banque Française Commercial Ocean Indien is on Rue Joseph Bedier. Banque de la Réunion is in the Centre Commercial and the BNP is along Avenue Republique. There is a tourist information office at 68 Rue Centre Commercial. Havas Voyages travel agents have a counter in the Centre Commercial, tel. 46.56.56. The chemist at Pharmacie Lacaille, on Rue de la Gare, can fill prescriptions and minister to minor medical problems.

No trip to Réunion can be regarded as complete without a visit to La Maison de la Vanille, 466 Rue de la Gare. Situated in the gracious gardens of a magnificent working estate, the home of vanilla provides a guided tour through the entire process of vanilla production. Visitors are able to see the vanilla creeper growing up bamboo sticks, watch the pods being marked, harvested and washed before being laid out on the drying tables. Once the highly informative 60 minute tour is over, you will be encouraged to visit the curio shop, with all its vanilla crafts and derivatives. Try not to balk at the prices; vanilla is one of the most expensive crops to grow and buy. La Maison de la Vanille is open Tuesday-Sunday 8h45-12h00 and 13h00-16h00.

Take the local bus from the gare routière to Champ Borne on the coast. In February 1962, Cyclone Jenny roared across the Indian Ocean and slammed into the north-east coast with winds exceeding 180 km/h. At the same time, 3 000 m below the sea, the ocean floor heaved and buckled from volcanic forces pushing upwards. The storm-battered villagers watched in horror as the sea first receded, then rushed back in an almost 20 m high wave. Known as a tsunami, the wall of water swept across the village, wreaking death and destruction at 100 km/h. When the wave finally receded, the only building left standing was the small church at Champ Borne. Most of its structure still remains. The locals make regular pilgrimages to this site, certain that it was saved by divine intervention.

On Rue de la Gare, strollers will pass a number of plantation houses set in carefully planned flower gardens with rolling lawns. Many of these homes are still inhabited, and the owners simply love showing interested tourists around the grounds and mansion. Just knock at the front door and ask to speak to the master or lady of the house – preferably in French of course!

If you have time, make an appointment to visit the orchid gardens of Mrs Audifax, on Chemin Rio, tel. 46.13.37. I doubt that anywhere, outside of the Seychelles, will visitors witness such a spectacle as the hundreds of bright colours of the orchids in this woman's hothouses. No fee is asked.

There is very limited suitable accommodation in St-André – few visitors ever stay overnight as St-Denis is less than 30 minutes away. If you need to stay over, try the *Pension Pluies d'Or and Chinese Restaurant* at 3 Allée Sapoties La Cressonniere, tel. 46.18.16.

Tasty meals may be chosen from a good menu at *Le Beau Rivage*, down at Champ Borne. *Chez Henry*, 258 Rue Bois Rouge, concentrates on seafood dishes, all at low prices. *Restaurant du Centre Oune Bive*, 52 Rue Deschanets, is expensive, but the restaurant most favoured by package tour operators on their whirlwind visits to the east coast. Its Creole and Chinese menu is large, but the servings a little too small for most travellers. *Restaurant Law Shun Jn*, 866 Avenue de Bourbon, is the best place for large plates of delicious Chinese food. The prices of food here are low when compared with the service and size of each meal. *Le Ficus Nitida*, 2 Rue Gauche, is popular with backpackers, but seems to have cashed in on the free advertising given it by budget travel guides, and now prices are far from competitive and the quality of food poor.

At the Tourist Office, 68 Rue Centre Commercial, shoppers can select from a wide range of grasswork, silk-screened clothing, vanilla products, postcards, local paintings and sculpture. The curio shop is open Tuesday-Saturday 8h00-12h00 and 13h30-16h30.

Less than 5 km south of St-André, travellers will see the turn-off, west, for the highland centre of Salazie. (The Cirque of Salazie is described in chapter 20.)

BRAS PANON

Home to the island's largest vanilla co-operative, Bras Panon is usually a way point on any tour of the east coast. Tourists should consider walking some of the wooded trails to the two waterfalls in the area.

You can reach Bras Panon by taking the bus that travels between St-Denis and St-Benoit. The post office is on Place Michel Debré in the village. Only Credit Agricole has banking facilities here, and even that is only an automatic teller machine. Tourist information concerning the region can be obtained from the maison at Ville Fleuri. It hands out free maps and offers detailed advice on what to see and do around Bras Panon.

The vanilla co-operative is at 21 Route Nationale 2. Visitors can take part in a guided tour or explore alone. Unless you can speak and read French, it is preferable to get a guide who will provide a tour in your own language. Whichever way you visit the facility, make sure to attend the film show about the vanilla industry shown every 30 minutes. Unlike La Maison de la Vanille, no growing takes place here. This is the processing side of the industry. The quills are brought here after harvesting, to be dried, graded and packed for shipment. To arrange a visit to one of the vanilla estates contact the Société Agricole, RN2 Paniandy, tel. 46.04.44. The future of vanilla production on Réunion looks bleak. With the invention of a much cheaper artificial flavouring called vanillin, the market has crashed for planters. The small estates on Réunion cannot hope to compete with the extensive plantings on Madagascar and the Comoros.

Those travellers keen to see the waterfalls along the Rivière des Roches, and feel that they would prefer a guide, should contact the Office Nationale des Forêts, Maison Forestières, in Bras Panon, tel. 46.61.75. It is, however, far more enjoyable and adventurous to do it alone. Take the road south from Bras Panon, and follow the signboards for St-Benoit. At the bridge across the Rivière des Roches turn west, up the road for **Beau Vallon**. Within 15 minutes you will reach the first waterfall, La Paix. Diving into the deep cold pool, surrounded by steep basalt cliffs, is wonderful after the walk through the thick forests. Another 30 minutes west, through even thicker vegetation and up a steep gradient, is the second, smaller, waterfall of La Mer. The pool at the base of the falls is dark and cold, casting an eerie atmosphere over the forested surroundings.

There are no tourist hotels in Bras Panon, and even travellers accustomed to *pensions* will not find anything advertised. Your best bet is to ask the police at the Gendarmerie Nationale on the N2. They are accommodating and will let you sleep in a cell or suggest a local family that might assist. Campers are permitted to pitch their tents in any of the forests, but should avoid camping too close to town.

There are three recommended restaurants in Bras Panon. All have low prices and extensive menus. *Le-Bic-Fin* restaurant, 66 Route Nationale; *Chez Nicolas*, 28 Chemin Bras Panon; *Restaurant Perle d'Asie*, 56 Route Nationale 2. No reservations are necessary, but try and get there before 19h30 if taking a family out. May I suggest that those visitors who stay with a local family, take them for a meal at one of these restaurants. They rarely eat out and will thoroughly appreciate the gesture.

Shoppers will find a captivating range of vanilla products at Parfums Vanille, 21 Route Nationale 2, next to the vanilla co-operative. It sells vanilla-flavoured rum, punches, sweets, vanilla quills and designs, a strange-smelling perfume, vanilla essence and oil, and a few local craftworks. The shop is open Monday-Friday 8h00-12h00 and 13h45-17h15.

ST-BENOIT

Completely destroyed by fire in the 1950s, St-Benoit, which was made almost entirely of wood until that time, has now been rebuilt in unattractive cement, concrete and asbestos. The once flourishing *bichique* fishing industry has now all but vanished, and, so it seems, has the town's vitality. The depressing housing estates, gangs of "punks", exotic flower gardens and a spectacular coastline produce a paradox that confuses most visitors.

St-Benoit is at the southern end of the blue-line bus route from St-Denis. There is a large bus depot and travellers will be able to catch buses to the west coast, the north and southern regions of Réunion from here. If coming from the west coast, take one of the two daily purple-line buses that leave from St-Pierre and cross the island via Plaine des Palmistes to St-Benoit. One leaves St-Pierre at about 9h30, the other at 13h30. From the south coast, take the yellow-line bus that stops at St-Joseph, St-Philippe, Ste-Rose and then St-Benoit. Several buses do this route through the day. Visitors using public transport are strongly advised to get a copy of the Alizes bus services' timetable.

The post office is at 12 Rue Georges Pompidou in the CBD. There is a traffic circle as you enter St-Benoit from the west. Just before this circle is a small tourist office that is able to arrange local tours, plus excursions to Grand Etang lake and further on to Plaine des Palmistes. All the banks are located along Rue Georges Pompidou. Credit Agricole is at 28 Rue Georges Pompidou, BNP is a little further along and Banque de la Réunion is at number 24. Emergency medical treatment is obtainable at Clinique St-Benoit, 2 Boulevard Prefecture.

Travellers camping in the area will find the supermarkets of St Benoit well stocked. *Score* supermarket on Rue Michel Debré has the biggest range of goods, followed by *Geant 2 000*, 61 Avenue Bouvet Le Butor. There is another, smaller, branch of Score on Rue Georges Pompidou. Remember that supermarkets are closed for lunch between 13h00-14h00.

There are no proper curio shops in St Benoit, but at nearby **Ste-Anne** there is a branch of the Maison de L'Artisanat, on Place de Eglise (next to the ornate church). This shop, which sells wooden crafts, T-shirts, vanilla products and local art, is closed on Sunday afternoon and Monday morning. During the rest of the week, it is open from 9h00-12h00 and 14h00-17h00.

Apart from hanging about the docks with out of work fishermen, the only other thing to do is visit the delightful flower gardens of Mrs Nauche, tel. 50.42.25. This floral wonderland is open Tuesday-Saturday 9h00-12h00 and 14h00-17h00. You do need to make an appointment first.

There is only one hotel that can be recommended in St-Benoit. *Hotel des Impots* (low-medium tariff), 4 Rue Beaulieu, tel. 50.06.27, has clean rooms but does not serve meals. Reservations are not necessary, and you will possibly be the only resident. The management is friendly, and will make every endeavour to make your stay as pleasant as possible. Though meals are not provided, if you supply the groceries, one of the owner's daughters will gladly prepare you dinner, at no extra fee – except perhaps a Friday night out at Le Palladium disco on Chemin Jean Roberts, which is a great rave anyway.

Light meals, takeaways and snacks are available from *Rest Snack Les Vacoas*, 1 Chemin La Paix. Chinese snacks and light Creole lunches can be eaten at *Café de Chine*, Place Marche. For midday sandwiches and spicy snacks, visit *Le Carrousel* snack bar, next to Score supermarket.

Comprehensive à la carte meals and daily specials are served at *Le St-Benoit* restaurant, 4 Rue Montfleuri, and from *Le Brasier*, 10 Chemin Îlet Danclas. High quality Chinese and Creole food, prepared in the traditional way with fried rice or noodles, can be tasted at *Le Lotus* restaurant, 61 Route Nationale 3.

West of St-Benoit, along the N3 highway, there are a number of sites to visit. **La Confiance** has the reputation as one of the most beautiful settlements on the island. It certainly is in a majestic setting at the foot of the highlands. The entire area is devoted to sugar production, and near La Confiance are the ruins of an old sugar refinery. In the village are several planters' houses from the 18th century. Most are in a state of decay, but a few are still lived in. South-west of the village, where the N3 is cut from north to south by the D3, turn north. At the end of this road, above the deep valley of Rivière des Marsouins, is a unique forest of ravinalas (traveller's tree). It is unclear how these Malagasy species got here, but the theory is that early French settlers from Tolanaro in Madagascar brought them across. Why they should have been planted in such dense profusion at this particular location is still a mystery. There is a wonderful panoramic view of St-Benoit and the coastal regions from up here.

About 10 km west of St-Benoit is Grand Etang lake. It takes quite a strenuous walk to reach the lake from the main road. The 5 km road leading to the start of the path is well signposted from St-Benoit. Get to the track early and persevere through the thick vegetation until reaching the lake edge. Swimming is allowed, but be warned, the water is very cold, even in mid-summer. Ancient tribal legends have assigned all manner of rituals, healing powers and curses to this remote mountain lake. According to the museum curator in St-Denis, it was one of the sacred lakes used by slaves for occult worship. At certain phases of the moon and seasons, they would sneak out of their quarters on the east coast plantations and journey to the forested lake, where they would wash and perform obeisance to their African gods and ancestors.

About 10 km south of St-Benoit is the village of Ste-Anne. As you cross the Ravine St-François bridge, going south, La Grotte de Lourdes is in the cliffs to the right. A shrine has been erected on this site. The shallow puddles that form from water seepage are claimed to have healing properties. In the settlement of Ste-Anne is the unusual church designed by Father Père Dobemberger in 1946. This intricately carved church is a triumph of human creativity and dedication. The priest died in 1948, and his tomb is inside the church, beneath the sculpted stonework and lattice roof that were the culmination of his dream. If you are in the vicinity on a Sunday morning, attend the mass held here at about 8h00. As the members of the choir raise their voices in song, the carved facades and tooled cornices collect the sound and broadcast it in a way that no stereo system ever has.

STE-ROSE

Ste-Rose lies on the very shoulder of the volcano. Built on the edge of the lava flow, her small populace live a life torn between acceptance and tension. The villagers survive mainly by fishing the rich waters beyond where the lava spilt into the sea. However, school leavers are moving to St-Denis or emigrating to France, where job prospects are better. Rural people in other parts of Réunion see Ste-Rose, especially **Piton Ste-Rose**, as places blessed by the Lord. Visitors to the church surrounded by lava at Piton Ste-Rose will understand why. Flanked to the east by a dramatic and savage coastline and the volcano to the west, Ste-Rose has several sites of interest. Its cheap restaurants are popular with holidaying Réunionnais, who are content to stay at the one place that provides visitors accommodation in Ste-Rose.

Travellers going to Ste-Rose need to catch the yellow-line bus that travels between St-Benoit and St-Pierre via St-Philippe. There is a regular daily schedule between the two towns, including all stops in between.

You will find two post offices in the area. One is in Ste-Rose, 184 Route Nationale 2. The other is 5 km south, at Piton Ste-Rose on Chemin Jardin. The Bibliotèque Municipal on Chemin Cimetière has a large collection of literature pertaining to volcanos and the eruptions on Réunion. This is an ideal place to do some research when the clouds roll down the volcano and hide all the sights. Basic medical problems can be diagnosed and treated at Pharmacie Boyer, 447 N2, Piton Ste-Rose.

Just before entering Ste-Rose from the north, travellers cross the new suspension bridge over the Rivière d'Est. If possible, stop and take a walk across the old suspension bridge, to the seaward side of the new one. The view is impressive, and already bungy jumpers are investigating the awesome fall. During the wet season, a raging torrent cascades from the volcano's sides to the sea. If you stand on the old bridge at that time there is a noticeable tremble and movement in the structure.

Near the Narayanin Store is a small waterfall worth seeing. Locals say that when the volcano is about to erupt, the water flowing down this cascade is coloured bright red, a warning to the inhabitants to flee. Between the banana plantations and coconut groves is the ruin of yet another sugar mill. There is not much to see at the mill, except crumbling walls, empty passages and rusting machinery. A monument to the defeated British naval commander Corbett has been erected at the fishing harbour. He was killed during a naval battle in 1809 with French admiral Bouvet. This is possibly the only British memorial on the island, despite the island once having belonged to the British Empire.

Tourists interested in the technical aspects of sugar production are welcome to view the technical centre for sugar cane and sugar milling on the N2 highway, Monday-Friday, 9h00-12h00 and 13h30-17h00. By taking the coastal path south, from La Marine harbour, walkers edge a coastline of plunging cliffs, forests and roaring ocean, to Piton Ste-Rose, about 5 km away.

Piton Ste-Rose's church, Notre Dame des Lavas, is the biggest tourist attraction of the area. On 12 April 1977, the volcano erupted. Spewing out molten rock and poisonous gas from a crater in its eastern flank, a wall of super-heated destruction rolled towards Piton Ste-Rose. Seeking safety, villagers ran to the church for sanctuary. It seemed as though they were doomed when the lava crossed the road west of the church. Then a miracle happened. For no apparent reason the lava flowed only as far as the door, separated and continued on either side of the church, leaving it and the people inside unharmed. There are photos and newspaper clippings describing the event on the back wall of the church. Also inside, is a subtly hued painting of Christ halting the lava before the church to protect His devotees. On the crest of the lava wave a log was borne. Unburned, it was carried to the doorway of the church, and now stands outside the church, as a memorial to that incredible day.

Between Piton Ste-Rose and the hamlet of **Bois Blanc** is Pointe des Cascades. Water running across the solidified lava falls from high black cliffs to the sea. Below the waterfalls is the little beach of L'Anse des

Cascades. Swimming here is unsafe, due to the rip currents, razor-like seabed and dumper waves. It offers great photo opportunities, especially at sunrise, when the sun's rays make the waterfall sparkle as though it were a cascade of glittering jewels. South of Bois Blanc, through the strangely silent forest of dead trees, is the blue statue of the Vierge au Parasol (The Virgin of the Parasol). The umbrella she holds over her head is to shield her from the fiery volcanic eruptions that may, at any time, rain down. The local Roman Catholic Father explains that it signifies the protection that the Virgin Mary provides for her worshippers who live in the volcano's brooding shadow.

On Friday and Saturday night, from around 22h30, the place to be in Ste-Rose is at the Disco Roz d'Zil, 317 RN2 Ravine Glissante. The partying, dancing and drinking continue until well after 2h00.

Ste-Rose only has one place that offers accommodation, *Auberge Touristique Les Refuges* (low-medium tariff). You must book your room at least three months before arriving. Over the island's holiday season, travellers should bring a tent if they plan on staying in the area. The Auberge will allow you to pitch your tent in its yard and use the washing and cooking facilities for free. Auberge Touristique Les Refuges, 503 RN2, Ste-Rose, tel. 47.21.76.

Restaurant Anse des Cascades, on Chemin Cascades, Piton Ste-Rose, has a decent set menu, and à la carte meals, at cheap prices. Over weekends, it is almost impossible to get a table without a reservation. Make sure you have booked by the previous Wednesday, tel. 47.20.42. *Les Deux Pitons* restaurant on the N2 is less popular, possibly due to its unrealistic prices, but the selection of Creole cuisine is large, and the wine list includes locally produced sweet wines from the Cilaos region. It is not necessary to reserve a table, unless you happen to want a meal on a public holiday or during the high season. At that time, call, just in case, tel. 47.23.16. *Les Marmottes*, 576 N2, Bois Blanc, is used mostly by package tours. The meals are excellent, with large helpings. It is always busy, and offers dishes from a Creole, Continental and seafood speciality menu. Independent diners must book at least 24 hours prior to arrival, tel. 47.24.67.

Snacks are sold at *Meti's Snack Bar*, near the post office in Ste-Rose. Tasty, cheap lunches are available from *Resto-Est*, in Piton Ste-Rose, which concentrates on delicious Creole and Chinese food. *Bar du Weekend*, also in Piton Ste-Rose, offers unimpressive lunches and snacks. The main items sold here are beer and rum. *Restaurant La Ste-Rose*, at Ravine Glissante, has a few traditional dishes that travellers will enjoy.

There are no high tourist prices and fancy crockery provided here. You eat enormous helpings of spicy Creole food from plastic plates.

At Couffin Rose, on Route Nationale 2, visitors can buy curios from a wide selection of locally produced handicrafts. Prices are surprisingly low and the items all from the region. The curio shop is open Monday-Sunday, 8h30-16h30.

The journey from Bois Blanc to St-Philippe crosses solidified flows, edges black beaches, forest reserves and the long lava slopes of Piton de la Fournaise, where you can see the results of recent lava activity. The vegetation grows to an enormous size, fed by the rich volcanic nutrients that are the very stuff of creation. South of Bois Blanc is a forestry reserve. The area is sprouting ferns, moss, lichens and conifer saplings. Near the aptly named village of **Tremblet**, take the turn-off for Symbiose pour Volcan et Oiseaux. It is quite a long walk up to the viewpoint, but the vista and oddly shaped sculptures are certainly worth the visit.

At the botanical centre, visitors can see the vegetative regrowth that takes place soon after the lava has cooled. Within a matter of years, pioneer plants take hold and then slowly begin to give way to invader species, then to sub-climax and finally to verdant climax vegetation. It is interesting and rather humbling walking about on the lava flows here.

Along the road which winds through the National Forestry Reserve is an information board. Maps show the various lava flows. The views up to the misty heights of the rim and down over the sea are impressive and expansive. The lava from the second 1986 eruption crosses the road a few kilometres south of the volcano information board. Visitors can walk on the bubbly rocks on either side of the road, and investigate the moss and fern tendrils that have already found a place to grow. At the first flow, Coulee de Lave 1986, snack vans have set up shop for the bus loads of tourists that arrive to walk about on the lava for a few minutes.

Close to St-Philippe is the Jardin Volcanique and Puits Arabe. The volcanic garden and Arab graves are a must if you come to this area. It is here that early Arab seafarers came ashore to dig for fresh water and bury their dead. There is a detailed map of the location at the car park. It is busy over weekends and public holidays, but visitors seldom go wandering along the black volcanic beach, onto the hollow lava pipes or even to the site of the 23 March 1986 eruption. This leaves the trail free for the more adventurous visitor. Study the map and then start a walk from the Puits des Arabes, south of the car park, among the palm trees behind the public toilets. From there walk out onto the crumbling basalt that continues north to meet the black beach at Pointe de la Table. This place is what many imagine the moon must look like. To the west, trees and bush crowd the edge of the lava, and to the east the sea launches consistent attacks against the brittle, cooled magma. A trail marked by white arrows takes visitors over the hollow chambers, where rivers of molten lava once raced to the ocean. Some of these chambers or pipes are large enough to crawl through. It can be a bit harsh on the knees, but an encounter with the inside of a volcanic chamber is something that few people on earth ever get the chance to experience. The trail leads to the site of the 23 March 1986 eruption. It is a startlingly small exit for the amount of lava that flowed out.

ST-PHILIPPE

The region around St-Philippe has intrigued anthropologists, archaeologists and geologists for decades. The pits supposedly dug by Arab sailors do not answer the many questions that researchers ask about the site. Why would the Arabs have landed on the south-eastern coast of the island, on what are surely the most inaccessible beaches available? Why are there distinctive Malayo-Polynesian engravings on some of the walls of the pits? Were they dug to search for water, or was there some other reason? The Puits Arabes are in the Jardin Volcanique, north of town, while Puits Anglais can be found south-west of St-Philippe. The markedly different Puits des Française are on the coastal shelf at Cap Mechant, between **Baril** and **Basse Vallee**. Most visitors to the wells and graves will, no doubt, also come away with unanswered questions and not a few theories of their own.

Travellers may take public transport, the yellow line bus, from either St-Benoit or St-Pierre, and ask the driver to put them out at St-Philippe or Le Baril. On weekends it is easy hitchhiking from the larger urban centres south to St-Philippe, but during the week, most transport takes the shorter route across Plaine des Palmistes, so you may have to do a considerable amount of walking.

La Poste (post office) is at 2 Cite Bouvet de Loziers. There are no banks at present in St-Philippe. Minor medical treatment is available at Pharmacie Manuel Mascart, 24 Rue Leconte de Lisle. An informative and helpful tourist office is at 69 Rue Leconte de Lisle, Hôtel de Ville, St-Philippe. For further information and details of the area, write to this office or phone them to send you information, tel. 37.10.43.

Every visitor to St-Philippe should spend some time in the Spice and Perfume Garden. Book onto one of the daily guided tours to see this marvellous garden. The plot is said to be about 200 years old and covers about 3 ha. In this busy garden tourists can see all of Réunion's endemic plants, fruit trees and several of the spices that now flourish on the volcanic island. Each plant is identified, its uses explained and its importance to the island's ecology carefully recorded by a dedicated team of botanists and gardeners. The garden has been set out in such a way that even independent visitors will be able to follow the different processes from traditional production to modern processing. Those fortunate enough to visit the garden between October and January will be able to see how delicate vanilla blossoms are hand pollinated. The Spice and Perfume Garden is open daily from 9h00-16h30. The reservation of guides and the purchase of tickets must be done at the Tourist Office, 69 Rue Leconte de Lisle, Town Hall, St-Philippe, tel. 37.10.43.

There used to be trails up the side of the volcano from St-Philippe, but these have now been sadly neglected, and it is advisable to rather hike to the volcano from Plaine-des-Cafres or St-Joseph.

The quaint little cave chapel of Notre Dame de la Paix can be visited west of St-Philippe. There are miniature pews, a shrine to the sacred Lady and a small altar in this Catholic site.

Accommodation in St-Philippe is available in one hotel and one *pension*. The hotel is called *Le Baril* (low-medium tariff). It has restaurant facilities that produce outstanding Creole meals, and a sparkling swimming pool to cool off in after a hike along the volcanic beaches and shelf zones. Book 30 days in advance if you plan on spending time at this pleasant hotel. Le Baril Hotel, Route Nationale 2, Baril, tel. 37.01.04, fax 37.07.62. There is a family *pension* at 55 RN2, Baril (low tariff). The sign outside states, "Chambres et Table d'hôte". Scrumptious Creole and French meals, comfortable rooms and clean ablution facilities are provided. This *pension* is even more popular than the hotel, so make reservations at least 60 day prior to departure, and confirm by telegram 15 days before arrival. Trebel Pension, 55 RN2, Baril, tel. 37.09.95.

Restaurant meals can be chosen from traditional and international menus along this section of the south-east coast. *Restaurant Le Cap Mechant*, 19 Rue Labourdonnais, in Basse Vallee, appears to be continually full of patrons. The view from the restaurant is astounding. A menu of Creole and French dishes is offered at reasonable rates. The 10% tip and 1% tourist tax is enforced here. It is recommended that you reserve a table 24 hours ahead, tel. 37.00.61. *Etoile de Mer,* also at Cap Mechant, Basse Vallee, has fresh fish daily and does wonders with shellfish and Creole spices. Guests who do not enjoy Creole cooking are able to select from a Continental menu. Weekend diners must book a table by Thursday afternoon, tel. 37.04.60. *Restaurant La Canot* is at 15A Rue Leconte de Lisle, as you enter St-Philippe from the west. Always busy, it serves lavish amounts of spicy food from an extensive menu that includes Creole, Continental, Indian and Chinese food. This medium-priced restaurant is ideal after a day's outing along the coast or through the forests, tel. 37.00.36.

20 HIGHLANDS OF RÉUNION

This is Réunion's most attractive region. In the highlands of this remarkable island you will discover an active volcano, forested cirques, water-filled calderas and a people who are still unaffected by the trappings of modern society. No visit to Réunion can be termed complete until one has ventured up into the mountains. Be prepared with warm clothing, good footwear, rain-gear and, where you feel it necessary, the services of a guide. Visitors in search of natural splendour should forego the large tour groups that are carted up to the highlands by buses every day. These trips are nearly always rushed, quickly returning to hotels on the coast.

LE TAMPON

North-east of St-Pierre, along the N3 highway, Le Tampon is the largest town on the way to the highland areas of Plaine-des-Cafres, the volcano and La Plaine des Palmistes. By Réunion standards, the urban centre is a large commune. It stretches from the south-west coast to meet the commune of Plaine des Palmistes, way up on the ridges around the volcano. Plaine-des-Cafres falls under the jurisdiction of Le Tampon, but is treated separately in this book. Visitors travelling from St-Pierre leave the sugar fields and climb steep roads, which edge dairy farms and flower-filled meadows until reaching Le Tampon.

There are two buses per day that travel all the way across the island from west to east. Several buses make the short journey from St-Pierre to Le Tampon. The first bus leaves from the gare routière in St-Pierre at about 7h45, and the last at 18h15. Take the purple-line bus from St-Pierre to St-Benoit via Le Tampon. A local bus leaves St-Pierre every 30 minutes and travels via all the villages and settlements – including Le Tampon – to **Grande Ferme,** at the start of the road to the volcano summit. The local bus leaves from the same depot as the Alizes buses on Rue François Isautier.

It is difficult hitchhiking to Le Tampon. The suburbs of St-Pierre stretch to the very foot of the hills and there are few places at which a vehicle can pull off. On the other hand, hitchhiking from St-Benoit, on the east coast, across the island to Le Tampon is relatively easy.

Most of the traffic using this route is going to St-Pierre anyway. The picturesque village of La Confiance, west of St-Benoit, is the best place to wait for a lift. Reasonably priced car hire is available from Central Automobile, 116 Rue Albert Frejaville, tel. 27.44.46.

Le Tampon's post office is at 46 Rue General de Gaulle. Four banks have branches in Le Tampon, all on Rue Hubert Delisle: Banque Française Commercial, BNP, Banque de la Réunion and Credit Agricole. Medical attention may be obtained from Dr Pierre Bourgeois, 237 Chemin Neuf Pont d'Yves, tel. 27.22.82 and Jocelyne Puget, 112 Rue General de Gaulle, tel. 57.67.57.

There is nothing to interest tourists in Le Tampon, and few visitors ever stay long in the urban centre. It is further to the north-east that the attractions are to be found.

Finding suitable accommodation in Le Tampon is not a problem. There are several hotels, *pensions* and chambres d'hôte. Travellers spending time in this area should book into accommodation in Le Tampon, and make bus trips to the surrounding area. Accommodation nearer the volcano is very expensive. The hoteliers in Plaine-des-Cafres are aware that people enjoy the mountain scenery and charge exorbitant prices for their somewhat shabby rooms and mediocre meals.

One of the best hotels in Le Tampon is *Hotel Outre-Mer* (medium-high tariff), 8 Rue Bourbon, tel. 57.30.30, fax 57.29.29. All meals are included in the rate at this 35-room hotel. All rooms have bathroom, television and mini-bar. There are reduced charges the longer you stay. Reservations are necessary and a deposit is required on confirmation.

Hostellerie du Paille en Queue (medium tariff). This hotel, with 14 rooms in bungalows, is a favourite with budget travellers. The management is jovial and attentive, arranging guides and transport to the volcano, or packing tasty lunches for those guests who are going hiking for the day. Breakfast and dinner can be taken at the hostel's French restaurant, and a television room and swimming are available. You can also leave your unnecessary luggage here if taking an overnight trail into the forests and mountains. Book well in advance, and confirm by telegram 15 days prior to arrival. Hostellerie du Paille en Queue, 14 Rue Paille en Queue, Le Tampon, tel. 27.47.60, fax 27.31.45.

Metro Hotel (medium tariff). Located near the busy CBD of Le Tampon, the Metro Hotel is well situated for visitors using public transport – it's close to the main Le Tampon bus stop. Breakfast and dinner are usually included in the rate. The hotel is a little austere and the staff not overly friendly or helpful. Service is however good, the meals tasty if somewhat small and the rooms comfortable. Make bookings about 30 days ahead. Metro Hotel, 102 Rue Marius et Ary Leblond, Le Tampon, tel. 27.07.90.

Hotel Les Orchidees (high tariff). This is Le Tampon's only two-star hotel. There are 16 rooms with washing facilities and television. A French restaurant offers an extensive menu that has a few Creole dishes as well. Hotel Les Orchidees, 3 Rue Jules Ferry, Le Tampon, tel. 27.11.15, fax 27.16.72.

For cheap accommodation with a local family, call in at *Roger Gîte Rural*, 163 Chemin Petit Tampon, tel. 57.04.71, about 5 km north-east of Le Tampon, in the hamlet of **Petit Tampon**. In Le Tampon, there is a wonderful *pension de famille* at 420 Rue Marius et Ary Leblond, tel. 57.08.56. The sign on the gate reads Ste-Gestion Exploitation Fond Commerce. During the tourist season a number of local families open a room or two in their homes for travellers. They are usually willing to accept visitors during the off-season as well. Approach the police on Rue Hubert Delisle. They are a helpful bunch who may even take you to lodgings in their blue Peugeot police car.

Patisserie Chan-Ky, 119 Rue Hubert Delisle, makes fresh cakes, pies and spicy snacks each morning. It also serves a delicious breakfast of hot bread, grape jam and black coffee for a few francs. *Restaurant Golden*, on Rue Roland Garros, has medium-priced Creole and French cuisine, plus a few rooms for overnight visitors. Seafood is a speciality of *Poisson Rouge*, 118 Rue Jules Bertaut. *Le Panda* has a large menu of traditional dishes and offers *plat du jour* at lunch time. You will find them at 226 Rue Marius et Ary Leblond. Out on Route Volcan, east of **Bourg-Murat**, is *La Bon Grillade*, popular with coach tours. It can be a problem finding a table here at lunch time, but the waiters are helpful and will set up an extra table or provide a meal as a takeaway, if necessary.

THE HIGH PLAINS

Plaine-des-Cafres

This little town located on the misty heights above Le Tampon is usually the starting point for journeys to the volcano, Piton de la Fournaise. Do not be in too much of a hurry to reach the volcano from this area. There are delightful walks and spectacular viewpoints around Plaine-des-Cafres to be enjoyed.

You can get to Plaine-des-Cafres from either St-Pierre or St-Benoit. Three buses travel daily up from St-Pierre, and two buses travel between St-Pierre and St-Benoit via Le Tampon. During the tourist season, an extra bus is put on this purple-line route. It leaves St-Pierre at about 16h30. The bus stop for Plaine-des-Cafres is outside the Lallemand Hotel, as you enter town from the south-west. There is also a local bus service that serves Plaine-des-Cafres and the mountain village of **Bois Court**, to the north.

There is a small post office on the N3 which passes through town. Credit Agricole has an exchange bureau and automatic cash teller on the N3, in the nearby settlement of **23e km**.

An interesting walk or drive can be taken north of the Lallemand Hotel. Turn north at the T-junction on the N3 national road, outside Tigre Store. Follow this road through several hamlets for about 4 km. At the small settlement above the gorges follow the narrow road to the right. Near the end of this district road is the Notre Dame Source d'Eau Vive shrine. Proceed past this shrine to the tarred viewpoint area. This has to be among the most beautiful views on Réunion. Overlooking the plunging gorges of the Rivière des Citrons, visitors gaze upon gorges, untouched forests, cloud-topped waterfalls and isolated settlements.

Turning left at the settlement near the Notre Dame shrine, visitors continue down a steep valley to **Grand Bassin**. There is a village on the river's edge here. The people are not only gentle and hospitable, but also thoroughly bemused by those active visitors who walk down from Plaine-des-Cafres. Take along some water and wet weather gear when doing this walk and if at all possible, try and get a ride back up the tortuous road to Plaine-des-Cafres. You are quite welcome to camp at the village, although it is more likely that a local family will offer you a room for the night.

The main reason people come to Plaine-des-Cafres is to see the volcano, Piton de la Fournaise. Take the N3 north-east until reaching the village of Bourg-Murat. Here visitors will find the Maison de la Volcan. It is highly recommended that people planning to visit the volcano first make a stop here. Visual displays, films, lectures and information brochures concerning the volcano are all available. The biggest problem is that nothing is in English. Still, it is fairly easy to get the gist of the information provided. An entrance fee must be paid. Armed with some prior knowledge of the volcano they are going to see, visitors proceed to the east and along the district road, RF5.

Climbing over a 2 136 m ridge and then skirting the plummeting valley of the Rivière des Remparts, you will get your first glimpse of the mighty volcano from the viewpoint known as Nez de Boeuf. Following the road across a tongue of rising land, visitors arrive at an escarpment above a wide, empty and sombre valley.

From the viewpoint above the red landscape of Plaine des Sables, the road drops to the plain's barren surface. It is easy to imagine yourself on some giant continent here. The humidity, forests and beaches of the Indian Ocean islands of the brochures are forgotten as you cross the heat and dust of Plaine des Sables. The road here is marked by white-painted stones. Passing collapsed craters, the road continues to climb to the viewpoint and gîte at **Pas de Bellecombe**, 2 311 m. You are now on the very shoulder of the rumbling, unpredictable monster. This is where most tourists stop. Basic accommodation and meals are provided in the gîte. It is necessary to book well in advance, about 60 days if possible, at one of the many tourist offices on Réunion. Contact the main office if making reservation from overseas. Réunion Tourism Board, 23 Rue Tourette, 97482 St-Denis, tel. 21.00.41, fax 41.84.41.

Start your ascent of the main cone of the volcano as early as possible. Come prepared with sufficient clothing, water, food and courage – the volcano often grumbles, as though complaining about the walkers on its back. From the viewpoint, take the paths and steps that drop to the outer crater. A clearly marked trail leads across the outer crater and up to the very rim of the frightening volcano. Several paths lead to the summit and around the rim. Along each one, visitors will encounter small cones, tiny eruptions and metre-wide flows. Finally, you arrive on the rim at 2 631 m. Take a big breath, step to the edge and peer into the crater. No adjectives can adequately describe the feeling and atmosphere of this primal place – you must go and experience it for yourself.

From the viewpoint, near the gîte, it is almost 13 km to the crater rim and back. Do not hurry in either direction. Expect to take about five hours of easy walking for the round trip. This journey is best done in the week, when there are few people on the route. The fewest people are to be found on Tuesday and Thursday – the ideal time for travellers to make the trek and witness a window on creation.

For such a remote place, there are two surprisingly vibrant nightclubs in this area. Along the road between Plaine-des-Cafres and Bois Court is L'Ouragan Disco. Youthful visitors should spend some time here, if in the area on Friday or Saturday night. The patrons are nearly all locals from the farms and remote villages in the mountains. Hiking boots, jeans and T-shirts are the norm. Initially reserved and almost suspicious of foreigners, they quickly accept you, if you take the first step towards meeting them. The doors open at 21h00 and close at around 2h00.

At Le Damier Bar, Restaurant and Dancing, near the turning for Grand Bassin, there is an older, more abandoned, more festive, crowd. The patrons are mostly farm labourers. The party starts at about 22h00 and continues until 4h00.

Two hotels, a guest lodge, campsite and four chambres d'hôte offer visitors a good selection of clean, but rather expensive, accommodation.

Lallemand Hotel (medium-high tariff)

Situated in Plaine-des-Cafres, the Lallemand is used by most tour operators travelling to and from the volcano. Unless you have made a reservation 60 days prior to arrival at this 17-room hotel, it is unlikely that you will find accommodation. The hotel is 1 600 m above sea-level and guests are advised to bring warm clothing if staying here. Its restaurant offers a selection of French and local dishes, with an excellent wine list that includes several overseas vintages. The owner-manager has spent several years working in southern Africa and is expert in arranging excursions for the more affluent tourist. Hotel Lallemand, 68 N3 – 23e km, 97418 Plaine-des-Cafres, tel. 27.51.27, fax 59.12.70.

Hotel La Diligence (medium-high tariff)

This secluded hotel has both rooms and bungalows for guests. All accommodation has ablution facilities and a heater. The staff is able to organise mountain bikes, hiking, tennis and horse riding for residents. A restaurant caters for visitors who enjoy Continental dishes. Reservations need to be made 30 days in advance. Hotel La Diligence, 28e km, 97418 Plaine-des-Cafres, tel. 59.10.10, fax 59.15.31.

Other tourist accommodation worth trying in Plaine-des-Cafres is along the road to Bois Court. *Auberge La Fermette* (low-medium tariff): This ski-lodge type place has friendly and attentive staff, who really endeavour to make visitors feel welcome. Its restaurant is, undoubtedly, the best in Plaine-des-Cafres. Although the menu is limited, all the meals are made to traditional Creole recipes, and served in a cosy wooden dining room. If I had to recommend accommodation in Plaine-des-Cafres, then this would be the place. Auberge La Fermette, 48 Route du Bois Court, 97418 Plaine-des-Cafres, tel. 27.50.08, fax 27.53.78.

Along the same road are a number of chambre d'hôte establishments which offer low tariff lodgings that include meals. Most are located between L'Ouragan Disco and Le Damier Bar. If you have difficulty in finding a place, speak to the barman at Le Damier; he can quickly arrange a room with himself or a friend.

Visitors with tents will find comfortable pitches and clean amenities at the campsite just off the Bois Court road. Turn left near the Chez Coco restaurant. Prices at the campsite fall into the low tariff category. The manager's wife gladly offers meals for a small fee. There are very seldom any travellers camping at this remote campsite, and the staff are eager to meet those who do stop for a few days. Camping is also available on the route to the volcano. You are permitted to camp outside the gîte on the volcano itself. With permission from the forest station, you may camp near the memorial to Josemont Lauret, who lost his life in 1887 trying to save a group of friends on the mountain.

Visitors to the area usually take meals at their accommodation, but simple, filling and cheap meals are available at lunch time and dinner at *Chez Coco Restaurant*, near the turning for the campsite. Expect large helpings of hot spicy food cooked with local ingredients. The chicken Creole is especially scrumptious and satisfying. *Le Damier*, on the road to Bois Court, is more of a bar and nightclub than restaurant, but it does serve set menus at reasonable prices. This is the only place that farm workers seem to visit for their evening tea.

Plaine-des-Palmistes

High above the east coast town of St-Benoit, the village of Plaine-des-Palmistes is visited by most cross-island travellers. The region around the village is full of dense forests, waterfalls, rivers and misty mountain ridges. Although some historians claim that the name of the town comes from the many palm trees that once grew in the area, the locals insist that the name was given by African slaves who, on first arriving here, thought that the giant cycads and ferns were some sort of palm tree. The district is still rich in lush vegetation, and a wonderland for those prepared to hoist on a pack and set off along forest trails.

Public transport to Plaine-des-Palmistes is provided by the daily Alizes bus service between St-Benoit and St-Pierre. There is no local bus route in the area. Travellers coming up from St-Pierre should hitchhike from Plaine-des-Cafres or from outside the Maison de la Volcan, at the end of the local bus service route. The road between the two settlements is busy with traffic from about 8h30-16h00.

Visitors will find the post office on Place Mairie, Rue Republique. Tourist information, including the hiring of mountain and hiking guides, can be obtained from the tourist office opposite the post office on Rue Republique. Exhibitions are often put on at this little office. They range from items of Réunionnais interest to displays from France and the USA. Recently, this tourist office published several maps and pamphlets detailing hiking trails and scenic walks around Plaine-des-Palmistes. Tourists who have a particular interest in the botanical species of the mountain forests should join one of the guided botanical tours that leave here twice a week.

In Plaine-des-Palmistes, which is actually two villages separated by Piton des Songes, visitors may view the memorial to the soldiers from this region who died for France in the Great War of 1914-1918. People with a fascination for shrines should consider the easy walk to Petit Grotte de Lourdes. Located south-east of Marie, there is a path off the N3 to the cave in the valley of the Dureau stream. The locals claim that the stream's water and cave give off healing gases that cure minor ailments. It is not unusual, over weekends, to see people with colds and flu fervently praying at the cave or along the stream bank. If you are willing to walk further, and possibly try and find accommodation at rural settlements in the area, there are other caves worth seeing. A cluster of them can be found south from the Sicalait bus stop, south-west of Plaine-des-Cafres.

By following the district road RF2, north of Plaine-des-Palmistes, tourists climb to the awesome views around Col de Bébour, before plunging into the enormous forests of Bébour. The road is in poor condition for most of the way, and hikers will find the going far easier than four-wheeled vehicles. There is a profusion of flowering trees and shrubs in these remote forests. Most of them flower in a riot of colour and fragrance from late May to early July. Guided walks can be arranged by the tourist office in town. Continuing to the end of this district road, visitors will find themselves above the Cirque de Salazie. The panorama of gorges and peaks is breathtaking. Those travelling with tents should consider following the mountain road that winds down to the hill village of Hell-Bourg, and from there east to the coast at St André.

Other walks on Plaine-des-Palmistes start near L'Hotel des Plaines. All are scenic and include paths through forests and along mountain ridges. Two of the best, though seldom used and therefore largely unspoilt, are to the gorges and waterfalls of Bassin Cadet, and Sources de Bras Cabot, where you can see the springs and cascades of this lonely site.

The tourist office recommends that all visitors take the 3 km stroll to the sparkling waterfall of Cascade Biberon. Go up Rue Raphael Babet to the cascade signboard on the left. The trail leads past several farm houses and over three bridges before reaching the falls in the forested Ravine Seche. You can walk down through the trees to the pool below the falls. The water is really cold, but the remoteness of the pool is a definite encouragement for skinny-dipping, particularly if you've walked the whole way from town. Despite the advertising by the tourist office, you are unlikely to encounter any other people at the Cascade Biberon.

The cheapest accommodation at Plaine-des-Palmistes is in one of the chambre d'hôte houses scattered about the area. None are advertised and you may have to spend a bit of time walking about looking for them. The women in the tourist office are helpful in this regard. Ask them for suitable accommodation, and remember to indicate your budget range. Their suggestions are often at places a little more expensive than those out of town, but saves the time and worry of hunting through the streets and alleys yourself.

There are two hotels, Hotel Les Azalées and Hotel Les Plaines.

Hotel Les Plaines (medium-high tariff). Three-star accommodation in 15 rooms, all with heaters, washing facilities and television. Mountain biking and hiking trips can be organised from the hotel reception desk. A cosy restaurant offers Creole and French meals at rather inflated prices, but with large helpings of food. Hotel Les Plaines, 156 Rue Republique, 97431 Plaine-des-Palmistes, tel. 51.31.97, fax 51.36.59.

Hotel Les Azalées (medium tariff). This self-catering holiday village provides guests with 36 bungalows. The location of the hotel, surrounded by towering peaks and green forests, is truly impressive. All accommodation has bathroom en suite, heater and telephone. A television and games room is the focal point at night, when music is played and residents get the chance to meet the manager and staff. Try and reserve accommodation about 30 days before arrival. Hotel Les Azalées, 80 Rue Republique, 97431 Plaine-des-Palmistes, tel. 51.34.24, fax 28.17.97.

Accommodation that will perhaps better suit visitors on a budget is located at *Pension Touristique Au Bon Refuge* (medium tariff). Rue Georges Lebeau, tel. 51.30.76.

Travellers are catered for by numerous families offering a room for a few nights. Breakfast and dinner are usually included in the tariff, and are cooked to traditional recipes by the mother or daughters. Reservations are seldom required and the owners operate on a first-come first-served basis. Two that are recommended are:

Plante Gîte Rural, 45 Rue Eugene Rochetaing, 97431 Plaine-des-Palmistes, tel. 51.33.45; *Gauvin Chambre d'hôte,* 2 Rue Raphael Babet, 97431 Plaine-des-Palmistes, tel. 51.31.48.

Fresh bread and cakes are sold from *Le Palmistes Bakery* on Rue Republique. Visitors who are camping or self-catering may obtain their groceries from *Chez Alexis* mini-supermarket, near the Shell fuel station on the N3. The local bar is Bar Latchimy on Rue Republique. This is where the town's youth and men gather on weekend evenings for drinks, card and domino games, loud music and a general celebration of life, that continues until well after 2h00.

South-west of the villages is *La Caverne des Fees* restaurant. Light lunches and dinners are available from a good menu that offers a variety of Creole dishes at reasonable prices. *Les Cryptomerias* restaurant, on Chemin Petite Plaine, tel. 51.38.15, has a small Creole speciality menu that concentrates on spicy seafood, saffron rice and tomato-based sauces. You are advised to make a reservation if you hope to taste the delights at this diner. At 167 Rue Republique is *Restaurant des Platanes,* tel. 51.31.69. The meals are costly and not that good. Service too seems to be lacking and guests are often left waiting for 30 minutes or more before receiving attention from a lackadaisical staff. In the settlement of **Bras des Calumets** – towards Plaine-des-Cafres – is the well-known *Escale des Calumets,* at 316 Rue Republique, tel. 51.35.08. The set menus and à la carte choice are a mouth-watering journey through Creole and Continental cuisine. The ambience and friendly service are a trade mark of this popular restaurant. It serves light lunches but it is the lavish dinners for which it is renowned. Order a bottle of wine, then sit back and relax while listening to soft music. Eating at this restaurant is a gourmet experience not to be missed.

CIRQUE DE CILAOS

Lying in an ancient caldera, scalloped by wind and water erosion, the Cirque de Cilaos has to be among the most beautiful places on earth. The drive up the twisting road from St-Louis is an adventure in itself. The volcanic amphitheatre is not only dramatic, but has thermal springs, numerous hiking and walking trails, indigenous forests and an invigorating climate.

Prior to the exploitation of the thermal springs at Cilaos (pronounced See-la-os), the area was home to escaped slaves and fugitives. Once you have seen the area it is easy to see why they chose this remote and beautiful mountain wilderness. In 1819, a French expedition sent to the area to recapture slaves and imprison outlaws, stumbled upon the hot, iron-rich springs. Despite accurate reports of their findings, nothing was done to develop the area until 1826, when the governor granted a freed slave by the name of Figaro settlement rights in the area that is now the village of Îlet a Cordes. From that time the development of the region has flourished.

Of the three cirques on Réunion, Cirque de Mafate, Cirque de Salazie and Cirque de Cilaos, the Cirque de Cilaos is arguably the most attractive and well-endowed with natural splendour. Reaching Cilaos from the west coast involves a drive up one of the most impressive feats of civil engineering on Réunion. Visitors using hired vehicles should drive to St-Louis and then take the N5 national road north-east. It is only 34 km from St-Louis, but the actual trip will take between one and two hours due to the steep inclines, hairpin bends and frequent stops for viewing. Travellers using public transport should take the Alizes red-line buses from St-Pierre to Cilaos that leave St-Pierre six times per day. The journey takes about two and a half hours.

Cilaos village

La Poste (post office) is at 76 Rue Père Boiteau. Tourist information is available from the tourist office, 2 Rue Mac Auliffe, tel. 31.78.03. For hiking or climbing guides contact La Maison de la Montagne on Rue Mac Auliffe, tel. 31.75.31. Details of the trails through the forests or across the mountains to the other cirques can be obtained from the other branch of La Maison de la Montagne on Rue Père Boiteau, tel. 31.80.54. Guided, driven tours of the area around Cilaos can be organised with Transport Touristique, tel. 31.75.81. Visitors wanting to explore the mountains by bicycle will find mountain bikes for hire from Location VTT, at 48 Rue Père Boiteau, tel. 31.81.95.

Banking facilities are non-existent. The best place at which to change traveller's cheques or hard currency is the elegant Hotel des Thermes. Handling charges are low and the service extended, even to non-residents, is exemplary. Emergency medical treatment is available from the local hospital at Les Mares, tel. 31.70.50. For non-critical medical matters visit the doctor who attends to out-patients, Paul Techer, 4 Rue Glycines, tel. 31.71.30. There are two pharmacies that can fill prescriptions: Pharmacie STAMM, 58 Rue Père Boiteau and Pharmacie des Thermes, 47 Rue Père Boiteau.

Things to do

The first thing that most visitors want to see is the thermal springs. Proceed north of the Hotel des Thermes along Route des Sources. About 150 m from the hotel there is a split in the road. On the corner is the new thermal springs spa and treatment centre, Irénée-Accot. Before visiting the modern site, take a trip to the original geothermal station in the deep valley to the south-west. Avoid the temptation to drive down. Instead, take a slow walk along the winding road to the thermal springs. Around each bend you will discover another waterfall, cascade of flowers and more inspiring views.

Turn left at the jumble of information and advertising boards and follow the tarred road down through dripping forests, past waterfalls, to the red-roofed thermal station at the very bottom of the steep valley. Before reaching the old site, there is a white pump house on the Cilaos side of the bridge. Turn left here and take the stairs which lead to the footbridge across the ravine. Although the original spa was closed in 1987, you can still peep in through cracks in the walls. It was supposed to be turned into a museum, but not much has been done. Beyond the geothermal station, the warm iron, sulphur and carbon water still flows down to the edge of the river. The banks of the stream are rust stained and bright orange in colour. Brightly coloured flowers and dark green conifers crowd in along the nutrient-rich river. The warm water's taste is not too pleasant, but it is apparently very healthy.

Back at the new thermal spa on Route Bras Sec, Établissement Thermal Irénée-Accot, a mineral-spring bath is recommended, especially for hikers. The health resort is open daily from 8h00-12h00 and 14h00-18h00, tel. 31.72.27, fax 31.76.57. One can simply turn up and pay at reception. Prices are reasonable.

If you do not take a thermal bath, then at least have a drink of the different flavoured waters at Source Veronique, outside the entrance of the new Établissement Thermal.

Hiking, rock climbing and mountain biking are some of the main reasons that visitors come to Cilaos. People wanting to try these activities should have a fairly good level of physical fitness, some knowledge of the outdoors and be confident in their ability. From Cilaos it is possible to reach the other cirques on the island.

There are two superb, well-marked routes for mountain biking. The first starts at Cilaos, crosses the Plateau des Chenes and ends at Roche Merveilleuse. The second, far more demanding route, commences at the remote village of **Bras Sec**, continues on to **Bras de Benjoin** and finishes in Cilaos.

Rock climbing is best done with a local guide who will be able to lead climbers to various cliffs that will suit their ability and level of experience. Hotel des Thermes is able to arrange for climbing guides. It offers one and two day circuits of the rocks around Cilaos.

Hikers are in for a bewildering choice of treks, distances and sights. Along the popular routes it is not necessary to hire a guide, but when exploring the mountain woodlands, a guide is recommended. The most walked route, and possibly the most scenic, is the three-day hike along Sentier Pays. Trekkers who would prefer doing this trip with a guide should contact Pays D'Accueil de Cilaos, 21 Rue Mac Auliffe, 97413 Cilaos, tel. 31.73.06, fax 31.78.18.

For a real encounter with Réunion's highland splendour, hikers should set off from Cilaos on a four to seven day hike to one or both of the other cirques.

Cilaos to the Cirque de Mafate: Take the road to the old thermal station and continue to the hamlet of Îlet a Cordes. From here follow the path straight up onto the forested hillside, to the right of the settlement. The path is steep and frequently slippery all the way to the summit of Col du Taïbit, in the shadow of Grand Benard peak (2 896 m). Below the col, on the edge of Cirque de Mafate and on the track to La Nouvelle, is the Marla gîte (mountain hut) where you may spend the night. From this gîte the trail continues north-west through forests and along mountain sides to the mountain hut below Piton Maïdo, at Roche Plate. By following the GR1 north from Roche Plate, trekkers proceed to the hut at Grand Place, before swinging east to the steep valley in which the village of **Aurère** is located. East of Aurère you can climb straight up the inner caldera to La Roche Ecrite (2 280 m). From here there are several paths going north to St-Denis and the coast.

Cilaos to Cirque de Salazie: From Cilaos follow the road north for Bras Sec. About 500 m from town there is a sign for the GR1 hiking trail north-east to Cirque de Salazie and Piton des Neiges. Take this track, which skirts the misty heights of Piton des Neiges (3 070 m). There is a mountain gîte near the Caverne Dufourg for those hikers wishing to climb to the summit of Réunion's highest peak. The gîte is at the juncture of the trails from the Bébour forests, the Salazie track and the path to the forests of Bélouve. Continue north-east on the GR1 until it splits below Mazerin peak (2 100 m). Here you have the choice of walking through the Bélouve forests and then down to Salazie, or turning north and taking the trail to pass Les Trois Cascades and exiting at the village of Hell-Bourg.

It is also possible to combine the cirques by walking south-east from the mountain hut at La Roche Ecrite above Cirque de Mafate to Grand Îlet on the northern edge of the Cirque de Salazie, around the base of Piton d'Enchaing and down through the dense forests and jumble of valleys to Salazie.

For those visitors to Cilaos who are not that interested in long treks, it is still recommended that you spend some time walking along the tarred road that links the town with several small villages and settlements in the area. The road behind Hotel des Thermes will take you through conifer forests to waterfalls and impressive viewpoints. Continue along this road to the village of **Bras Sec**. Here you can buy locally grown and matured wine, lentils and legumes from roadside stalls. Proceeding on the road that dips to the right, south-west of Bras Sec you will arrive at a truly spectacular viewpoint. Back along the road to Cilaos, take the steep road to the mountain viewpoint at La Roche Merveilleuse.

Le Noctambule nightclub, 6 Chemin Trois Mares, is open on Friday and Saturday evening, and Thursday during summer. The young mountain people descend from the hills and forests in denims, checked shirts and hiking boots for a long evening of fun, drink and laughter.

Movies are shown at the dilapidated cinema on Place de Eglise on Tuesday at 17h45, Wednesday and Saturday at 21h00.

Things to buy

Shopping for curios is fun in Cilaos. In Cilaos town try the tourist office on Rue Victor Mac Auliffe, for a selection of local and Réunionnais crafts. The Centre Artisanal, along Rue Père Boiteau, sells traditional farm items such as pickles, jams, vetiver, legumes, lentils and local wine. This centre is open Monday-Saturday 9h00-18h00. One place that all tourists must visit is La Maison de la Broderie (House of Embroidery), on the corner of Rues Victorine Sery and des Ecoles. Started in the early 1900s by Angèle Mac Auliffe, the craft has grown to the point where some of the works are now exported and compete favourably with those from Venice and Chantilly. The Maison de la Broderie is both a school and workshop. Casual visitors may wander about observing the techniques and skills required to create these delicate artworks. Most of the items are for sale, and pieces are made to order, provided you give adequate time to complete the project. The site is open Monday-Saturday 9h00-12h00 and 14h00-17h00; Sunday 9h00-12h00.

One of Réunion's most celebrated artists, Philippe Turpin, has his studio in Cilaos, at 10 Rue Winceslas Rivière. He specialises in copper engravings of local scenes and daily aspects of the hill-people's lives. Although his prices are high, the amount of work that goes into the art warrants them. His studio is open Monday to Friday 9h30-16h30; Saturday only until 12h00 and very rarely on Sunday.

Out in the mountain villages, walkers can buy wooden carvings, tapestries, woollen jerseys and local alcohol brews that include wine and rum.

Accommodation

Top-class accommodation in Cilaos is only available at one hotel, Hotel des Thermes. There are other, lower graded hotels, holiday villages, *pensions* and campsites in and around the town.

Hotel des Thermes (high tariff)

Despite the high tariff, this is the recommended accommodation for visitors to Cilaos. The old mansion overlooks the settlement of Cilaos, near the thermal baths. There are 28 exquisite rooms, all fitted with elegant bathroom en suite, heater, television and telephone. The owner, a gracious Parisian, has brought the culture and charm of that great city to her hotel in the forested mountains of Réunion. The restaurant is a gourmet's delight with French cooking, fine wine and delicate island herbs.

From the hotel, visitors can arrange for guided trips on mountain bikes, canyoning, rock climbing and hiking. There are tennis courts on the hotel grounds. The management of the Hotel des Thermes has a programme for those guests who are visiting for recuperative reasons.

It schedules thermal baths and monitors each visit. Over weekends, there are indoor games, theme evenings and dinner parties. Baby-sitting is also provided free of charge. There is secure parking in the grounds. Make certain to book about 60 days in advance. Hotel des Thermes, 8 Rue des Sources, 97413 Cilaos, tel. 31.70.01, fax 31.74.73.

VVF Cilaos (medium tariff)

Huddled below the towering peak of Piton des Neiges, this VVF village is the cheapest of the three on Réunion. The atmosphere is decidedly relaxed. Guests have the choice of bungalows, studios or apartments. The studios and apartments have their own washing facilities, while the bungalows share a communal ablution block. There are restaurants, a television room, small library and a curio shop. Baby-sitting is also offered. The staff can organise group outings, guides and the hire of mountain bikes for residents. It is very popular during summer and reservations should be made at least 30 days ahead. VVF Cilaos, Rue Fleurs Jaunes, 97413 Cilaos, tel. 31.71.39, fax 24.05.77.

Other hotels worth considering include:

Hotel du Cirque (high tariff). 20 rooms with washing facilities and heater. A bar and restaurant, plus a courtesy bus to the start of hiking and mountain bike trails. 27 Rue Père Boiteau, 97413 Cilaos, tel. 31.70.68, fax 31.80.46.

Le Vieux Cep (high tariff). Popular with package tourists. As a result the hotel is noisy and the staff not too friendly. There are 20 rooms with bath, heater and television. A restaurant serves expensive French and Creole meals from a limited menu. 2 Rue des Trois Mares, 97413 Cilaos, tel. fax 31.71.89.

For budget accommodation try the local *pensions*, or the even cheaper camping facilities. Recommended low tariff lodgings, that usually include breakfast and dinner in the rate, can be found at:

Gardebien Gîte Rural, 50 Rue St-Louis, tel. 31.72.15

Auberge du Hameau, 5 Chemin Seminaire, tel. 31.70.94, fax 31.70.22.

No reservations are required. If you phone them on arrival they will usually send someone down to meet you. The latter *pension* is located in the old Catholic seminary, and is quite an eerie place when you are the only resident.

Inexpensive camping is available at Camping des Eucalyptus, at nearby **Matarum**, tel. 31.77.41. You have the choice of using the dormitory-style bungalows and eating in the cafeteria. The weather around Cilaos is unpredictable, and if you do go camping, make certain that you have sufficient clothing and a warm sleeping bag.

Places to eat

While the hotels offer à la carte menus and extravagant meals, you can just as easily get by on cheaper, but no less filling or tasty meals from the snack vans that park around the school on Rue des Ecoles. Pizzas, with a variety of toppings, are sold at *Le Triton Pizzeria*, on Rue Père Boiteau. *Boulangerie*, near the Esso fuel station, bakes fresh bread daily and has a wonderful selection of pies and spicy Creole snacks. Self-catering visitors only have the *Oke Supermarket* on Rue Père Boiteau at which to shop. Its selection is limited and expensive, and it is a far better idea to do your shopping in St-Pierre or St-Denis before going to Cilaos.

On the way to the village of Bras Sec, there are a number of table d'hôte establishments open for lunch and early dinner. Their prices are always good and the set menu food exceptional. On Rue Père Boiteau is *Chez Noe*, which sells fresh fruit, legumes, lentils, local wine and vegetables. All prices are negotiable for the fresh produce, and visitors will be pleasantly surprised when they compare the prices to those in the coastal cities.

L'Auberge du Lac Restaurant, 13 Rue Mare A Joncs, tel. 31.76.30, has a decidedly tourist-orientated menu that includes several Creole dishes. It is expensive to eat here, but the view and top-notch service is worth it. *La Grange Restaurant*, on the edge of the lake at 2 Chemin Saules, tel. 31.70.38, offers a good selection of reasonably priced meals from an à la carte menu. *La Terrasse*, 73 N5, Bas du Village, is a little way out of Cilaos. It has awesome views of the mountains and waterfalls, and a delicious range of Creole dishes at low prices, with huge servings and second helpings.

CIRQUE DE SALAZIE

Salazie has always been the most popular cirque to visit due to its accessibility from the capital of St-Denis and the east coast. In the path of the warm monsoon winds, Salazie has lush vegetation, spectacular waterfalls and rivers that are fed almost daily by light rain. Although Salazie is the main settlement in the cirque, it is linked to the village of Hell-Bourg, further into the cirque. The name Salazie comes from the Malagasy word *Salazane*, which means "sentry post" or "mast".

Travellers visiting the area by public transport will find buses going to Salazie from the coastal town of St-André. Five buses travel the route. The first departs from St-André at 7h15 and the last leaves at about 15h10. The trip can take anything from two to four hours, depending on road and weather conditions. Over weekends it is a pleasure hitchhiking up from the coast. Wait at the off-ramp onto the D48 district road, signposted for Salazie and Rivière du Mat.

The road up to Cirque de Salazie passes through litchi and banana plantations as far as Îlet. Then mountain vegetation takes over into the cirque. At one point the tarred road actually passes through a waterfall on its tortuous climb. The architecture changes as well. From flat-roofed adobe wall houses there is a gradual change to more Alpine homes of steep-pitched roofs and wooden walls, with flower boxes. Many of these houses have table d'hôte signs on their gates. The cheap meals they serve are nearly always delicious. Lunches seem to be their forte, and a plate of Creole rice and fish, washed down with a bottle of white Cilaos wine, is a satisfying experience. On the way from Salazie to Hell-Bourg, stop for the incredible views over the waterfall of Voile de la Mariée.

Salazie and Hell-Bourg villages

The post office in Salazie is at 59 Rue Georges Pompidou, while that in Hell-Bourg is on Rue General de Gaulle. There are no banks serving either of the settlements, and visitors should cash their cheques at one of the tourist-class hotels. Tourist information is obtainable from the tourist office in Salazie, 75 Rue Georges Pompidou, tel. 47.50.14. Medical attention is available from Dr Christian Bettoum, **L'Îlet A Vidot**, tel. 47.83.79. There are two pharmacies in the area, Pharmacie de Salazie, 73 Rue Georges Pompidou, in Salazie, and Pharmacie Hell-Bourg, Rue General de Gaulle, Hell-Bourg.

Things to do

It is highly recommended that visitors to the Cirque de Salazie bring day-packs, good walking shoes and both wet and cold weather gear. There is no need for a guide when walking or hiking the cirque. All the GR hiking trails are clearly signposted, and the routes well marked.

The other cirques can also be reached from Salazie or Hell-Bourg. At Gîtes de France, as you enter Hell-Bourg, the manager will give hikers a detailed map with routes that link the three great cirques of Réunion. Shorter hikes are recommended for those visitors not wanting to spend days on the trail, sleeping in wet tents and eating dehydrated food. A pleasant four hour trip can be made from Salazie to the remarkable waterfall of Voile de la Mariée. Follow the tarred road southwest from Salazie, and about 2 km further is the route to the viewpoint. A track leads down and to the side of the viewpoint. The climb down can be slippery and visitors should pay particular care when crossing the moss-covered wet rocks in the ravine.

From Hell-Bourg, there is a 2 km walk east into the Bélouve forests. There is an overnight mountain gîte east of the Mare à Poule d'Eau viewpoint. South-west of Hell-Bourg, a day hike can be made on a relatively easy 2 km walk. This route will lead to Les Trois Cascades. From here, there are views – on rare cloudless days – to the highest mountain on Réunion, Piton des Neiges (3 070 m). The water in the shallow pools at the bottom of the waterfalls is icy cold and invigorating after the forest walk. About 3 km north of Hell-Bourg, on the GR1 hill trail, is Piton d'Enchaing. The walk to the summit can be dangerous in wet weather but the effort is rewarded with unbelievable views across the Cirque de Salazie and down the Rivière du Mat valley.

Other sites worth visiting while in the Cirque de Salazie are the Chez Nous Soyez Reine church and the quaint homes and colourful flower gardens of the Salazie hill-folk. At Le Parc Piscicole d'Hell-Bourg, visitors can try their hand at trout fishing from the dams and brook, at a price, or just buy from the kiosk.

Things to buy

Curio hunters will find offerings on sale from Cazanou, on Rue General de Gaulle, in Hell-Bourg. It sells traditional Salazie wood carvings, grass and straw products, hand-woven cloths, durable clothing and farm produce in the form of bottled jams and pickles. The shop is open Monday-Friday 9h30-18h00; Saturday 9h00-12h00.

Accommodation

Lodgings in Cirque de Salazie are much more expensive than high-grade accommodation in Cirque de Cilaos. However, the service is of a higher standard. There is some form of accommodation for everyone to the cirque. It is important to note that with the popularity of the destination, visitors should make their room reservations a minimum of 60 days before arrival.

Hotel Le Relais des Cimes (high tariff). 15 rooms with washing facilities, heater and telephone. Built in the manner of a traditional Creole village, Le Relais des Cimes also has a restaurant that specialises in Creole and Malagasy dishes – which means lots of rice on your plate. Hotel Le Relais des Chimes, Rue Charles de Gaulle, Hell-Bourg, tel. 47.81.58, fax 47.82.11.

For budget travellers, the best bet is to try any of the numerous *chambres d'hôte* that open their doors to visitors in Salazie. One of the most rustic is at *Mare a Vieille Place*, about 3 km from Salazie, tel. 47.51.10. For hikers arriving for or departing from a circuit of the cirques, spend the night at the home of Madeleine Laurent in Hell-Bourg, tel. 47.80.60. Also in Hell-Bourg is the picturesque chambre d'hôte of Madeleine Parisot, 17 Rue General de Gaulle, tel. 47.81.48. 17 km from Salazie, deep in the shadows of the cirque at Grand Îlet, is the alpine chambre d'hôte of François Boyer, tel. 47.71.62.

Even cheaper accommodation can be had at the *Auberge de la Jeunesse d'Hell-Bourg*, on Rue Cayenne, Hell-Bourg, tel. 47.82.65. Visitors ought to be card-carrying International Youth Hostel members, or first buy such membership from the manager before being permitted to stay here. But neither age nor membership appears to be a criterion, and this is certainly one place worth staying at – especially if you are only in the area for a day or two. If you call the youth hostel from Salazie, the manager will send someone down by car to collect you. The staff at the hostel is a joyous bunch who will arrange all manner of outings into the area. Self-catering is *de rigueur* and you are advised to do all your grocery shopping before arriving. Often it is impossible to find a bed here, but the staff are usually able to make some sort of plan to accommodate you. Bookings are better than just arriving. Make your reservations about 30 days before arrival. La Federation Réunionnais des Auberges de Jeunesse, BP 127, 97460 St-Paul, tel. 45.53.51, fax 45.61.07.

Places to eat

Most of the chambres d'hôte also provide meals, while several table d'hôte establishments serve delicious lunches. The best way of finding a place to eat is to just wander down the lanes and up the alleys of

Salazie and Hell-Bourg. You will not have to walk further than 1 km
before finding at least one suitable place. Cheap restaurants are hard
to find. *Les Lilas* restaurant, near the Esso service station, has a good
Creole menu of mainly vegetarian dishes. *Restaurant Le Voile de la
Mariée*, along the D48 out of Salazie, has a selection of French and
Continental dishes at reasonable rates.

Up at **Mare à Poules d'Eau**, there is a small bar and stall, and the
well-known *Hong Kong Saigon* restaurant. The meals are expensive but
the quality of food is high. It is frequented by day-trippers and is
popular with tour groups. Make a table reservation about two days in
advance, tel. 47.58.34.

In Hell-Bourg, the *Restaurant Chez Alice* on Rue General de Gaulle
has a good reputation and is often full of islanders over weekends. The
food is spicy and well prepared, served with vegetables, followed by
crisp salads and the offer of a glass of home-brewed rum punch. At
the *Ti'Chouchou Creole Food Restaurant*, 25 Rue General de Gaulle, visitors may try the local speciality in greens, chou chou. This queer-
tasting, mango-shaped vegetable is added to most of the traditional
meals eaten in the Cirque de Salazie.

Light meals and snacks can be bought from the pizzeria in Hell-
Bourg. On the roadside you will often see youths selling wild honey.
The combs drip with delicately flavoured honey, and it is a wonderful
way of spoiling yourself. Do not accept the first price they ask; bargaining is expected. At the *Salon de The Bakery*, in Salazie, you can
choose from cabinets full of rich cream cakes, light pastries and fresh
bread, and then feast while sipping thick espresso coffee.

INDEX

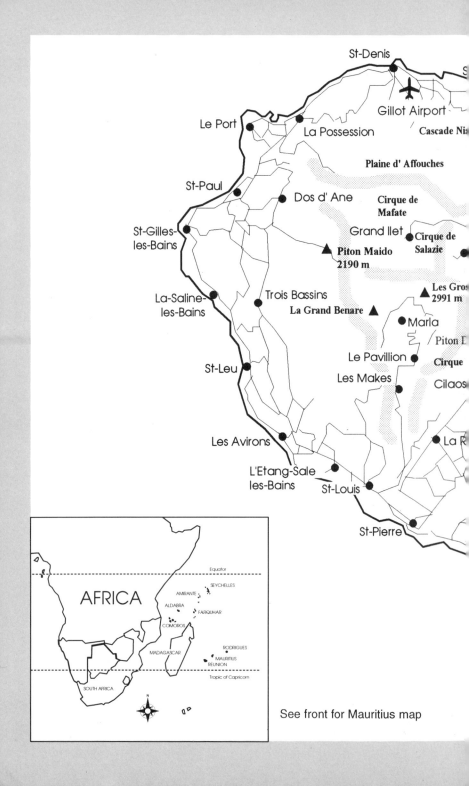

See front for Mauritius map